doing the days

A Year's Worth of Creative Journaling, Drawing, Listening, Reading, Thinking, Arts & Crafts Activities for Children Ages 8-12

by
Lorraine M. Dahlstrom

edited by
rosemary wallner

free spirit
PUBLISHING®
Works for kids®

TETON COUNTY LIBRARY
JACKSON, WYOMING

Copyright © 1994 by Lorraine M. Dahlstrom
All rights reserved. Unless otherwise noted, no part of this book may be reproduced in any form, except for brief reviews, without written permission of the publisher.

Library of Congress Cataloging-in-Publication Data
Dahlstrom, Lorraine M.
      Doing the days : a year's worth of creative journaling, drawing, listening, reading, thinking, arts & crafts activities for children, ages 8–12 / by Lorraine M. Dahlstrom ; edited by Rosemary Wallner.
          p.   cm.
      ISBN 0-915793-62-8
      1. Language arts (Elementary) 2. Language experience approach in education. 3. Education, Elementary—Activity programs. I. Wallner, Rosemary, 1964–   . II. Title.
LB1576.D14 1994
372.6—dc20   93-38119
                                                                                                          CIP

Cover and book design by MacLean & Tuminelly
Editorial direction by Pamela Espeland
Text illustrations by Lisa Wagner

12 11 10 9 8 7 6 5 4
Printed in the United States of America

Dear Teacher: We hope that you will enjoy using *Doing the Days* in your classroom. We ask that you *not* photocopy the entries and assignments to give to your students. As teachers and former teachers, we understand that your budget for classroom materials may be tight. As publishers and authors, we ask you to respect our rights. We're working hard to bring you the best possible books at the best possible prices. If you plan to make *Doing the Days* part of your curriculum, call us at 1-800-735-7323 and ask about our quantity discounts for teachers. We want to help!

Free Spirit Publishing Inc.
217 Fifth Avenue North, Suite 200
Minneapolis, MN 55401-1299
(612) 338-2068
help4kids@freespirit.com
www.freespirit.com

The following are registered trademarks of Free Spirit Publishing Inc.:

FREE SPIRIT®
SELF-HELP FOR TEENS®
WORKS FOR KIDS®

FREE SPIRIT PUBLISHING®
SELF-HELP FOR KIDS®
THE FREE SPIRITED CLASSROOM®

dedicAtioN

To the young people who share and surround my life. . .
past, present, and future.
To Jay, Joel, and David—a mother's dream.
To Lori and Marci for masterfully guiding and
supporting my journeys.

Acknowledgments

Special appreciation to Nikki Johnson and Jean Holt, Scott Highlands Middle School's library aides. Their support, knowledge, assistance, and perseverance often kept me looking. Thanks to Wild Rumpus Book Store in Minneapolis (a place to visit and seek) for special generosity. Special blessings to Doris, Gene, Fran, and Dorothy—a fine support staff and family. Thanks to Pamela Espeland and Judy Galbraith for patience and understanding. And to Rosemary Wallner, an outstandingly talented young woman who has gained my deepest respect for her craft. Thank you.

Contents

iNtroductioN

Conduct a survey. Write about something you think should be invented. Create your own passport. Make a list of things to do the next time you're bored. These are only four of the almost 1,500 activities you'll find in these pages—activities created from your students' experiences, hopes, feelings, and knowledge. Most of them are based on subjects you might not have thought of before and can be accomplished within one class period.

I wrote this book after receiving feedback from my first book, *Writing Down the Days: 365 Creative Journaling Ideas for Young People.* Some early elementary teachers told me that they had adapted the writing activities from that book to fit the skills of their younger, beginner writers. They encouraged me to put together a sequel. I took their suggestions and expanded them—as a result, this book is not only filled with writing activities, but is also packed with additional things to do, ranging from questions to discuss with classmates to crafts and drawing projects.

I've filled this book with celebrations, inventions, origins, explorations, political events, holidays, festivities, observances, people's birthdays, and anniversaries. In choosing the people, ideas, and events, I kept a few goals in mind. One was to bring as much cultural literacy, thought-provoking activities, and interesting fun to the classroom as I could. You'll find a large supply of creative, easy-to-use ideas for all areas of the curriculum. Another goal was to instill a love of learning into young students—to help them develop a love of literature, art, music, athletic excellence, and history.

In today's teaching environment, classroom strategies such as whole language skills, cooperative learning, critical thinking, interdisciplinary units, continuity of study, and interactive involvement are all important. I made every effort to provide as many varied activities as possible. I wanted to make sure that *all* students could participate in the daily events at some level.

How to use this book

The way to become a good writer is to write. Sometimes, young students feel unsure when their teacher asks them to write, especially if they feel that they don't have creative ideas. With that in mind, for each day of the year you'll find a paragraph about something that happened (or something that was invented or someone who was born) followed by a writing activity connected to that idea (or invention or person). These questions and statements are meant to ignite your students' imaginations, get them thinking about an idea they hadn't known existed, or look at a situation from a different point of view.

But that's not all.

Each day also includes three *more* activities—including addresses to write to, books to read, music to listen to, ideas to talk about, and problems to solve. Some of these activities are based on the information from the main paragraph; others include new and different tidbits.

As the professional in the classroom, you're the expert. Adjust the materials to fit your students' needs; there's no single right way to work on a day. I suggest that you read an entry's first paragraph aloud and talk about the idea (or invention or person) with your class. Then let your students write using the journal activity as inspiration. Pick and choose from the remaining activities as time, materials, and interest allow. With encouragement and a few simple materials, you'll stimulate enthusiasm for writing, creativity, history, and research.

Read ahead and connect the activities to classroom, school, and community projects and events. Encourage your students to investigate and extend the given information. Provide newspapers, news magazines, almanacs, encyclopedia yearbooks, phone numbers, and other resources for your students to page through, read, and research. Urge your students to apply their research skills and learn more about the things they want to know more about. Be flexible; let your students guide you. Accept alternative projects.

Help your students to write to the addresses given in the book. They'll probably get a quicker response if they include a self-addressed, stamped, business-sized envelope every time they send for information.

To supplement and expand on an entry's facts, I searched for books, poems, videos, and music recordings. To help you locate these materials, I included author or composer names, publishing houses or recording studios, and publishing dates at the end of the entry. I tried to find items that are easily available to you. If you can't find them in your own school library, try the public library. If you've found other materials, add that information in the margin so you'll remember that resource next year.

A Writer's Notebook

■ Your students will need something to write in. Encourage them to create, use, and keep a Writer's Notebook. My students keep three-ring binders that allow for expansion and change. Index dividers are useful; students can easily create them by using folder labels (heavy cardboard folders also work well).

■ It's best to keep the notebooks in the classroom. That way, they're more likely to remain available and in good condition. Plastic crates make great classroom notebook holders.

■ In grading your students' work, use your own grading system. For the journaling activities in this book, I recommend using a plus for a job well done, a check for an adequate, passing job, and a minus when additional effort is needed. Try to avoid letter grades for the writing assignments.

I am sure that many of the topics mentioned in this book will lead you to create your own timely and appropriate activities. I'd like to hear your ideas and suggestions. You may write to me at the following address:

Lorraine M. Dahlstrom
c/o Free Spirit Publishing
217 Fifth Avenue North, Suite 200
Minneapolis, MN 55401-1299

I continue to be amazed at the cultural, historical, and entertaining people, places, and ideas waiting to be discovered. I hope you and your students enjoy this compilation of discoveries.

Lorraine M. Dahlstrom
January 1994

key to icons

Before each activity in *Doing the Days*, you'll find an icon that identifies it.
Following are the icons and their meanings.

 WRITE in your journal

 LISTEN to music or someone reading a story or poem

 ACTIVITY, such as run, jump, sing, or dance

 LOOK; study something or watch a movie

 CONTEST; challenge a classmate just for fun

 READ a book, story, or poem

 DO; make something, experiment (extra materials may be needed)

 TELL, talk about, discuss, debate

 DRAW or paint

 THINK about, solve, contemplate

 FIND more information; take a survey

 WRITE or make a list

 LETTER; write a letter to someone

JaNUaRY 1

Happy New Year! This is New Year's Day. Many countries have special customs for celebrating this day. One custom is to make New Year's resolutions. Resolutions are promises you make to yourself to do certain things during the coming year. *Examples:* You might resolve to make your bed every day without being told. You might decide to read more books. Some people resolve to go swimming. In colder regions of the country, Polar Bear Clubs take an icy dip today.

 Describe the wintry sights, sounds, and feelings you'd experience if you were to take a swim on a chilly January day in a snowy place.

 Try a New Year's custom from another country. *Examples:* In Japan, people clean their houses thoroughly on New Year's Day. Dirt and dust from last year are believed to be bad luck. In Russia, Grandfather Frost comes to parties held under fir trees. In Hungary, it's considered good luck to touch a pig on New Year's Day.

 Create a time capsule. Include articles from current events magazines, pictures, a sample of your handwriting, and any souvenirs you may have collected. Include anything that will remind you of the past year. Put the items in a large plastic or metal container. Seal the container with tape or glue. Put a label on the outside of the container. Figure out the month and year when you will graduate from high school. On the label, write "Do Not Open Until _____." Fill in the month and year of your graduation. Take the container home and put it in a special place.

 Read *New Year's Poems*, selected by Myra Cohn Livingston and illustrated by Margot Tomes. Pick your favorite poem. Share it with your classmates.

....
R E S O U R C E
New Year's Poems, selected by Myra Cohn Livingston, illustrated by Margot Tomes (New York: Holiday House, 1987).
....

JaNUaRY 2

Today is the birthday of Isaac Asimov. He was born in Petrovichi, Russia, in 1920. When he was three, Asimov and his family came to the United States. Five years later they became U.S. citizens. Asimov was an author, scientist, and astronomer. He wrote many articles, some short stories, and over 300 books. He also put together collections of fantasy and science-fiction stories. Asimov died in 1992. He once said, "I do not fear computers. I fear the lack of them."

 Write down your feelings about computers.

 Draw your own science-fiction character. Look at creatures from science-fiction movies or TV shows to get ideas. Invent a unique figure of your own. Give your character special skills or talents.

 Since January is a time of new beginnings, make a decision to learn something new, try something new, or start something new— maybe a hobby. Write down your decision as a promise to yourself.

 Look through magazines and newspapers for words and pictures that have something to do with time or ways to measure time.

Examples: hour, day, clock, birthday cake, anniversary. Cut out your words and pictures and paste them on tagboard or create a collage.

january 3

On this day in 1894, Norman Rockwell was born in New York City. Rockwell was an artist who painted pictures of people doing everyday things. Many of his paintings showed people living and working in small towns and farms in the United States. His paintings were realistic, funny, and sometimes sad. Rockwell also painted more than 300 covers for *The Saturday Evening Post*. He died in 1978.

 If you could paint a picture, what would you paint? Describe the people and things you would include in your painting.

 Norman Rockwell painted people, animals, and things just as they appeared in real life. He wanted his paintings to be accurate. Look at a painting by Norman Rockwell. Notice the small details the artist added to his painting.

 Alaska became the 49th state of the United States on this day in 1959. It's the largest state in terms of its area, but it has a small population. Vitus Jonassen Bering, a Danish explorer, discovered Alaska in 1741. He sailed from Russia to see if North America and Asia were connected by land. The body of water that is between the two continents was named the Bering Strait in his honor. In 1867, the United States bought Alaska from Russia for $7.2 million. Look at a map of the United States. Compare Alaska's size to other states.

 John Ronald Reuel Tolkien, also known as J. R. R. Tolkien, was born on this day in 1892. Tolkien was an author. One of his most popular stories is *The Hobbit*. In this book, Tolkien writes about a place called Middle-earth where dwarves, elves, and hobbits fight dragons and discover treasures. One of the hobbits, Bilbo Baggins, finds a ring that makes him invisible when he puts it on. Ask someone to read part of *The Hobbit* to you. Draw a picture to illustrate that part of the story.

RESOURCE

The Hobbit by J. R. R. Tolkien (Boston: Houghton Mifflin, 1984).

january 4

People who are blind or visually impaired rely on the Braille alphabet to read books and write letters. This special alphabet was invented by Louis Braille, who was born on this date in 1809. Braille was a French inventor. When he was three years old, he was blinded in an accident. He invented the alphabet of raised dots for readers and writers who are visually impaired.

 Close your eyes. Listen to the sounds around you. Write a description of what you heard.

 Each letter in the Braille alphabet is made up of one to six dots. A special typewriter prints out the dots so they're raised and feel like small bumps. People who are visually impaired feel the dots and read the letters with their fingertips. This is what the Braille alphabet looks like:

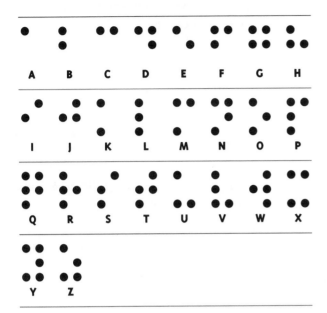

A B C D E F G H

I J K L M N O P

Q R S T U V W X

Y Z

Use the Braille alphabet to translate this message:

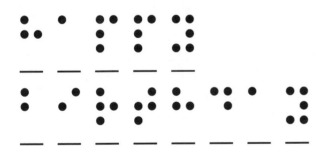

 Write your name using the Braille alphabet.

 Discover how people who are visually impaired rely on their other senses. Form teams of two. Have one person wear a blindfold while the other person acts as a guide. Take turns leading and being blindfolded. When you're blindfolded, use your other senses to determine where you are. Go around the classroom and identify familiar objects by touch. Identify classmates by the sound of their voice. Try to find something in your desk.

january 5

George Washington Carver died on this day in 1943 near Diamond Grove, Missouri. Since no one knows for sure when Carver was born, he is remembered on the day of his death. Carver loved to take care of plants. He decided to study botany, the science of plants. While in college, he met another student named George Carver. Many people got the two students mixed up. To avoid confusion, Carver used Washington as his middle name.

 Write about your middle name. Tell why you like it or why you don't like it. If you don't have a middle name, choose one and tell why you like it.

 In 1896, Carver began to teach at Tuskegee Institute in Alabama. He also began to experiment with common plants. His research created many products from peanuts, potatoes, and wood. One of his products is peanut butter. Celebrate Carver's delicious creation with a new sandwich. You'll need peanut butter, two slices of bread, and a cookie cutter. Spread peanut butter in the middle of a piece of bread. Cover with the other slice. "Stamp" your sandwich with a cookie cutter to create a shaped sandwich.

 To find out more about George Washington Carver, read *A Weed Is a Flower: The Life of George Washington Carver* by Aliki. You could also read *A Pocketful of Goobers: A Story about George Washington Carver* by Barbara Mitchell.

 There is an old proverb that says: "When nuts have thick shells, it will be a hard winter." Do you think this winter has been a hard one? Ask your classmates about other winters they remember.

RESOURCES

A Weed Is a Flower: The Life of George Washington Carver by Aliki (New York: Simon & Schuster, 1988).

A Pocketful of Goobers: A Story about George Washington Carver by Barbara Mitchell (Minneapolis: Carolrhoda Books, 1986).

jaNUarY 6

On this date in 1794, Rebecca Pennock Lukens was born. In 1825, after her husband died, Lukens took over the responsibilities for the Brandywine Iron Works in Pennsylvania. At the time, women were not expected to be the heads of large companies. Although the business had not been managed well, she turned it into a profitable one. Lukens became one of the only female industrialists in her time. The company's name was later changed to Lukens, Incorporated.

 Write about a company you'd like to be in charge of—perhaps a soft drink or toy company. Would you want to start your own business?

 Carl Sandburg was born on this date in 1878. He was an American poet, biographer, historian, and folklorist. Sandburg wrote a poem called "Fog." In his poem, he compares fog to a cat. His poem begins, "The fog comes on little cat feet...." Sandburg describes the fog's silence and its quiet arrival.

Have someone read the poem "Fog" to you. Use finger paints, crayons, or markers to make a picture of fog rolling in. Will your fog look like a cat?

 Prepare a scientific explanation of fog. Use reference books to find out how fog is formed. Read about why it appears. When you have finished, compare your scientific facts with Sandburg's description.

 For many years, Sandburg researched facts about Abraham Lincoln. He wrote a set of six books called *Abraham Lincoln: The Prairie Years and the War Years*. He searched libraries and read many books to find out information about Lincoln.

Think of three people you'd like to know a lot about Write down their names. How would you find out more about them?

RESOURCE

"Fog" may be found in *Early Moon* by Carl Sandburg (New York: Harcourt, Brace & World, 1958).

jaNUarY 7

On this day in 1929, Tarzan first appeared in a comic strip. Author Edgar Rice Burroughs had created the character in his book, *Tarzan of the Apes*. Tarzan lived in the jungle and could communicate with the animals. He had many adventures as he swung from vines and yelled his famous Tarzan yell.

 Write about your favorite jungle animal.

 Can you duplicate Tarzan's call? Aaah-AhAh-Aaah-AhAh-Aaah!

 A jungle is land covered with a dense growth of trees, vines, and bushes. You can usually find a jungle in warmer, tropical climates. Look through the maps in an atlas to find the locations of the world's jungles. (Atlases show vegetation types using different colors for forests, farmland, and desert.)

Johnny Weissmuller was an actor who played Tarzan in the movies. He was also an athlete who participated in the Olympics. Find out the sport Weissmuller competed in. Find out if he won a medal. Investigate and then draw a picture of Weissmuller competing.

january 6

Fanny Bullock Workman was born in Worcester, Massachusetts, on this day in 1859. Workman and her husband, Dr. William Hunter, traveled through many countries on their bicycles. They studied the places they visited and became fluent in many languages. Throughout Europe and the United States, Workman gave many lectures about her explorations. In 1903, she became the first woman to climb Mount Koser Gunya in the Himalayas.

 Write about where in the world you'd like to ride your bicycle.

 Elvis Aaron Presley was born on this day in 1935 in Tupelo, Mississippi. In the 1950s and 1960s, he was a popular American singer. "Love Me Tender" and "Hound Dog" are two of the songs that made Elvis a superstar. He has been called "The King of Rock and Roll." Elvis died at Graceland, his home, in 1977.

Write down what you'd like to be the king or queen of. *Examples*: Would you be the King or Queen of Computer Games? of Soccer? of Math Class?

 Elvis' middle name was spelled incorrectly as "Aron" on his birth certificate. He had it legally changed to "Aaron." Spell your name in as many different ways as you can.

 Some early rock-and-roll songs had unusual titles. "Teen-Age Crush," "Love Potion No. 9," and "Endless Sleep" were popular songs in the 1950s. "Fun Fun Fun" and "Doo Wah Diddy Diddy" were popular in the 1960s. With your classmates, make a list of song titles. Talk about the most unusual titles. Which song is the class favorite?

january 9

On this day in 1793, a Frenchman named Jean Pierre Blanchard made the first hot air balloon flight in U.S. history. That first flight took place in Philadelphia, Pennsylvania. President George Washington was there to witness the event.

 Imagine that you're taking a ride in a hot-air balloon over your neighborhood. Write about what you see as you lean over the side of the basket.

 Paint or draw a picture of yourself riding in a colorful hot air balloon.

 Experiment with a balloon. You'll need a small narrow-mouthed bottle, a balloon just large enough to fit over the bottle's top, a pan filled with cold water, and a pan filled with hot water. Slip the end of the balloon over the top of the bottle. The balloon should fit securely over the top. Let the balloon hang on the side of the bottle.

Place the bottle in the pan of cold water for five minutes. (You could add a few ice cubes to the water to make sure it's very cold.) After five minutes, take the bottle out of the cold water and put it in the pan with the hot water. Watch what happens to the balloon. Return the bottle to the cold water for five minutes. Then put it back in the pan of hot water. Warm up the hot water if necessary.

Did your balloon get larger when you put the bottle in the hot water? As air warms, it expands. Placing the bottle in hot water warms the air in the bottle. The expanded air goes into the balloon. When you put the balloon in cold water, the air leaves, and the balloon shrinks.

 Fly a bread wrapper kite. You'll need an empty plastic bread bag, a hole punch, a sharp pencil, and some kite string.

Open the bread bag. Two inches from the bag's opening, punch four holes each about the same distance apart. Cut four pieces of kite string. Each piece should be about six inches long. Tie one end of each piece to one of the four holes in the bag. Tie the four strings together at the other end. Tie the rest of your kite string to the four tied strings. With a very sharp pencil, poke four holes in the closed end of the bread wrapper. Then go fly a kite!

jaNUary 10

On this day in 1776, Thomas Paine anonymously published a pamphlet titled "Common Sense." In the pamphlet, Paine encouraged American colonists to fight for independence from Great Britain.

 Write about how your life would be different if a king or queen ruled the United States.

 On this day in 1911, for the first time, a photographer flying in an airplane took a photograph of the ground. In honor of this first, draw a picture of your school as though you were flying in an airplane looking down at it.

 January is National Soup Month. What's your favorite soup? Make a list of the things you like to eat with your soup. *Examples*: a sandwich, salad, or breadsticks.

 Some brands of soup have labels that everyone recognizes. Invent your own soup brand. Draw a can of soup and create your own label. Include a list of ingredients. Make your soup something silly. *Examples*: "Cream of Dandelion" or "Bubble Gum Noodle." Share your new brand of soup with your class.

jaNUary 11

On this day in 1921, Juanita Morris Kreps was born in Lynch, Kentucky. In 1972, she became the first woman to head the New York Stock Exchange Board of Directors. In 1976, President Jimmy Carter appointed her to the position of Secretary of Commerce. She was the first woman to be appointed to this position. Kreps wrote many books about economics, the science that studies how money and goods are produced and used.

 Write about what would happen if there was no money.

 Milk was delivered in glass bottles for the first time in Brooklyn, New York, on this date in 1878. Today, we buy milk in waxed paper cartons or plastic bottles. Which do you think is better and why—glass, paper, or plastic?

 Read *The Milk Makers* by Gail Gibbons to learn more about how cows produce milk. This book also tells the processes milk goes through before it reaches the grocery store.

 Milk is one of the foods in the dairy group. The dairy group is one of the five food groups. Cut out pictures from newspapers or magazines that show milk and other foods in the dairy group. Mount your images on a piece of tagboard.

R E S O U R C E

The Milk Makers by Gail Gibbons (New York: Macmillan Children's Group, 1987).

jaNuary 12

For centuries, people have delighted their children by telling them fairy tales. But one man, Charles Perrault, decided to write them down so they wouldn't be forgotten. Perrault was born in France on this day in 1628. He wrote down the fairy tales to amuse his children and their friends. In 1697, he published the *Tales of Mother Goose*. Some of the stories in this book were "Sleeping Beauty," "Little Red Riding Hood," "Cinderella," and "Puss in Boots."

 If Charles Perrault hadn't written down the fairy tale stories, they might not be remembered today. Write a short letter to this author thanking him for your favorite fairy tale.

 People in countries around the world tell their children fairy tales. Read the book *Lon Po Po* by Ed Young. It's a Chinese fairy tale

that may remind you of "Little Red Riding Hood." After you read the story, tell your classmates how the two stories are alike and different.

 Many fairy tales end with "They lived happily ever after." But what do you think happens after the story ends? Continue your favorite fairy tale. Write a paragraph about what happens to the characters the next day. *Examples:* Finish the story of "Cinderella." What happened after she married the prince? Complete "Little Red Riding Hood." What did she do the day after her walk to Grandma's?

 Hold a dress-up day in January. Have everyone dress in a costume that represents a favorite fairy tale character.

R E S O U R C E

Lon Po Po: A Red Riding Hood Story from China, translated and illustrated by Ed Young (New York: Putnam, 1989).

jaNuary 13

Michael Bond was born on this date in 1926. He created Paddington, the little bear that wears the yellow hat and blue coat. On Christmas Eve in 1957, Bond saw an unsold stuffed bear on a store shelf. He felt sorry for the bear and bought it for his wife. Bond lived near Paddington Station in London, England. Because of this, he named the bear Paddington. Since that time, Bond has written many stories about Paddington Bear.

 Paddington always wears a coat with pockets so that he can have a place to keep things. Write about what you keep in your pockets.

Michael Bond's stories about Paddington Bear include *Paddington Abroad*, *Paddington On Top*, and *Paddington's Storybook*. Volunteer to read your favorite passage from a Paddington Bear story out loud.

 Create a Paddington Bear party. Bring your own favorite bear or stuffed animal. Have cookies and juice for treats.

 Paddington is always seen in his yellow hat and blue coat. Why not design a new outfit for Paddington to wear? What could he wear to a birthday party? to the zoo? at bedtime? Draw Paddington in an outfit you've created.

....

RESOURCES

Some books by Michael Bond:

Paddington Abroad, Paddington On Top, Paddington's Storybook (Boston: Houghton Mifflin).

....

jaNUary 14

On this date in 1841, writer and cooking expert Juliet Corson was born in Roxbury, Massachusetts. She wrote newspaper and magazine articles and cooking manuals. In 1876, she founded the New York Cooking School, which many people think was the first cooking school in the United States. The next year, she wrote a pamphlet called "Fifteen Cent Dinners for Families of Six."

 Write down your ideas for fixing a family meal for very little money. What dishes would you include?

 On this day in 1886, author Hugh Lofting was born in England. His most famous works were part of his Doctor Dolittle series. Dr. Dolittle was a veterinarian who talked to animals. He used grunting noises

to communicate with pigs. He understood what a dog's barking meant.

Lofting's first book in his series was published in 1920. It was called *The Story of Dr. Dolittle*. He wrote other adventures for this special vet including *The Voyages of Dr. Dolittle*, *Dr. Dolittle & the Green Canary*, and *Dr. Dolittle & the Secret Lake*. To celebrate Lofting's birthday, read one of the Dr. Dolittle books today.

 The earliest veterinary schools were founded in France in the mid-1700s. Today, students who want to become vets study chemistry, physics, and zoology. They learn how to prevent and treat diseases. If you'd like information on how to become a veterinarian, write to:

The American Veterinary
Medical Association
1931 North Meacham Road, Suite 100
Shaumburg, IL 60173-4360

 If you and your class are interested in veterinary medicine, ask a local vet to come in and talk to your class about the work he or she does. Write a list of questions to ask the veterinarian. *Examples*: What kinds of animals does the doctor treat? What was the most unusual animal the doctor treated? What does the doctor like most about being a vet?

....

RESOURCES

Some books by Hugh Lofting:

The Story of Dr. Dolittle and *The Voyages of Dr. Dolittle* (New York: Delacorte Press).

Dr. Dolittle & the Green Canary and *Dr. Dolittle & the Secret Lake* (New York: Harper & Row).

....

jaNuary 15

Dr. Martin Luther King, Jr., was born on this day in Atlanta, Georgia, in 1929. King wanted people to be treated equally. He thought that people of all races should live together peacefully. King once said, "Many men cry 'Peace! Peace' but they refuse to do the things that make for peace." He won the Nobel Peace Prize in 1964. In 1986, people began observing King's birthday as a national holiday on the third Monday in January.

 Write about what you can do to help people live together in peace.

 When King was a boy, he had many heroes. He read about Frederick Douglass, Harriet Tubman, Booker T. Washington, George Washington Carver, and Jesse Owens. Pick one of these people and do some research. Find out what that person did to promote peace. Why do you think King admired this person? Share your findings with your class.

 Dr. Martin Luther King, Jr., gave a speech on August 28, 1963. He told a crowd of 200,000 people, "I have a dream." He dreamed of a United States free of hatred and unfairness. King wanted people to treat each other fairly. He felt people could and should work for peace.

Draw a picture of people living together in peace.

 To learn more about Dr. King, read *I Have A Dream: The Story of Martin Luther King* by Margaret Davidson or *Martin Luther King, Jr., Free at Last* by David A. Adler. You will also find more information in *Martin Luther King: The Peaceful Warrior* by Ed Clayton.

RESOURCES

I Have A Dream: The Story of Martin Luther King by Margaret Davidson (New York: Scholastic, 1991).

Martin Luther King, Jr., Free at Last by David A. Adler (New York: Holiday House, 1986).

Martin Luther King: The Peaceful Warrior by Ed Clayton (New York: Simon & Schuster, 1986).

jaNuary 16

Dian Fossey was born in San Francisco, California, on this day in 1932. In 1966, she began to study gorillas in the forests of Rwanda, a country in south central Africa. Through living and working among the gorillas, she gained their trust. They let her touch them and allowed her to be a part of their family gatherings. In 1985, Fossey was killed; no one was able to find out how she died. She was buried in the gorilla graveyard next to her favorite gorilla, Digit, who had been killed by poachers.

 Write about an animal you'd like to study. What could you do to earn that animal's trust?

 Fossey worked for many years to get close to the gorillas in their natural habitat. She worried that gorillas might become extinct as people drove them out of their habitat and poachers killed or captured them.

Talk with your classmates about why you think it's important to study animals in their natural habitat. What would happen if no one studied these animals?

 Today is National Nothing Day. This day was the idea of Harold P. Coffin, a newspaper reporter, who observed the first National

Nothing Day in 1973. He created this day so that Americans had one day when they could just sit. Coffin wanted one day when nothing was celebrated and no one was honored.

Have a class contest. See who can sit for ten minutes doing nothing. This means no talking, laughing, squirming, or making noise. The winners win. . .nothing!

 List activities you can do the next time you feel you have nothing to do. *Examples:* Visit a friend. Run around the block. Read a book or magazine. Start a hobby. Clean out your closet. Keep your list and pull it out the next time you're bored.

jaNuarY 17

"**E**arly to bed and early to rise, makes a man healthy, wealthy and wise." That saying is from a book called *Poor Richard's Almanac*. The author was Benjamin Franklin, who was born on this day in 1706. An almanac contains facts on many different subjects. Franklin first published his almanac in 1732. He filled it with sayings about friendship, money, and love. Many of his sayings are still remembered today.

 Write how you feel about going to bed early and getting up early.

 Ben Franklin had 57 pseudonyms. (A pseudonym is a made-up name used in place of a real name.) Some of his silliest pseudonyms were "Anthony Afterwit," "The Busybody," and "Mrs. Silence Dogwood." Make a list of pseudonyms for yourself. Make them as silly as you can.

 Franklin was a writer who also had many other jobs. In his lifetime, he was a states-

man, diplomat, inventor, publisher, philanthropist, philosopher, scientist, and printer. Look up these words in a dictionary. What do they mean?

 Read *What's the Big Idea, Ben Franklin?* by Jean Fritz. This book will give you more details about Franklin's life. Discover a different point of view about Franklin in *Ben and Me* by Robert Lawson. In this book, Amos the mouse reveals that many of Franklin's inventions were really invented by Amos.

RESOURCES

What's the Big Idea, Ben Franklin? by Jean Fritz (New York: Putnam, 1982).

Ben and Me by Robert Lawson (New York: Dell Publishing Company, 1973).

jaNuarY 18

Today is the birthday of Alan Alexander Milne. He was born in 1882. A. A. Milne was a British author who created Winnie-the-Pooh, a friendly bear that lives in the Hundred Acre Wood. Piglet, Kanga and Roo, Eeyore, Tigger, Rabbit, and Owl are some of Pooh's friends. Pooh is also friends with a little boy named Christopher Robin. Milne got the idea for his stories after his son received a stuffed bear for his birthday. Milne wrote about Pooh and his friends in *Winnie-the-Pooh* and *The House at Pooh Corner*.

Write a mini-adventure story that includes one of your stuffed animals.

Make Pooh and his friends into stick puppets. You'll need some heavy paper or cardboard, crayons or markers, scissors, glue, and some sticks. (You can use Popsicle sticks or twigs from outside.)

Draw Pooh and his friends on the paper. Cut out your drawings. Glue the figures onto the wooden sticks. Use your puppets to dramatize one of the stories from A. A. Milne's books.

 A. A. Milne thought about new stories and new characters all the time. He once said, "Nowhere can I think so happily as in a train. . . . I see a cow, and I wonder what it is like to be a cow, and I wonder whether the cow wonders what it is like to be me." Have you ever wondered what a cow thinks about? Use your imagination and make a list of the noises, smells, tastes, and sights a cow experiences. What would a cow think of all these things?

 Milne thought that it was okay to be messy sometimes. He said that when he looked through his stacks of papers, he would find things that he hadn't seen in awhile. He said, "One of the advantages of being disorderly is that one is constantly making exciting discoveries." Clean out your school desk or locker. List the exciting discoveries you find.

. . . .

RESOURCES

Some books by A. A. Milne:

Winnie-the-Pooh and *The House at Pooh Corner* (New York: Dutton).

. . . .

E dgar Allan Poe was born in Boston, Massachusetts, on this day in 1809. He was an American poet and short-story writer. He was famous for his tales of mystery. Poe's stories often included scary

and gruesome things. One of his most famous poems is "The Raven." That poem begins, "Once upon a midnight dreary, while I pondered weak and weary...."

 Write about something scary.

 Look up "raven" in an encyclopedia or bird book. Learn more about this interesting bird.

 Write a list of words that you'd use to describe something scary. Can you think of more than 10 words?

 You can help crows, chickadees, and other winter birds find food by making a bird feeder. You'll need a plastic soda bottle, scissors, a ruler, sturdy wire, and a 10-inch dowel. (A dowel is a smooth round stick that isn't very thick.)

About three inches from the bottom of the bottle, carefully punch a hole through the plastic with the scissors. Make another hole on the opposite side of the bottle. Push the dowel through the holes so it sticks out. The birds will sit on the ends of the dowel while they feed. Now use the scissors to cut feeding holes about 1 1/2 inches above each perch. Fill the bottle with bird seed. Wrap one end of the wire around the neck of the bottle. Attach the feeder to a tree or pole with the other end.

jaNuarY 2o

In Bulgaria, people celebrate Babin Den, or Grandmother's Day, today. Grandmother's Day started a long time ago when a woman who helped deliver babies was called a *baba*. (Baba means grandmother.) Some people believed that a baba passed her knowledge to the children she helped deliver. Today, Bulgarians remember this day with celebrations and festivities.

 Write down some of the nicest things about grandmothers.

 What did people do for fun 50 years ago? Interview your grandmother or grandfather to help you with this question. If you don't have a grandparent, ask another older person about what they used to do. Share your findings with your class.

 Make a wall plaque for your grandmother or another special person in your life. You'll need plaster of Paris, water, a coffee can lid, some toothpicks or a sharp pencil, and a large paper clip.

Joey 1993

Mix the plaster and the water according to the directions. Pour the plaster into the coffee can lid. Wait a few minutes. When the plaster is almost hard, press your hand into it. Use a toothpick to write your name and the date on the plaque. Push a large paper clip halfway into the top edge of the plaster plaque. The paper clip can be used to hang the plaque on the wall. Let your plaque dry overnight and then give it away to someone special.

 In 1987, Clayton Ary was an eighth grader who lived in Lyons, Illinois. On this day in that year, Clayton's grandmother fell and started turning blue. Clayton called the operator because the 911 emergency number was not in service where he lived. The operator explained how to give mouth-to-mouth resuscitation. Clayton followed the operator's instructions. His grandmother finally started breathing on her own.

Does your community have the 911 emergency service? If so, design a card that lists your address and phone number. Put the card next to your phone so someone calling 911 has the right information to give to the operator.

If your community doesn't have the 911 emergency service, write a letter to your mayor or other city council member and ask them to consider adding the service to your area.

jaNuarY 2I

John Charles Fremont was an American surveyor. He was also an army officer. Fremont's nickname was "The Pathfinder." He was famous for leading expeditions to explore the early West. The Pathfinder was born on this day in 1813.

On this day in 1824, Thomas Jonathan Jackson was born. Jackson was a Confederate General in the Civil War. During the Battle of the First Bull Run, he stood still watching his enemies. One of his men said that Jackson was like a stone wall. From that day, he was nicknamed "Stonewall" Jackson.

Be a nicknamer. List five people you know and give them unusual—but nice—nicknames. Explain why you gave them those nicknames.

 Conduct a survey. Ask your classmates about their nicknames. Ask them if they have one that only their family knows about. Find out if they wish they had a nickname. If they don't have one, ask them what they'd want it to be.

 This is National Hugging Day! Some people believe that everyone needs at least six hugs a day.

Make a hug coupon for someone in your family. Use a small piece of paper and label it with the words "Hug Coupon." Make it small enough to carry and give away easily. After you've created your coupon, give it away. That way, the person you give it to can use the coupon the next time they need a hug.

 Today is the birthday of actor Telly Savalas. He was born in 1924 and played a TV character named Kojak. On his series, Kojak asked people, "Who loves ya, baby?" List all the people who love you.

jaNuary 22

January is named after the Roman god Janus. In ancient times, people believed Janus was the god of all passages and the spirit of all beginnings. As a god of passages, the ancient Romans dedicated gates and arches to him. Because he was also the god of beginnings, the first day of each month was sacred to him. The Romans named the first month of the year *Ianuarius* in his honor. That Latin word led to our word January.

 Are you named after somebody? Who? If you have a child someday, will you name him or her after somebody you know or admire? What name would you choose?

 Look up the word for each month in an encyclopedia or other reference book and find out who the other months are named after.

 Today is National Popcorn Day. To celebrate, create some popcorn flowers. You'll need blue and green construction paper, popped white popcorn, scissors, glue, and a brown marker.

With the brown marker, draw a large tree trunk on the blue paper. Draw some leaves on the green paper and cut them out. Glue the leaves on the blue paper above your tree trunk. Now glue pieces of white popcorn over the leaves to create apple blossom flowers.

 For more information about popcorn, send a letter to:

The Popcorn Institute
401 North Michigan Avenue
Chicago, IL 60611-4267

jaNuary 23

On this day in 1918, Gertrude B. Elion was born in New York City. During World War II, while many men became soldiers, many women began working in jobs that had previously been only open to men. As a result, Elion became a laboratory assistant to Dr. George Hitchings. Over the next 40 years, Elion and Hitchings worked as research partners and developed drugs that helped cure diseases. In 1988, the two scientists won the Nobel Prize for physiology.

Write about something you'd like to invent a cure for—would you like to invent a cure for a cold or for sadness?

Today is the birth date of John Hancock. He was born in Braintree, Massachusetts, in 1737. Hancock was an American patriot and politician. His signature was famous—he was the first person to sign the Declaration of Independence.

In John Hancock's honor, today is National Handwriting Day. Write about your handwriting. Is it neat? messy? big? small? Do you like your handwriting? Why or why not?

A signature is the way people sign their names. When you write your signature, you sign your "John Hancock." Write your name in a different signature. *Examples:* Create fancy loops around the letters. Decorate it with flowers or funny faces. Write your name very small or very big. Fill up a whole piece of paper with your fancy signature.

To find out more information about John Hancock, read the book *Will You Sign Here, John Hancock?* by Jean Fritz.

···

RESOURCE

Will You Sign Here, John Hancock? by Jean Fritz (New York: Putnam, 1982).

···

jaNuary 24

Maria Tallchief was born on this date in 1925 in Fairfax, Oklahoma. Tallchief was a ballerina for 18 years. She toured the country and appeared on TV promoting ballet. In 1947, she joined the Ballet Company, which became the New York City Ballet. Tallchief was one of the first American ballerinas to gain fame throughout the world.

Do you like to dance? Write about your feelings when you dance.

Tallchief's father was an Osage Native American. Her mother was Scotch-Irish. Tell your class about your family's ethnic background. Are there certain things your family does because of where family members came from? *Examples:* Does your family like to prepare certain foods? Do you and your family celebrate special festivals and holidays?

Today begins the Alacitas Fair. The Aymara Indians of Bolivia celebrate this three-day event. The fair honors Ekeko, the Aymara's god of prosperity and well-being.

Ekeko looks like a little man with a very big belly. His mouth is open and his head is back. His arms are spread out wide. He carries an empty pack on his back. During this celebration, people put small items in Ekeko's pack. If they want something, they put a small copy of it in Ekeko's empty pack. They believe that Ekeko will give them what they want.

Demonstrate how you think a statue of Ekeko looks. Stand up, spread your arms out, put your head back, bulge your stomach out, and open your mouth.

Today is also the anniversary of the discovery of gold. John Sutter discovered it in California's Sacramento Valley in 1848. Early prospectors panned for gold. They took a clump of mud and some water and swished the mixture around in a shallow pan. They looked for gold by sifting out the mud and water.

Pretend you're John Sutter or another gold prospector. Write a letter to a friend telling about your discovery.

january 25

Robert Burns is Scotland's most famous poet. He was born on this day in 1759 in Ayrshire, Scotland. Burns wrote a poem called "Auld Lang Syne." The title means "long ago." About ten years after Burns wrote the poem, someone added music to his words. The song is about remembering old friends and is usually sung on New Year's Eve.

 Write about some friends you remember.

 Robert Burns wrote over 300 songs. He used the melodies of old Scottish tunes and added his own words. Compose a song using a familiar tune and your own words. *Example*: "Row, Row, Row Your Boat" could become "Fly, Fly, Fly Your Kite."

 One of Robert Burns' most famous poems was called "The Cotter's Saturday Night." His poem tells of the happiest time in his home life. It's about Saturday night, when his family relaxed, read books, talked, and played simple games. What does your family do for fun? Tell your class. Find out what your classmate's families do.

 On this day in 1915 a famous telephone call was made. Alexander Graham Bell, who was in New York, New York, called Thomas Watson, who was in San Francisco, California. The call was the first one made across the country. With a partner, pretend you're making the first coast-to-coast call. What would you say to each other?

january 26

In 1919, millionaire William Randolph Hearst hired Julia Morgan to design his new home. Hearst gave Morgan a list of all the things he wanted in his San Simeon, California, mansion. He wanted 100 rooms, 31 bathrooms, 2 libraries, and a garage for 25 limousines. Using the list, Morgan created one of the most famous architectural projects of the twentieth century. Morgan was born on this day in 1872.

 Write about your dream house.

 G' Day Mate! Today is Foundation Day or Australia Day. On this day, Australians honor Captain Arthur Phillip. Phillip and his crew were the first Australian settlers. In 1788 they landed on the southeast side of this continent. Today, the city of Sydney stands at that first landing site.

Find out which animals live only in Australia. Discuss with your class how the animals are different from those of other continents. (Read about one of them, the kangaroo, in the next activity.)

 One of the unusual animals in Australia is a kangaroo. There are over 47 species of kangaroos. Kangaroos are marsupials; they have pouches in which to carry their young. One of the things that kangaroos do best is jump. Have a kangaroo hopping contest. Pretend everyone in your class is a kangaroo. Who can jump the highest? the farthest? Create a kangaroo obstacle course with small hurdles or barriers. Who is the fastest kangaroo? Remember that kangaroos don't run. They jump.

A large portion of Australia is called the *outback*. The outback is a vast area where sheep and cattle graze. The country also has dry desert areas and rich farming land. For more information about Australia, read D. V. Georges' book *Australia*.

RESOURCE

Australia by D. V. Georges (Chicago: Childrens Press, 1986).

jaNuary 27

On this date in 1888, the National Geographic Society was founded. It was formed to gather and spread information about geography to everyone in the world. The society awards money to scientists so that they can explore and report on places around the world. The society publishes magazines and books about the places scientists have found. It produces TV specials and videos. The National Geographic Society makes it possible for people to travel to places they might never have even heard of before.

 Write about a place you hope to travel to someday.

 Many National Geographic specials are available on video. Find out if your school has some of these specials in the media center. If it doesn't, rent one from your public library. Watch it with your class.

 Today is the birthday of Charles Lutwidge Dodgson. He was born in Cheshire, England, in 1832. He was an English mathematician, author, and photographer. Dodgson wrote *Alice's Adventures in Wonderland* and *Through the Looking Glass*. When he wrote them, he used the name Lewis Carroll. Draw a picture of your own wonderland.

 Wolfgang Amadeus Mozart was born on this day in 1756 in Salzburg, Austria. Mozart started composing music when he was only five years old. He was considered a child prodigy. (A prodigy is a child with exceptional talent.) During his lifetime, he wrote hundreds of musical works—operas, symphonies, songs, piano pieces, and much more.

Listen to a piece of music by Mozart. As you listen, write about or draw a picture of what you see in your mind as you hear the music.

RESOURCES

Alice's Adventures in Wonderland and *Through the Looking Glass* by Lewis Carroll (New York: Bantam Books).

Mozart's Greatest Hits recording (CBS Masterworks, 1984).

jaNuary 26

Ballet dancer Mikhail Baryshnikov was born on this date in 1948. When he was 21 years old, he became a member of the Kirov Ballet in Leningrad in the former Soviet Union. In 1974 he left his homeland to become a U.S. citizen. Baryshnikov performed with the American Ballet Theatre and the New York City Ballet. He once said, "The essence of all art is to have pleasure in giving pleasure."

 Write about something you do that pleases other people. *Examples*: Do you draw pictures that others like to look at? Do you do errands or chores for others?

 Today is the National Day of Excellence. Demonstrate something you can do with excellence. If you can't do something excellently quite yet, show how good you are now.

Claes Oldenburg was born in Sweden on this date in 1929. He is famous for his giant sculptures. He creates gigantic, soft sculptures from common objects. He has made huge hamburgers and monstrous telephones. He created enormous light switches and jumbo ice cream cones. Celebrate his birthday by designing your own large creation.

 Today is National Kazoo Day. Do you know what a kazoo is? It's an instrument that makes a buzzing sound when you hum through one end of its tube. Can you make the sound of a kazoo? Create a kazoo chorus in your class. Pick a song that everybody knows, then "play" it with kazoo sounds.

january 29

On this date in 1929, Seeing Eye, Incorporated, was founded. This company trains dogs to help people who are visually impaired. The trainers teach their dogs to obey commands and recognize unsafe obstacles. When the guide dogs are fully trained, they help people who are visually impaired cross busy streets and move through crowded stores.

 Pretend you're a seeing eye dog. Write about the things you watch for and how you help your master.

 January is National Eye Care Month. Preserving your sight is important. Three people who care for your eyes are an optician, ophthalmologist, and optometrist. Look up these words in a dictionary. Find out how these people help their patients.

 According to statistics, nearly one in two Americans wear eyeglasses or contact lenses. More people need them than wear them. In the three- to sixteen-year-old age group, more girls than boys wear glasses, but that changes as they get older. Take a survey of students in your class. How many girls wear glasses or contacts? How many boys? Do the figures you gathered agree with the national statistics?

 Learn more facts about eyes and eyeglasses. Read about the history of glasses, how different cultures use eye wear, and how to keep your eyes healthy in *Look How Many People Wear Glasses: The Magic of Lenses* by Ruth Brindze.

RESOURCE

Look How Many People Wear Glasses: The Magic of Lenses by Ruth Brindze (New York: Atheneum, 1979).

january 30

Today is the birthday of Franklin Delano Roosevelt. He was the 32nd president of the United States. Roosevelt was born in Hyde Park, New York, in 1882. He was the only U.S. president to serve more than two terms. During Roosevelt's second term, World War II began. Roosevelt once said, "Far more than an end to war, we want an end to the beginning of war."

 Write about what you think people should do to prevent wars.

 Franklin Roosevelt suffered from polio. In 1938, he founded the National Foundation for Infantile Paralysis to research and treat the disease. Today, the organization is known as the March of Dimes. Find out more information about the March of Dimes. What can you do to support its work?

Roosevelt collected stamps as a hobby. To get materials and information about stamp collecting, write to:

Benjamin Franklin Stamp Club
475 L'Enfant Plaza SW, Room 4485 E
Washington, DC 20260-6757

 A hobby is something that people do regularly in their spare time. *Examples*: Sewing, playing football, collecting baseball cards, raising tropical fish. Promote the hobby of your choice. Make a poster showing your hobby. Include reasons why you like your hobby.

january 31

On this day in 1961, Ham, a chimpanzee, was sent into space. Scientists wanted to test the Project Mercury capsule. They didn't want to risk a human life so they chose Ham to ride in the capsule first. (Ham's ride was a success.) Today, many companies try to test their products without endangering animals in any way.

 What's your opinion on the use of animals for testing products? Write about why you think some companies use animals in their testing. What else do you think they could do instead of using animals?

 In Whitehorse, Canada, the temperature reached minus 62 degrees Fahrenheit on this day in 1947. It was the coldest temperature ever recorded in Canada.

When the weather is cold, some people warm up with a breakfast of oatmeal. January is National Oatmeal Month. List the things you like to put in your oatmeal. Compare your answers with your classmates.

On this day in 1709, Alexander Selkirk was rescued. He was marooned for five years on a small island in the South Pacific Ocean. Daniel Defoe read an article about Selkirk's rescue and created a character called Robinson Crusoe. His story, *Robinson Crusoe*, tells how Crusoe was shipwrecked on an island and how he salvaged materials from the ship, built a home, grew crops, made clothes, and tamed animals. Crusoe also rescued and befriended a character named Friday.

Have someone read part of *Robinson Crusoe* to you. Draw a picture to illustrate that part of the story.

 Today is the last day of January. Tomorrow is the first day of February. Can you think of three ways that January and February are alike? How about three ways they're different? Tell the class your ideas.

RESOURCE
Robinson Crusoe by Daniel Defoe (New York: Airmont Publishing Company, 1964).

february 1

February is Children's Dental Health Month. Throughout this month, dentists encourage children to learn how to take care of their teeth.

 Write about why you think it's important to take care of your teeth.

 Practice the right way to brush your teeth. Pretend your pointer finger is a toothbrush. Brush the top parts of your teeth by moving your brush back and forth. Now practice brushing the sides of your teeth. For the bottom teeth, move your brush upward

along the sides of the teeth. For the top teeth, move your brush downward.

 Look through David Macaulay's book *The Way Things Work*. Find out how a dentist's drill works. Explain to your classmates how a drill works.

 Different animals have different types of teeth. Create a display that includes animals and their teeth. Write a short description of each animal. Tell how it uses its teeth to eat its food.

RESOURCE

The Way Things Work by David Macaulay (Boston: Houghton Mifflin, 1988).

 Today is Groundhog Day. According to one story, if a groundhog sees its shadow today, it'll burrow back into its hole and winter will continue for six more weeks.

 Write a description of what the weather is like today. How long do you think winter will last? Do you think it will last six more weeks?

A groundhog is a small animal with a plump body, short legs, and a bushy tail. Groundhogs live underground in holes that they dig themselves. They eat leaves and grass. During the winter, these animals hibernate. Draw a picture of a groundhog peeking out of its burrow. What's the weather like outside its hole? Is the groundhog happy or sad?

 If it's sunny outside, play a game of shadow tag. The person who's "IT" must tag other people by stepping on their shadows.

 Tell a joke or a riddle about the weather. For examples of some of the wackiest weather jokes, read *Weather or Not: Riddles for Rain and Shine* by Rick and Ann Walton.

RESOURCE

Weather or Not: Riddles for Rain and Shine by Rick and Ann Walton (Minneapolis: Lerner Publications, 1989).

Elizabeth Blackwell was the first woman in the United States to become a doctor. She was born on this date in 1821 in England. In 1857, she founded the New York Infirmary. Eighteen years later, she started the London School of Medicine for Women.

 Write advice to someone who is about to go to the doctor's office or the hospital for the first time.

 When you visit a doctor's office or the hospital, the nurse or doctor might take your pulse. Your pulse is the throbbing that your heart produces as it pushes blood through your body. Pulse points are the places on your body where the throbbing is easy to feel. One pulse point is at the front of your neck right next to your Adam's apple. Feel your pulse. Keeping your index and middle fingers together, press gently on your neck. Move your fingers around until you can feel your pulse.

 Taking your pulse means counting the number of throbs that occur during one minute. Your pulse will be different depending on what you're doing. Feel for your pulse on your neck. Sit still and relax for a few minutes. Have someone time one minute. When they say, "Go," start counting the number of throbs. Write down that number. Now jump up and down for one minute. Run in place for another minute. Take your pulse again. Write down that number next to the first pulse. Which number is higher? The harder your heart is working, the higher your pulse.

 For more information about taking your pulse, read the book *Hear Your Heart* by Paul Showers.

RESOURCE

Hear Your Heart by Paul Showers (New York: HarperCollins Children's Books, 1985).

Charles Lindbergh was the first person to fly across the Atlantic Ocean by himself. He was born on this day in 1902. In 1927, Lindbergh took off from Long Island, New York. He flew 33 1/2 hours in his plane named *The Spirit of St. Louis*. When he landed at Le Bourget airport in Paris, France, a huge crowd gathered to welcome him.

 Write about how it would feel to ride in an airplane. If you've ridden in an airplane, write about what you remember from the ride.

 Charles Lindbergh was called "Lucky Lindy." Think of a time you were lucky. Tell the class about it.

 Do you know how to fold paper to make an airplane? If you do, teach someone how to make a paper airplane the special way you do. Experiment with different tails and wings. Hold a paper flying contest.

 If you don't know how to fold a paper airplane, find the book *Instant Paper Airplanes*

by E. Richard Churchill. You could also find *Paper Airplane Book* by Seymour Simon or *Paper Airplanes to Make and Fly* by Jim Razzi. These books have pictures and instructions to show you how to fold a paper airplane.

RESOURCES

Instant Paper Airplanes by E. Richard Churchill (New York: Sterling Publishing, 1990).

Paper Airplane Book by Seymour Simon (New York: Viking Children's Books, 1971).

Paper Airplanes to Make and Fly by Jim Razzi (New York: Scholastic, 1990).

Today is Weather Forecaster's Day. On this day people honor John Jeffries, America's first weather forecaster. He was born on this date in 1744. Jeffries was a doctor who lived in Boston. He kept careful track of the weather and wrote about what happened each day.

 Write about how weather affects you every day, no matter where you live.

 Without watching or listening to weather reports for tomorrow, predict the weather. Tell why you feel the weather will be that way tomorrow. Write down your prediction and see if it comes true.

 Explore how people use animals to predict the weather. (See the February 2 entry for a story about how people use groundhogs to predict the end of winter). Look at two books in the *What Will the Weather Be?* series. Read *No. 1: A Folk Weather Calendar* or *No. 2: Animal Signs*. Share what you learn with your classmates.

Did you know that clouds are made up of billions of water drops? Research the different types of clouds. *Examples*: *cumulonimbus*, *nimbostratus*, and *cumulus*. People who study the weather look at these cloud types and the speed the wind pushes them. They use their findings to predict the weather.

Make a poster showing how clouds are different. Use cotton balls for a three-dimensional look. Display your poster in a weather information center in your classroom.

RESOURCES

What Will the Weather Be?: No. 1: A Folk Weather Calendar and *No. 2: Animal Signs*, both by Hubert J. Davis (Blacksburg, Virginia: Pocahontas Press).

Play balloon baseball indoors. You'll need a blown-up balloon and some paper. Roll up the paper to make a bat. Find an indoor spot to play your game, such as the gym or an empty room. Let everyone have a turn being the pitcher and hitting the balloon ball. It's not as easy as it sounds!

Share a baseball card collection or special autograph collection with your classmates. Tell why you started your collection. If you don't have a collection, tell the class about one you'd like to start.

RESOURCE

Babe Ruth, Home Run Hero by Keith Brandt (Mahwah, New Jersey: Troll Associates, 1985).

American baseball player George Herman "Babe" Ruth was born on this day in 1895 in Baltimore, Maryland. He began playing professional baseball when he was 19 years old. For 15 years, Ruth played baseball for the New York Yankees and broke many baseball records. When he first started playing baseball, older players called him "Babe" because he was so young.

Are you too little or too young to do something you'd like to do? Write about one thing you'd do if you were bigger or older.

Babe Ruth was left-handed and hit 714 home runs. He played for 22 major league seasons and was in 10 World Series. His nickname was "The Sultan of Swat." Find three more facts about Babe Ruth in an encyclopedia or in the book *Babe Ruth, Home Run Hero* by Keith Brandt.

Today is the birthday of Laura Ingalls Wilder. She was born in 1867 in Pepin, Wisconsin. Wilder and her family were pioneers; they were one of the first families to explore and settle the American Midwest. Laura and her sisters went to school in a one-room schoolhouse. They helped their mother churn butter and make soap and candles. When she was 65 years old, Wilder wrote about growing up as a pioneer in the "Little House" books.

Write a short story about something you did when you were younger.

Little House in the Big Woods is the first book in Laura Ingalls Wilder's series. In that book, she describes frontier life in Wisconsin. Find out the titles of the other books Wilder wrote. If you haven't read any of her books, begin *Little House in the Big Woods* today in honor of her birthday.

Charles Dickens, another famous author, was born on this day in Portsmouth, England, in 1812. One of his famous stories is *Great Expectations*. It's about a boy named Pip who hopes to be a rich gentleman someday. Tell your class about something you hope to be someday.

 Charles Dickens' father was sent to prison because he could not pay his bills. Because his family needed money, Dickens began to work in London when he was only 12 years old. Today, laws say that young people can't be forced to work at that age anymore. Make a list of the jobs you'd do if you had to get a job today.

RESOURCE

Little House in the Big Woods by Laura Ingalls Wilder (New York: HarperCollins Children's Books, 1971).

february 8

Today marks the birthday of author Jules Verne. He was born in Nantes, France, in 1828. Verne wrote more than 50 adventure novels. In his novels, he wrote about fancy gadgets and incredible machines. In his novel *20,000 Leagues Under the Sea*, Verne writes about a submarine named the *Nautilus*. The first submarine wasn't even invented at the time Verne wrote his book.

Verne wrote about many other machines before they were invented. He was one of the first authors to write about air conditioning, remote control units, oxygen tanks, TV, and blimps.

 Write about something that you think should be invented.

 Geography was Jules Verne's favorite subject at school. In his novels, he described many different parts of the world. In 1873, Verne wrote a story called *Around the World in Eighty Days*. In it, his characters travel to many cities and have many adventures. Make a list of your favorite places. Create a story title about your favorite place.

 With your class, use a world map to trace an imaginary trip around the world. How long would the trip would take? Ask your classmates which countries they'd like to include in the trip. What supplies would your class need for the around-the-world trip?

 Jules Verne kept a writer's notebook. In it he jotted down every idea or bit of information that he thought would be useful in his stories. Think about the information you could keep in a writer's notebook. *Examples*: Write down a funny saying you heard. Cut out a funny comic strip and paste it to one of the pages.

february 9

On this day in 1964, Arthur Robert Ashe, Jr., became the first African-American on the U.S. Davis Cup tennis team. Four years later he became the U.S. singles champion. In 1979, Ashe had heart surgery, which ended his tournament career, but the next year he became the nonplaying captain of the U.S. Davis Cup team. In April 1992, Ashe announced he had AIDS. He had contracted the disease in a blood transfusion during heart surgery. He died on February 6, 1993.

 Write a few sentences on what you like or dislike about the sport of tennis. Is this a sport you'd like to play? Why or why not?

To learn more about Arthur Ashe, read *The Tennis Book* by Larry Lorimer. You can also find information about Ashe in the book *Famous Tennis Players* by Trent Frayne.

 The most prestigious tennis tournaments include Wimbledon, held in Great Britain; Forest Hills, held in the United States; and the singles championships of France and Australia. For many nations, the most coveted prize is the Davis Cup, which is played each year on tennis courts around the world.

Draw a tennis trophy or a trophy a winner might receive in some other sport or game.

 Play pantomime tennis. With a partner, pretend that you have tennis rackets, a net, and a ball. Be silly. Pretend to hit the tennis ball through your legs or with your eyes closed.

··

R E S O U R C E S

The Tennis Book by Larry Lorimer (New York: Random House, 1980).

Famous Tennis Players by Trent Frayne (New York: Dodd, Mead, 1977).

··

In 1933, the first singing telegram was delivered. A telegram is a note sent by telegraph, one of the systems used to send messages over long distances. The message is sent in code from one station to another. Then a messenger delivers the message to the person it's for. Most of the time, messengers deliver the telegram in envelopes. On this day in 1933, however, the messenger sang the message.

 Write down a message you'd like to sing to someone.

 People who send telegrams use *telegraphese* (pronounced tel-uh-graf-eez). That's the language or speech that leaves out all but the necessary words. *Example:* "Come over to my house tomorrow for dinner" could be rewritten as "My house tomorrow dinner." Write down your own message. Now see how few words you can use while still saying what you need to say.

 Deliver a singing telegram to celebrate Valentine's Day. (You have four days to practice.) With some friends, think of a simple melody ("Row, Row, Row Your Boat" or "Twinkle, Twinkle Little Star" are good choices). Now think of your own words to go along with the song. Decide who in your school would deserve a special message. *Examples:* the principal, your teacher, the school secretary, custodian, or special bus driver. Practice your song and send this special Valentine.

 E. L. Konigsberg was born on this day in 1930. Read *From the Mixed-Up Files of Mrs. Basil E. Frankweiler* by Konigsberg. It's an adventure that takes place in the Metropolitan Museum of Art in New York City.

··

R E S O U R C E

From the Mixed-Up Files of Mrs. Basil E. Frankweiler by E. L. Konigsberg (New York: Macmillan Children's Book Group, 1972).

··

On this day in 1802, Lydia Maria Frances Child was born in Medford, Massachusetts. In 1826, she began publishing *Juvenile Miscellany*, the first magazine for children in the United States. Child also wrote articles about her views against slavery. Because of her opinions, people who supported slavery avoided her. Child's magazine sales suffered and she was forced to discontinue *Juvenile Miscellany*.

 Write about your favorite magazine. Why is it your favorite?

 Thomas Alva Edison was born on this day in 1847. He was responsible for more than 1,200 different inventions. Edison often could not get to sleep at night. He invented the electric light so that he could read better after dark.

While looking for the right materials to burn in the light bulb, Edison tried 6,000 different materials. He finally found one that worked the way he wanted. To find out more about Edison, read *Edison's Electric Light: Biography of an Invention* by Robert Friedel.

 Many people thought that Thomas Edison accidentally discovered his inventions. But he worked long and hard to make his ideas a reality. In 1931, he said, "There is no substitute for hard work." What do you think Edison meant when he said this? Talk about Edison's quote with your class.

 On this day in 1990, Nelson Rolihlahla Mandela was released from prison. He had been in prison since 1963. That year, the South African government had imprisoned Mandela for fighting against apartheid. (Apartheid is the South African system of segregating the races.) You can find more information by looking up "Nelson Mandela" or the term "apartheid" in an encyclopedia.

∙∙∙

R E S O U R C E

Edison's Electric Light: Biography of an Invention by Robert Friedel (New Brunswick, New Jersey: Rutgers University Press, 1987).

∙∙∙

On this day in 1809, Abraham Lincoln was born in a log cabin in Kentucky. Lincoln worked as a lawyer and then was elected to the Illinois congress. In 1861, he was sworn in as the 16th president of the United States. Lincoln strove to be truthful and honest. Because of this, he was called "Honest Abe."

 Write about a time when it was hard for you to tell the truth.

 Use a penny to make a rubbing of Abraham Lincoln. Put a plain piece of paper over a penny with Lincoln's face on top. Using the side of a pencil lead, rub back and forth over the penny until the picture of Lincoln appears on your paper. Experiment with different colored pencils and colored paper.

 Learn more about Lincoln's life by reading *Lincoln: A Photobiography* by Russell Freedman. This book contains many photos of Lincoln and his family. Share the photographs with your classmates.

 Create a log cabin. You'll need a brown paper grocery bag, pencil, paper plate, scissors, glue or tape, and construction paper.

Cut the paper bag into 16 strips that are each 4" x 2 1/2". To make a log, place the pencil along the longer side of the paper. Roll the paper loosely around the pencil. Glue or tape the paper to make the log stay and pull it off of the pencil. Do this again for each log. You'll use the 16 logs to make the cabin's base.

On the paper plate, make a square using four logs. Overlap the logs at the corners and glue or tape them in place. Add four more logs onto your base and glue or tape them in place. Continue adding logs until you've used all 16 logs. To create the house's roof, take a piece of construction paper and fold it in half. Open the paper up a bit and place it on top of the logs.

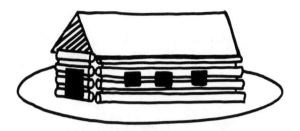

Draw windows, shutters, chimney, and a door on the brown bag or on construction paper. Cut out the drawings and glue or tape them onto the cabin.

....

RESOURCE

Lincoln: A Photobiography by Russell Freedman (New York: Ticknor and Fields, 1987).

....

february 13

In his lifetime, Johann Strauss, Jr., wrote almost 500 pieces of opera and dance music. People loved to whirl and glide across the dance floor as the orchestra played his waltzes. Dancers loved his music so much that they called this Austrian composer "The Waltz King." One of Strauss' most famous waltzes is *The Blue Danube*. It was first performed in public on this day in 1867.

 Write about your favorite kind of music. Does it make you feel like dancing?

 Johann Strauss was born in Vienna, Austria. He wrote *The Blue Danube* to honor one of the waterways in his country. If you were to write a song about a certain place, what place would you choose? *Examples:* the sidewalk in front of your house, the school playground, your room. Make a list of places you could write a song about.

 Listen to *The Blue Danube* or another waltz by Johann Strauss. As you hear the waltz music, listen to the one-two-three, one-two-three count. What did the music make you think about?

 Look through a book on how to dance. (*Waltz Made Easy* and *Dance! A Complete Guide to Social, Folk and Square Dancing* are two good ones.) Notice how the authors use footprints to show how dances are done.

Create your own dance instructions. You'll need six sheets of plain paper, a pen or marker, tape, and your shoes. Put one sheet of paper on the floor and place your left foot in the middle of it. Trace your shoe and label that sheet of paper "L" for Left. Trace two more sheets of paper using your left shoe. On the other three sheets of paper, trace your right foot and label those sheets "R" for Right.

Think of a dance move using six dance steps. Tape one sheet of paper to show where your left foot begins and another to show where your right foot begins. Tape another sheet of paper to show the next step. Keep going until all six dance steps are taped to the floor. Now number the dance steps from 1 to 6. Ask a classmate to follow your steps. Try someone else's dance steps.

RESOURCES

The Blue Danube in *Johann Strauss' Greatest Hits* recording (London Label, 1971).

Waltz Made Easy in the Ballroom Dance Series (New York: Revisionist Press, 1985).

Dance! A Complete Guide to Social, Folk and Square Dancing by J. T. Hall (Salem, New Hampshire: Ayer Company Publishers, 1980).

february 14

Happy Valentine's Day! Today is the most widely observed unofficial holiday in the world. People in the United States, England, France, and other nations celebrate this day. They give cards, flowers, and candy to people they like very much.

Write about someone you like.

Hold a paper-heart tearing contest. Have your classmates hold a piece of paper behind their backs. Now have everyone tear the paper into a heart shape—without looking at the paper. See who can create the shape that looks most like a heart.

On some construction paper, draw the largest shape of a heart that will fit on the paper. Inside the heart, write words you think about on this day. *Examples*: friendship, love, hearts, red. When you're finished, cut each word out into puzzle pieces. Mix up the pieces and give the puzzle to a classmate. Can your classmates put it back together?

On this day in 1838, inventor Margaret Knight was born. In 1871, she was granted a patent for the square-bottomed paper bag—but that wasn't her first patent. She also had received patents for other items including window frames, rotary engines, and numbering devices. She received up to 87 patents for her inventions.

Square-bottomed bags are used to hold many things. Write a description of the most creative way to use a paper bag.

february 15

Galileo Galilei, an Italian scientist and mathematician, was born on this day in 1564. He improved the telescope and was one of the first people to see the mountains on the moon. Galileo also discovered new stars and saw the rings of Saturn. He inspired other astronomers of the 1600s to explore new planets and new ideas. Galileo died in 1642.

Write a letter to Galileo telling him about space discoveries that have occurred since the 1600s.

My **V**ery **E**xcellent **M**om **J**ust **S**erved **U**s **N**ine **P**izzas. That sentence might not be true, but it's a way to help remember the names of the nine planets. (**M**ercury, **V**enus, **E**arth, **M**ars, **J**upiter, **S**aturn, **U**ranus, **N**eptune, and **P**luto.) In the first sentence, the first letter of each word stands for another word. Write your own sentence to help you remember the planet names.

Look up the words "astronomy" and "astronomer" in the dictionary or encyclopedia. What are their definitions? What kinds of things would you have to learn in order to be an astronomer?

Galileo taught mathematics at the University of Pisa. While in Pisa, Italy, he performed one of his famous experiments. He went to the top of the Leaning Tower of Pisa and dropped two balls of different weights off the balcony. To the surprise of most people, the balls hit the ground at the same time. The old idea, that heavy objects fell faster, was found to be incorrect.

Recreate Galileo's experiment. You'll need two objects. One object should be light. *Examples:* a piece of chalk, a pencil, a ruler. The other object should be heavier. *Examples:* a book, a full pencil case, a large eraser. Stand on top of a chair and hold one object in each hand. Drop the objects at the same time. Record what happens. Try the experiment with different objects. Were your results the same as Galileo's result?

february 16

Tutankhamen became the king of Egypt in 1348 B.C and died when he was only 18 years old. He was buried in a tomb filled with Egyptian treasures. On this date in 1922, British archaeologist Howard Carter broke through an inner door of King Tut's tomb. As he peered into the dark tomb, he saw golden beds, couches, and jewelry. The contents of King Tut's tomb became the most famous and valuable archaeological find in history. It was the most complete and untouched royal tomb ever to be examined.

 Pretend you're Howard Carter. Write a journal entry describing the thoughts you had as you opened the silent, still tomb of King Tut.

 Today is the birth date of Edgar Bergen, who was born in 1903. Bergen was an actor, ventriloquist, and radio entertainer. As a ventril-

oquist, he was the voice of the puppet Charlie McCarthy. (A ventriloquist can speak so that the sound seems to come from a different place. Good ventriloquists can speak clearly without moving their lips.)

Create your own puppet. You'll need washable markers and your hand. Make a loose fist. Use your thumb as your puppet's bottom lip. With the marker, draw a small bottom lip on the side of your thumb. Draw the top lip on your finger above the thumb. Now draw eyes just above the mouth. Move your thumb up and down to make your puppet talk. Try to keep your lips still as you make your puppet talk.

Also on this day in 1896, the first comic strip appeared in a newspaper. One panel of Richard F. Outcault's creation "The Yellow Kid" appeared in the *New York World Newspaper*. A year later, Rudolph Dirks was the first cartoonist to put several cartoon panels together to tell a story.

Using a comic strip from a newspaper, cut out all the words. Paste the comic strip on a blank sheet of paper. Make up new words and sentences for the characters and write them in the blank spaces. If you need more space, create bigger bubbles.

 Create your own cartoon character. Make some of its features extra big or extra small to create an interesting creature. Use your character to create your own comic strip or comic book.

february 17

Rene Theophile Laennec was born on this day in 1781. Laennec was a doctor who invented the stethoscope in 1817. A stethoscope is used to listen to the heart and other organs inside the body. At first, Laennec used paper tubes to make his stethoscope. Later, he used hollow wooden cylinders. Laennec used his stethoscope to listen to body sounds. He wrote detailed descriptions of what he heard. His writings were so detailed that other doctors used his descriptions to identify diseases.

 Write a paragraph about a familiar sound. *Examples:* your bike riding across gravel, your gerbils scratching in their cage, your baby sister waking up.

 Use a cardboard tube from the center of a paper towel roll as a stethoscope, or create a more complex stethoscope. You'll need a short piece of tubing (from a rubber hose) and a funnel. Attach the funnel to one end of the tubing. Put the funnel against someone's chest. Place the end of the tubing to your ear. Keep very quiet and listen. Sounds usually spread out in every direction. With a stethoscope, the sound energy is directed along the tubing to make it possible to hear quiet sounds.

Your brain weighs about 3 pounds. You have 206 bones in your body. What other facts can you find out about your body? Look up "human body" in an encyclopedia or other reference book for more information.

On this day in 1876 in Eastport, Maine, sardines were first canned. A sardine is a small ocean fish that is packed tightly into flat cans.

Play hide-and-seek with a few different rules. Ask one person to be "IT." That person hides and all the other players hunt for her. As players find the hidden person, they have to pack into the same hiding place—like sardines. When only one player is left looking for the "sardines," the game ends.

february 18

Clyde W. Tombaugh discovered the planet Pluto on this day in 1930. Pluto is the ninth planet in our solar system. It's 4.65 billion miles from Earth.

When Tombaugh discovered the planet, he was a young astronomer at the Lowell Observatory in Flagstaff, Arizona. An 11-year-old British girl read about the discovery. The girl's uncle, who was an astronomer, encouraged her to think of a name for the planet. She sent her idea to the observatory where Tombaugh worked. Tombaugh like the girl's suggestion and named his new discovery Pluto, after the Roman god who ruled over darkness.

 Write about the things you see when you look up at the sky.

 Scientists believe that there is another planet beyond Pluto. Write an imaginary description of this planet. Include its size (is it smaller or larger than Earth?) and its weather (is it a very hot or very cold planet?). Name your planet. Describe the type of creature that could live there.

 Create your own planetarium light show. You'll need a flashlight, paper, ruler, pencil, scissors, empty juice can, and a rubber band. To help make an accurate light show, refer to a book on star constellations such as *Point to the Stars* by Joseph Maron Joseph and Sarah Lee Lippincott.

With the ruler, draw a square whose sides are six inches long. Using a star book, draw a constellation pattern in the center of the square. Carefully punch out the stars with the tips of the scissors. Remove the top and bottom from the juice can. Place the complete star map over one end of the juice can. Use the rubber band to hold the map in place.

Make the room as dark as possible. Shine the flashlight at an angle in the inside of the can. Aim the star map at the ceiling.

 In June 1977, Tiger the cat wandered away from his owners. His owners had taken Tiger on vacation with them to Wausau, Wisconsin. On this date in 1978, Tiger arrived at home. Home was in Dubuque, Iowa, 250 miles south of Wausau, Wisconsin. It's also on the other side of the Mississippi River. Tiger had traveled eight months and crossed this river to get home. Draw some pictures of Tiger trying to get home. Show your ideas of how Tiger made the journey.

RESOURCE

Point to the Stars by Joseph Maron Joseph and Sarah Lee Lippincott (New York: McGraw-Hill, 1977).

february 19

On this day in 1968, the TV show "Mister Rogers Neighborhood" aired for the first time on PBS. Fred Rogers stars in this show for young kids. Every day, Mr. Rogers introduces people from his neighborhood to his audience. His trolley takes viewers to the Land of Make Believe. There, a whole cast of characters sing, solve problems, and laugh together.

 Create your own Land of Make Believe. Describe your imaginary place and how you could get there. Tell what you'd do and who lives there.

 Draw a map of your neighborhood. Include the streets near your home and any parks and stores. Show your map to your class. Point out all the special things in your neighborhood.

 Nicolaus Copernicus was born on this date in 1473. He believed that Earth rotated around the sun. At the time, other people thought the sun spun around Earth. In the 1400s, most people also thought that Earth was the center of the universe. Copernicus, however, felt that our planet was only one of several planets.

Pretend you're Copernicus. Convince your classmates that you're correct about how the solar system works. Remember that you're the only one who thinks this way. Everyone else thinks the sun and the stars go around Earth.

 Before the phonograph, no one had ever heard a machine "talk." On this day in 1878, Thomas Edison received the patent for his phonograph invention. Edison's invention led to the invention of the tape recorder.

The tape recorder led to today's compact disc players.

People use modern versions of the phonograph to listen to music, poetry, speeches, and books. Listen to a book on tape. *Example*: Many *Frog and Toad* stories can be heard on cassettes.

RESOURCE

Frog and Toad Are Friends (book and tape set) by Arnold Lobel (New York: HarperCollins Children's Books, 1985).

On this date in 1962, John Glenn became the first American astronaut to orbit Earth. He circled Earth three times in *Friendship 7*, a small space capsule. His journey took 4 hours and 55 minutes.

During the early 1960s, the National Aeronautics and Space Administration (NASA) sent up many test flights into space. But no one was sure what would happen when a human spent several hours traveling around our planet. After Glenn's successful flight, NASA sent astronauts into space for longer and longer periods of time.

 Write what you think it would feel like to blast off into space.

 Ansel Adams was born on this day in 1902. He photographed many scenes of the western United States. His black-and-white images capture the hugeness of the Grand Canyon and the smallest, most fragile flower. Ansel also loved to photograph huge natural formations in California's Yosemite National Park. Adams once said, "Not everybody trusts paintings, but people believe photographs."

To see some of his photographs, look through his book *Ansel Adams, Classic Images 1923-1974*. Think about things in nature you'd like to photograph.

 On this day in 1895, Frederick Douglass died in Washington, D.C. He was born a slave in about 1817. He eventually bought his freedom with the help of some British friends.

As a free man, Douglass wrote articles and spoke out against the slavery of black people. He published an antislavery newspaper that urged people to oppose slavery. By the end of his life, he had become involved in education, civil rights, and women's rights. To find out more about Douglass, read *Frederick Douglass Fights for Freedom* by Margaret Davidson.

 In 1880 on this date, the Metropolitan Museum of Art opened in New York City. In the years since it was started, the museum has obtained more than 3 million works of art. It's the largest art museum in the United States.

Create an art corner in your classroom. Ask your classmates to bring in their own drawings, sculptures, paintings, and other works of art. Set aside one corner of your classroom and display the artwork on tables.

RESOURCES

Ansel Adams, Classic Images 1923-1974 by Ansel Adams (Boston: Bulfinch Press, 1986).

Frederick Douglass Fights for Freedom by Margaret Davidson (New York: Scholastic, 1989).

february 21

The Washington Monument, which was built to honor George Washington, was dedicated on this day in 1885. The monument stands in Washington, D.C., and measures 555 feet, 5 1/8 inches high. Over 1 million people visit the monument each year.

 Write a paragraph about your favorite hero or heroine. What kind of statue would you build to honor that person?

 To learn more about the Washington Monument, read *Incredible Constructions and the People Who Built Them* by Mel Boring.

 E. H. Land demonstrated the first instant camera on this day in 1947. Land's camera took a photograph, developed it, and printed it.

Have fun with some photographs of your classmates. Ask everyone in your class to bring in their baby pictures. Mount each photograph on a bulletin board and include a number next to each one. Have a contest to see who can identify the most babies. Include your teacher's baby picture, too.

 February is National Heart Month. Walking is a healthy activity for your heart. Celebrate National Heart Month by going for a winter walk.

RESOURCE

Incredible Constructions and the People Who Built Them by Mel Boring (New York: Walker and Company, 1985).

february 22

On this day in 1892, poet Edna St. Vincent Millay was born in Rockland, Maine. She published her first poem when she was only 14 years old. As she grew older, she became more interested in writing poetry with social and political themes. In 1923, she became the first woman to win a Pulitzer Prize in poetry. She won the award for her book *The Ballad of the Harp-Weaver*.

 Would you want to be a poet? Why or why not?

 George Washington, the first president of the United States, was born on this date in 1732.

Using a one dollar bill (which has a picture of George Washington on it), find these six things:

- The Roman numerals for 1776 (they look like this: MDCCLXXVI)
- A single eye in a triangle
- The word "tender"
- 13 arrows
- 13 stars
- A key (Hint: Look on the front of the bill, over the word ONE. The key is part of the Treasury Department seal.)

 How many words can you make from the name GEORGE WASHINGTON?

 Did you know that there are 119 grooves around the edge of a quarter? Quarters also have a picture of George Washington on them. Trace a quarter. Draw a tiny picture inside the shape of the quarter. It can be a picture of anyone (or anything) you want.

february 23

Aviator Ruth Rowland Nichols was born on this day in 1901. Nichols began flying when she was 21 years old. Five years later, she earned her pilot's license. Soon after, she began to break flying records. In 1930, she was the first female pilot to fly from Los Angeles to New York. She held the women's altitude record, the women's speed record, and the women's world distance record. In 1932, she became the first woman to work as a commercial passenger airline pilot.

 Would you want to fly a plane? Why or why not?

 On this date in 1991, U.S. soldiers began a land attack on Iraqi troops during the Gulf War. Six months earlier, Iraq's president, Saddam Hussein, had invaded Kuwait, a small country in the Middle East. To free Kuwait from Iraq, President George Bush ordered U.S. troops to launch a land attack. General H. Norman Schwarzkopf was the commander of Desert Storm, the code name for the armed force's ground attack. Four days later, on February 27, the war ended. The U.S. soldiers had liberated Kuwait.

Look at a map of the Middle East and identify the countries located there. Why do you think the area is important to the rest of the world?

Samuel Pepys (pronounced Peeps) was born in Cambridge, England, on this date in 1633. He was the author of one of the most famous diaries in the world. Pepys wrote about the gossip and politics of his time. But he wrote the diary using his own secret code. No one figured out what his code was until 1825.

To create a simple code of your own, write out the alphabet. Underneath it, write the alphabet again, backwards. Put the A under the Z. Put the B under the Y. Continue writing out the full alphabet like this:

A B C D E F G H I J K L M N O P Q R S T U V W X Y Z
Z Y X W V U T S R Q P O N M L K J I H G F E D C B A

Write out a sentence using this code. Instead of using the letter that spells the word correctly, use the letter below it. *Example*: SCHOOL would be coded to HXSLLO. You can create other codes. Write out the alphabet and assign numbers or shapes to the letters. When you write your message, it'll look like a list of numbers or silly designs.

 Play Mixabet. Divide into teams of two. acEh aemt eirstw a ceeennst. (Each team writes a sentence.) enhT eht aemst aceeghnx ceeennsst. (Then the teams exchange sentences.) The team that decodes the sentence first wins.

Here's how to mix up a sentence the Mixabet way: Put the letters of each word in alphabetical order.

february 24

James Otis gave a speech on this day in 1761. Otis was an American political leader during the Revolutionary War. In his speech, he protested against the British who felt it was all right to enter a person's home without permission. He didn't like how British soldiers barged into a colonist's home and took things whenever they felt like it. He said that the owner's rights should be respected. In his speech, he declared that people's homes are their castles.

Write about your home.

 Wilhelm Carl Grimm was a German author. He was interested in the study of myths and where they came from. He was born on this day in 1786. He and his brother Jacob wrote *Grimm's Fairy Tales*.

The Brothers Grimm didn't make up these fairy tales—many of them had been around for along time. They simply wrote them down for people to enjoy. "Rapunzel," "Hansel and Gretel," and "Rumpelstiltskin" were some of the stories they retold. In 1983, *The New York Times* reported that another tale by Wilhelm Grimm had been found. The story was written in a letter that Grimm wrote to a little girl. If you'd like to read the newest Brothers Grimm story, you can find it in the book *Dear Mili*, illustrated by Maurice Sendak.

 Take a trip to a library or your school media center. Find more stories by the Brothers Grimm. Draw a picture to illustrate one of the stories.

 The Winter Olympics of 1980 was held at Lake Placid, New York. On this date, the U.S. hockey team won a gold medal. They defeated the talented Russian hockey team. After the U.S. victory, the team had a great celebration. Tell about a time you celebrated something special.

···

RESOURCES

Dear Mili by Wilhelm Grimm, illustrated by Maurice Sendak (New York: Farrar, Straus & Giroux, 1988).

Grimm's Fairy Tales by Jacob Grimm and Wilhelm Grimm (Teaneck, New Jersey: Sharon Publications, 1981).

···

Herbert Marx was born on this day in 1901. When he was young, he was better known as Zeppo. Zeppo had four brothers and each of them had nicknames, too. His brothers were Chico, Harpo, Groucho, and Gummo. Together the family was known as the Marx Brothers. In the early 1900s, the Marx Brothers sang, danced, and told jokes in shows around the country. Although Zeppo and his brother Gummo left the family act, the other brothers continued performing in shows and movies.

 Write about your favorite TV comedian. Tell why that person makes you laugh.

 The Marx Brothers performed in vaudeville shows. In these shows, people performed many different acts. In one vaudeville show you might be entertained by a comedian, a singer, a magician, and an actor with a trained dog. Actors and actresses put on vaudeville shows in small theaters in the country and in large halls in the cities. By the 1930s, many successful performers, like the Marx Brothers, left the vaudeville shows to appear in movies and on the radio.

Tell your class about the type of act you'd perform for a vaudeville show. *Examples:* Would you play the piano? Tell jokes? Sing your favorite song? Ask your classmates what they'd do.

 On February 25, 1873, in Naples, Italy, Enrico Caruso was born. He became the world's most famous opera singer. Even today, many people consider him the greatest operatic tenor who ever lived. In an opera, the actors and actresses tell a story by singing their lines. For the next few minutes, don't say anything. Just sing it.

Artist Pierre Auguste Renoir (pronounced Wren-wah) was born on this day in 1841 in Limoges, France. As Renoir grew older, severe arthritis disabled him. He became unable to hold a paintbrush. But Renoir loved to paint so he figured out a way to use a brush and continue his work. He strapped a brush to his hand and painted that way. Try to paint a picture the way Renoir did. Use a piece of string or some tape to attach a paintbrush or marker to your hand. Now try to draw using that paintbrush or marker. Be patient. This type of drawing takes practice.

february 26

William Frederick "Buffalo Bill" Cody was an American pioneer. He was also a buffalo hunter, a U.S. Army scout, and the star of his Wild West Show. People heard many tall tales about Cody. They heard amazing stories of how he tamed wild animals and fought outlaws. Buffalo Bill was born on this date in Scott County, Iowa, in 1846.

 Stretch the truth a bit. Write a tall tale about yourself.

 When he was 14 years old, Buffalo Bill became a Pony Express rider. After that, he hunted buffalo and organized his own traveling show. Ned Buntline made Cody famous by writing dime novels about him. Buntline's stories were not always totally true, but they sold well. Dime novels often had exciting scenes drawn on the cover so more people would buy them. If the words "Buffalo Bill" appeared on the cover, the book was sure to be a success.

Design your own dime-novel cover for a Buffalo Bill adventure. Include an exciting western scene. Put the words "Buffalo Bill" on your cover.

 Buffalo Bill's Wild West Show was a fancy rodeo that featured people showing off their riding and shooting skills. One of the show's stars was Annie Oakley.

Oakley was a sharpshooter who could hit a dime in the air with shots from her gun or rifle. In 1885, when she was 25, she joined the Wild West. One of her favorite tricks was asking someone to throw a playing card into the air. She would shoot it full of holes before it landed on the ground. Find out more about Annie Oakley by looking up her name in an encyclopedia.

 With your class, make a list of all the words you think of when you hear stories about the Old West.

february 27

Henry Wadsworth Longfellow was born on this day in 1807 in Portland, Maine. Longfellow was an American poet who wrote long storytelling poems. In the late 1800s, families would gather by the fireside and read Longfellow's poems aloud. His poems included "Paul Revere's Ride," "The Courtship of Miles Standish," and "The Village Blacksmith."

 Write a story that you think would make a good poem. Try writing a few lines of the poem.

 Find one of Henry Wadsworth Longfellow's poems. You might look in the book *The Poetical Works of Longfellow*. Ask someone to read one of the poems aloud.

Illustrate one of Longfellow's poems. Draw Paul Revere, a blacksmith, or Hiawatha.

February is Canned Food Month, a month for companies to promote the usefulness, nutrition, and convenience of canned foods. Write about your favorite canned food. Describe the way it smells, tastes, and looks when it's on your plate ready to be eaten.

RESOURCE

The Poetical Works of Longfellow (Boston: Houghton Mifflin, 1975).

february 28

On this day in 1797, U.S. teacher and educator Mary Lyon was born in Buckland, Massachusetts. In 1837, she founded the Mt. Holyoke Female Seminary, the first women's college in the United States. A woman could attend the school and learn about history, science, and math. These were subjects that women back then weren't supposed to study.

Write about your favorite school subject.

Sir John Tenniel was born on this date in 1820. Tenniel was an English caricaturist and illustrator. A caricature is a drawing of a person where parts of the body are exaggerated for a comic effect. Tenniel is famous for his illustrations for Lewis Carroll's *Alice's Adventures in Wonderland* and *Through the Looking Glass*.

If a caricaturist drew a caricature of you, what part of your face or body would the artist exaggerate? Would the caricature exaggerate your beautiful hair? Or your nice hands? Or your pretty smile?

Draw a caricature of one of your classmates. Ask your friend to sit in a chair facing you. Study that person's face and pick out a nice feature that person has. Now draw that person and make that one feature stand out.

Today is the birthday of Tommy Tune. He was born in Wichita, Texas, in 1939. Tune is an actor, singer, and dancer who has performed in many plays. He is also a choreographer and musical theater director. If you'd like more information about Tommy Tune, write to him at:

Tommy Tune
International Creative Management
8899 Beverly Boulevard
Los Angeles, CA 90048

february 29

Today is Save the Rhino Day. Every four years, people bring attention to the efforts made to protect these pachyderms. Rhinoceros are massive, horned and hoofed, herbivorous mammals native to Africa and Asia. Depending on the species, they have either one or two horns on the snout. They have thick skins and poor eyesight. Rhinos are on the verge of extinction because hunters kill them for their horns, which some people believe have magical powers.

Why is it important to protect the rhinoceros from extinction? Write down your opinion on this issue.

To learn more about the Save the Rhino Day, send a letter to:

Really Rhinos!
P.O. Box 1285
Tucson, AZ 85702-1285

The rhinoceros is one of the heaviest of all land animals. A large male may weigh up to 3 1/2 tons (that's 7,000 pounds). A rhino's horn could reach a length of three feet. Use an encyclopedia to find out three more facts about rhinos.

Since 45 B.C., people have been adding an extra day to their calendars. In that year, the Roman emperor Julius Caesar decided exactly how many days and hours would make up one year. He said one year would be 365 days and 6 hours long. In fact, Earth doesn't take quite that long to revolve around the sun. Every four years, we add an extra day to the calendar to use up those extra minutes.

If this year is a leap year, celebrate today in some special way. Tell your class how you plan to celebrate this extra day.

March 1

In 1912 on this day, Captain Albert Berry of the U.S. Army made the first parachute jump from an airplane. But people had been thinking about and testing parachutes for a long time before that. In the early 1500s, Italian artist and inventor Leonardo da Vinci had drawn his ideas for a parachute. That was long before airplanes were built. In 1785, a dog became the first parachute jumper. His master harnessed him to a parachute and dropped him from a hot-air balloon. The dog landed safely, but quickly ran away.

Describe what you think it would be like to parachute from an airplane.

Create your own miniparachute. You'll need a handkerchief or a similar-sized piece of cloth, four pieces of string, and a small "jumper" (a rubber eraser, small pencil sharpener, or pencil.) Tie each string to a corner of the cloth. Now tie the four strings around the small object. Toss your parachute into the air and watch it return.

Today is National Pig Day. The highest price ever paid for a pig was $56,000. The heaviest pig ever recorded was a hog named Big Bill. He weighed 2,552 pounds. The height to Big Bill's shoulder was five feet. He was nine feet long. Pigs are considered the most intelligent domestic animal. Did you know that a pig stops eating when it's full? Did you also know that humans and pigs are the only mammals that can get a sunburn? Look in an encyclopedia or other reference book for more information about pigs.

On this date in 1872, President Ulysses S. Grant signed a bill to establish Yellowstone National Park. Yellowstone is located in parts of Wyoming, Idaho, and Montana. It covers more than 2 million acres of land and is the world's largest wildlife preserve. But Yellowstone has more than just animals. There are more geysers in Yellowstone National Park than anywhere else in the world.

A geyser is a hot spring that erupts and shoots steam and hot water. One of Yellowstone's most famous geysers is called "Old Faithful" because it erupts every 65 minutes. Imagine a geyser suddenly spouting up in your backyard. Draw a picture of the geyser and name it.

March 2

Theodore Seuss Geisel was born in Springfield, Massachusetts, on this date in 1904. He was better known as Dr. Seuss. During his writing career,

Dr. Seuss sold more than 100 million copies of his books. He wrote more than 80 different titles. You may be familiar with some of his books: *The Cat in the Hat*, *And to Think That I Saw It on Mulberry Street*, and *Green Eggs and Ham*. Dr. Seuss died on September 24, 1991.

 Write about what you'd do if someone made you green eggs and ham for breakfast.

 Sneetches, grinches, wockets, gacks, and ooblecks are just some of Dr. Seuss' characters. Create your own unusual character. Close your eyes and draw a shape on a piece of paper. Open your eyes and finish the drawing any way you want. Make up an unusual name for your character.

 Hold a Dr. Seuss Trivia Contest. Gather as many Seuss books as you can and divide your class into teams. Have each team look through the books and write up ten questions about the people, places, and things in them. *Example*: Little Cindy Lou Who is a character from which book? Answer: *The Grinch Who Stole Christmas*. After you've written the questions, have the teams quiz each other.

 Talk with your classmates about your favorite Dr. Seuss books. Ask your teachers or other adults about the Dr. Seuss books they remember. They might have some special memories about one of the books. If they aren't familiar with Dr. Seuss' books, share your favorite.

March 3

On March 3, 1847, Alexander Graham Bell was born in Edinburgh, Scotland. He became a scientist and educator in the United States. Bell worked with his father to develop ways to help teach people who are hearing impaired.

In his spare time, Bell worked on his inventions. He wanted to invent a telegraph that could send two messages at the same time. When he discovered that he could send electric speech, he changed his mind and decided to invent a machine that could carry human speech instead. In 1876, Bell patented the first telephone.

 Write about a time when you changed your mind.

 "THE PHONE'S FOR YOU!" Is that the way you get someone to come to the phone? Although that might work, try a nicer way next time. What are your rules for answering the telephone courteously? If you don't have any guidelines, list some possibilities. *Examples:* If the phone call isn't for you, place your hand over the receiver before calling the other person's name. When you're through talking on the phone, gently hang up the receiver.

 Investigate Elisha Gray. He claimed that he invented the speaker phone first. The U.S. Supreme Court decided that Bell patented the invention first. What other information can you find about Gray?

 Have you ever noticed that there are letters—not just numbers— on a phone's key pad? Above each number are the letters of the alphabet. The number and letter combinations are:

2 A-B-C; 3 D-E-F; 4 G-H-I; 5 J-K-L; 6 M-N-O; 7 P-R-S; 8 T-U-V; 9 W-X-Y

Write out your phone number and substitute the numbers for letters. Does your phone number create a word? (If it doesn't, try some of the other possible letters. Remember, each number has three letters.)

Did you notice that there are two letters missing from the number and letter combinations? Which two?

March 4

On this date in 1947, Richard and Betty James received a patent for an unusual toy. The toy was made of thin, coiled wire and could "walk" down stairs end over end. It was called a Slinky. Richard had invented the toy in 1943. Betty thought it would be a great toy and tried to get people interested in buying it. When she asked a major department store to display their invention, all 400 Slinkies sold out in 90 minutes.

 Write about your favorite toy. Where have you seen it advertised?

 Have you ever heard of President David Rice Atchison? He was president of the United States for 24 hours. In 1849, March 4—the official inauguration day at the time—fell on a Sunday. Zachary Taylor, the elected president, refused to take his oath of office on a Sunday. Atchison was a senator from Missouri and president *pro tem* of the Senate. According to the U.S. Constitution, the president *pro tem* was next in line to become president. Atchison automatically held the office of president until Taylor took the oath on March 5.

Some reference books say Atchison slept most of the day. Many books don't even include his name. Look through some reference materials to see what information you can find on this president for a day.

 On this day in 1976, John Pezzin set a record. He bowled 33 strikes in a row. A strike in bowling means that you knock all the pins down the first time you hit them with the bowling ball.

Make your own bowling game. Collect empty plastic containers and use them as the pins. Use a tennis ball to knock them down. Roll the tennis ball, don't throw it. How many strikes can you bowl in a row?

 On this day in 1873 the first illustrated daily newspaper was published in New York City. It was called the *Daily Graphic*. Look through your local newspapers and find a graph, chart, or other illustration. Does that illustration help you understand the story? How?

March 5

On this day in 1512, Gerardus Mercator was born in Rupelmonde, Flanders. Mercator worked as a cartographer (mapmaker) for the Emperor Charles V. He popularized the name "atlas" for a bound collection of maps. At the beginning of his map collection, Mercator put an illustration of the Greek god Atlas supporting a globe.

 Pretend that someone has hired you to make a map of your neighborhood. Write about how you'd explore your neighborhood to create an accurate map. What would you include in your map?

Create a simple map to help new students find their way around your school. Include your classrooms, restrooms, and the school office. Your map could also include the cafeteria and gym.

 Take a good look at a world map. On the map, mapmakers draw the lines of latitude from left to right. They draw the lines of longitude from top to bottom. People use these lines to find certain points on the Earth's surface. Find where you live on the map. What latitude and longitude are you near?

 Crispus Attucks was the first person killed in the Boston Massacre on this date in 1770. He became the first casualty of the American Revolutionary War. Read the book *Days of Slavery: A History of Black People in America 1619-1863* by Stuart Kallen to find out more about Crispus Attucks and the Revolutionary War.

RESOURCE

Days of Slavery: A History of Black People in America 1619-1863 by Stuart Kallen (Minneapolis: Abdo and Daughters, 1990).

Sarah Caldwell is an American opera director and conductor. She was born on this day in 1924 in Maryville, Missouri. In 1957, she helped to found the Opera Company of Boston. Under her direction, the company became noted for its new and modern productions. In 1976, she became the first woman to conduct the Metropolitan Opera.

 Would you like to see an opera—where the actors and actresses sing their lines instead of saying them? Why or why not?

 Conductors guide musicians and singers through the musical notes. They most often lead orchestras and choirs. It's their job to make sure all the instruments and voices play or sing together correctly. To help them keep time to the music, many conductors hold onto small, slender rods called *batons*.

Listen to some music and pretend you're a conductor. Use a pencil as your baton.

 On this day in 1475, Michelangelo di Lodovico Buonarroti Simoni was born. Michelangelo was an Italian sculptor, painter, architect, and poet. He created many famous works, including his paintings in the Sistine Chapel and his marble statues of Moses and David. He died on February 18, 1564, at the age of 89.

Write about the kind of work you'd like to do when you're older. Would you like to sculpt, paint, design buildings, and write poetry as Michelangelo did?

 In 1508, Michelangelo began to paint the walls and ceiling of the Sistine Chapel in Rome, Italy. He built platforms that rose high above the chapel's floor. He lay on his back on the platforms and painted the ceiling. For four years he worked on the ceiling and walls.

Try to paint while lying on your back as Michelangelo did. Tape a piece of paper to the underside of your chair or desk. Take a marker and lie flat on your back under the paper. Create your own masterpiece.

In Sweden, people celebrate Vasaloppet today. In 1520, a Swedish nobleman named Gustav asked the men in the town of Mora to drive out the Danish king. No one volunteered. The Danish soldiers found out about Gustav's plan so he headed for Norway to escape the soldiers. When the townspeople changed their minds, they sent a group of skiers to find Gustav. Together, Gustav and the townsmen drove the Danes out of Sweden.

The people elected this brave man King Gustav I Vasa. On this day in his honor, thousands of people ski the route of Gustav's journey from Salen, Sweden, back to Mora.

 Pretend you're skiing down a mountain of snow on a crisp sunny day. Write about the sights, sounds, and smells you'd experience.

 Sweden is an independent nation located on the eastern half of the Scandinavian peninsula. Its neighbors are Norway to the west and Finland to the northeast. Denmark lies across the Kattegat, which is part of the North Sea. Sweden is the most heavily populated Scandinavian country and is one of the most prosperous countries in the world. To learn more about Sweden, read *Sweden in Pictures* by the Lerner Publications Department of Geography Staff.

 Today is Burbank Day. It may also be Bird Day or Arbor Day because these holidays are sometimes combined. This day marks the birthday of Luther Burbank who was born in Lancaster, Massachusetts, in 1849. Luther Burbank was an American naturalist and plant breeder. He was responsible for discovering 600 different plant varieties. He died on April 11, 1926. To celebrate Burbank Day, draw a colorful flower or a leafy green tree.

 Use an avocado pit to grow a plant. You'll need an avocado pit, three toothpicks, and a jar of water. Peel off the pit's brown covering. Stick three toothpicks halfway into the top of the pit and suspend it over the top of the jar. Carefully fill the jar with water until the water covers the bottom part of the pit. Add more water as it evaporates. The pit will send out roots, a stem, and leaves. When these appear, transplant the pit into a pot of dirt.

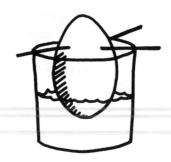

....

R E S O U R C E

Sweden in Pictures by the Lerner Publications Department of Geography Staff (Minneapolis: Lerner Publications, 1990).

....

March 8

Since 1910, people have celebrated International Working Women's Day on this date. Women attending a special conference in Helsinki, Finland, established this day. People in China and the former Soviet Union enjoy a national holiday. They give flowers and gifts to working women.

 Write about a working woman you know. Include a list of all the jobs she does in one day.

 Celebrate International Working Women's Day by reading a book about a famous woman. Ask your school librarian to help you find a good one.

 Joseph Lee was born on this day in 1865. He was one of the first people to develop playgrounds for children.

Write about your favorite place to play.

 What is your favorite piece of playground equipment? Do you like slides, swings, tunnels, see-saws, or jungle gyms? Take a survey of your class members and find out their favorite pieces of playground equipment.

Robert James "Bobby" Fischer was born on this date in 1943 in Chicago, Illinois. In 1972 in Reykjavik, Iceland, he played chess against a Russian-born French citizen named Boris Spassky. Fischer won the match, but three years later he refused to defend his world title. In 1992, Fischer claimed to be the World Champion of chess even though he had spent 20 years away from the international chess rounds. Fischer and his old rival Spassky played a rematch in Sveti Stefan, Yugoslavia, in 1992. Fischer won.

 Do you have an old rival? If you do, write about how you could make up with that person. If you don't, write about an old friend.

 Chess is a board game for two players. It is considered a "pure" game because no luck or dice are involved. The object of the game is to trap, or checkmate, the opponent's king. The game of chess originated in India in the sixth century. Write about your favorite game. Who taught you how to play it?

 Yuri Alexseyevich Gagarin was born on this day in 1934. On April 12, 1961, Gagarin traveled 187 miles above Earth's surface; his flight lasted 108 minutes. Gagarin was a Soviet cosmonaut and the first man to travel in space.

Find the book *Famous First Facts* by Joseph Nathan Kane. It may be located in the reference section of the library. Use the book to find other "firsts."

 According to *Famous First Facts*, the patent for the first pair of artificial teeth was granted on this day in 1822. It was given to Charles M. Graham of New York City. Also on this date, Robert Arthur and R. Covington Mackall received the first degrees from the Baltimore College of Dental Surgery.

To help you remember to brush your teeth after each meal, chart how many times you brush your teeth. Across a sheet of paper, write down the days of the week. Underneath each day, write an "X" for each time you brush your teeth. At the end of the week, look back at how many "X"s you have. Do you need to brush your teeth more often?

······································

R E S O U R C E

Famous First Facts (Fourth Edition) by Joseph Nathan Kane (Bronx, New York: H. W. Wilson Company, 1981).

······································

Today is Harriet Tubman Day. Harriet Tubman was an American abolitionist who led people to freedom through the Underground Railroad. Tubman was born into slavery in 1820. She died on this date in 1913 at the age of 93.

 Write a letter to Harriet Tubman thanking her for helping people escape to freedom.

 In the 1800s, people in the south who did not like slavery set up a secret roadway known as the Underground Railroad. These people helped slaves escape from their hard life to freedom in the north. They hid people in their basements and barns and gave them clothes and food. These hiding places were known as "stations." The runaway slaves were called "passengers." After Harriet Tubman escaped from slavery, she acted as a guide and led hundreds of slaves to freedom. She traveled at night and depended on the Underground Railroad to help her reach safety. There was a $40,000 bounty for her capture, but she was never caught. Write about what it means to live in a free country.

 On this date in 1974, citizens of the Philippine Islands were surprised to see a Japanese soldier come out of the jungle. The man was still wearing a World War II uniform. It seems no one had told him that World War II had ended 30 years before. The soldier had never left his post because, he said, "I had not received the order." Talk with your classmates about how long you wait before giving up on something. Do you give up easier if the assignment or job is harder? What could you do to encourage yourself to try harder?

 The first telephone call was made on this day in 1878. Alexander Graham Bell called his assistant, Thomas Watson. Thomas Watson was in the next room. Bell said, "Mr. Watson, come here, I want you."

Play a telephone game. The first person in the group whispers a short phrase or story to the second person. The second person whispers the story to the third person and so on. The last person tells the story out loud. Did the story change at all?

zra Jack Keats was born on this date in 1916. He lived in a poor neighborhood in Brooklyn, New York. When he was young, Keats found a library not far from his home. He spent many hours there studying the art books. When he returned to that same library years later, he found many of his own children's books on the shelves. *The Snowy Day* was the first book he wrote and illustrated. In 1963, it won

a Caldecott Medal, a prize awarded to the best American picture book.

 Write about your favorite part of the library.

 A legendary blizzard hit the Northeastern part of the United States on this date in 1888. The severe cold, strong winds, and heavy snowfall ended three days later. The blizzard killed 400 people.

In late winter and early spring, many parts of the country experience drastic changes in the weather. At that time, a warm, moist wind sometimes blows from the Pacific Ocean. As the wind crosses the Rocky Mountains, it gets warmer and drier. People called this weather the Chinook Wind because it always came from the same direction as the Chinook Indian settlements. The Chinook Wind is also called the "snow eater" because the wind melts snow as it passes over the ground. Draw a picture of an imaginary "snow eater" as it passes over snow-covered ground.

Build a wind chime and use the wind to make music. You can make chimes from wood, metal objects (such as washers, nails, or thin metal pipes), or shells.

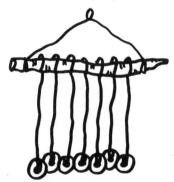

For your wind chime, you'll need some string or fish line, a large metal ring or a branch, scissors, and six of the wind chime objects mentioned above. Cut your string into six even pieces. Attach the string to each of your objects. Tie the other end of the string to the metal ring or branch. Cut a long piece of string to tie onto the ring or branch to help hang your wind chime.

 Read a story or poem about the wind. A good source for wind poems is *Wind Song* by Carl Sandburg. You can find a story of a girl and her grandfather who are snowbound by the strong wind of a blizzard in *Anna, Grandpa and the Big Storm* by Carla Stevens.

RESOURCES

Wind Song by Carl Sandburg (New York: Harcourt, Brace & World, 1960).

Anna, Grandpa and the Big Storm by Carla Stevens (New York: Penguin Books, 1986).

On this day in 1945, Anne Frank died at a concentration camp called Bergen-Belsen. She was 15 years old. Frank and her family had gone into hiding because they were Jewish people living in Amsterdam, Holland, during World War II. When soldiers discovered the family, they took the Franks to a guarded concentration camp. Two years after the war ended, the diary Frank wrote while she was in hiding was published. In spite of her young age and the things that happened to her, Frank had remained hopeful.

 Write about a time in your life when you felt hopeful.

 To learn more about Anne Frank, read the book *Anne Frank: Life in Hiding* by Johanna Hurwitz.

 This is Moshoeshoe Day in Lesotho, a small country surrounded by the Republic of South Africa. In the 1800s, Lesotho was

called Basutoland and Moshoeshoe I was the country's young chief. Moshoeshoe helped his people fight against the Zulus and then against the Europeans. In 1966, Lesotho became an independent country. The Basotho honor Moshoeshoe I on this day. The celebration includes sporting events and traditional music.

On a map, find the country of Lesotho on the southern tip of the African continent. What other information can you find about this country?

 On this day in 1912, Juliette Gordon Lowe organized the first Girl Scout troop. Her group was originally called the Girl Guides. The name was changed to Girl Scouts in 1915.

Ask your class members if any of them are Girl Scouts. Ask them why they joined the Girl Scouts and what they do. If you don't know any Girl Scouts, contact people with the Girl Scout organization in your area. Ask them to speak to your class about their group.

RESOURCE

Anne Frank: Life in Hiding by Johanna Hurwitz (New York: The Jewish Publication Society, 1988).

March 13

Bertha Mahoney Miller, who was born on this day in 1882, introduced an early version of the bookmobile. Large public libraries usually sponsor bookmobiles, which take books to people who aren't able to get to the library. Miller was also a cofounder of the first magazine devoted only to reviews and criticisms about children's books.

Write about the library you go to. What does it look like?

Chester Greenwood patented "ear mufflers" on this date. He received his patent in 1877. Draw your own ear muff design. Make them creative, unusual, and toasty for your ears.

In 1884 at an international conference in Washington, D.C., a world system of standard time was established. Standard Time is based on Greenwich Mean Time (the time it is in Greenwich, London, England). The conference divided the earth into 24 Standard Time zones. The United States has six time zones. Find out which one you live in.

On this date in 1798, Abigail Powers Fillmore was born in Stillwater, New York. She was the wife of Millard Fillmore, the 13th president of the United States. When the Fillmores moved into the White House in 1850, the mansion did not have a library. Abigail Fillmore, who had been a teacher, turned a second-floor room into a library. Within a year, Congress had set aside $250 for the president to add books to the White House's library.

Write about the kinds of books you'd add to a library of your own.

Kirby Puckett was born on this day in 1961. He was raised in a poor, southside Chicago neighborhood. Puckett was the youngest of nine children. His father worked at two jobs to support the family. Puckett's high school baseball coaches remember that he smiled a lot and played hard. In 1984, Puckett began to play professional baseball in the major leagues. He

started his career with the Minnesota Twins. In 1991, he was named the American League Championship Series Most Valuable Player.

Write about your favorite baseball player. If you don't have a favorite baseball player, write about someone you know who plays baseball.

On this date in 1879, Albert Einstein was born in Ulm, Germany. In 1939, Einstein wrote a letter to President Franklin Roosevelt. Einstein told the president that research should be done on an atomic bomb. This letter, along with the opinions of other scientists, brought about the Manhattan Project. The Manhattan Project was a code name for the United States' atomic bomb research. What do you think about atomic and nuclear weapons? Share your views with your class.

When Einstein was younger, adults labeled him a problem child. But as an adult, he performed such amazing calculations that people labeled him a genius. What labels do people use to describe you? Would you use the same ones to describe yourself? Make a list of these labels and write about how they are true or untrue for yourself.

Today is the birthday of Casey Jones. He was a railroad engineer and the hero of a song and poem. Casey's real name was John Luther Jones. He was born near Cayce, Kentucky, in 1864. He died in a railroad accident on April 30, 1900. To learn more about Casey Jones, read the book by that name written by Jan Gleiter and Kathleen Thompson.

....

RESOURCE

Casey Jones by Jan Gleiter and Kathleen Thompson (Milwaukee, Wisconsin: Raintree Publishers, 1987).

....

Today is Buzzard Day. Tradition says that on this day in Hinkley, Ohio, the buzzards return to raise their young. Although the buzzards spend their winters in the Great Smokey Mountains, they fly east back to Hinkley every spring.

 Buzzards (also called turkey vultures or carrion crows) are considered to be one of the ugliest birds. Describe something you think is ugly.

 The Roman emperor Julius Caesar was assassinated on this day in 44 B.C. Caesar had named himself Dictator for Life of the Roman Empire and many people were upset. Some of Caesar's friends formed a secret group to stop his reign. One of the group's members stabbed Caesar to death.

In Caesar's time, freeborn citizens wore garments called togas. They looked like sheets that were wrapped loosely around the body. Men wore plain white togas. Young boys and important government ministers wore purple ones with fancy stitching. Draw your own creative toga. Decorate it in any color. Add fancy buttons, snaps, or bows.

 On this date in 1909, 71-year-old Edward Weston took a walk. He decided to walk from New York to San Francisco. The journey took him 104 days. Using a map, find New York, New York, on the east coast. Now locate San Francisco, California, on the west coast. Figure out how many miles Weston walked.

 On this day in 1820, Maine became the 23rd state. For some information on the early history of this state, read *The Sign of the Beaver* by Elizabeth George Speare. It's the story of how 13-year-old Matt survived with the help from local Native Americans. The story takes place in the wilderness of Maine in the 1700s.

R E S O U R C E

The Sign of the Beaver by Elizabeth George Speare (Boston: Houghton Mifflin, 1983).

Today is St. Urho's Day. On this day, people remember St. Urho, the patron saint of Finland. When a swarm of grasshoppers invaded the country and began to eat the grape crop, St. Urho drove out the insects and saved the crop.

 Write about a time you were bugged about something.

 Finland is in northern Europe and is about the same size as the state of Montana. In the early 1990s, over 4 million people lived in this country. The northern part of Finland is in the Arctic Circle, which means that in the summer, the sun shines until midnight. In winter, however, the sun doesn't come out at all. The southern city of Helsinki is Finland's capital. Find Finland on a map. What else can you find out about this country?

 The third week in March is National Poison Prevention Week. The purpose of this week is to encourage people to learn the dangers of accidental poisoning. If you would like more information on how to prevent accidental poisoning, send a letter to:

Poison Prevention Week Council
P.O. Box 1543
Washington, DC 20013

Ammonia, bleach, carpet cleaner, and laundry detergent are some of the poisons found in almost every household. Even though these chemicals help keep houses clean, they can be dangerous if someone swallows or inhales them. Discuss the poisons found around your home. Think about every room in your house, including the kitchen, laundry room, and bathroom. Talk about ways to keep these poisons out of reach of young children.

March 17

Nathan Adam Coles began his musical training in his father's church. When he was 12 years old, he played the church's organ. Later in his musical career, Nathan dropped the "s" from his last name and was known as Nat "King" Cole. He was born on this day in 1919 in Montgomery, Alabama. In the 1940s and 1950s, Cole was one of America's most popular recording artists. Besides singing, Cole liked to take photographs and collect phonograph records. He died on February 15, 1965. His daughter Natalie has also become a famous entertainer.

 Write about something your parent or other favorite adult likes to do. Is that something you'd like to do someday?

 Today is also St. Patrick's Day. Bishop Patrick lived from A.D. 389 to 461. About 432, he began to travel across Ireland introducing Christianity to the people. St. Patrick's Day is a holy day in Ireland. People in other countries around the world celebrate this day by wearing green. To find more information about St. Patrick's Day, read *Shamrocks, Harps, and Shillelaghs: The Story of Saint Patrick's Day Symbols* by Edna Barth.

 Blarney Castle is located in Ireland. On the castle grounds is the Blarney Stone. Some people say that if you kiss the Blarney Stone, you'll develop a great skill in flattering people. Flattering means to say something pleasant about another. Flattering can turn into exaggerated compliments about someone, too. *Example*: Instead of saying you have nice hair, someone who has kissed the Blarney Stone might say you have the most wonderful hair in the whole world. Pretend everyone in your class has kissed the Blarney Stone. Take turns saying things a person might say if the Blarney Stone legend is true.

 Draw a green shamrock to wear today. Did you know that a shamrock is not the same as a clover? Find out what the difference is.

RESOURCE

Shamrocks, Harps, and Shillelaghs: The Story of Saint Patrick's Day Symbols by Edna Barth (New York: Houghton Mifflin, 1977).

March 18

Colonel Aleksei Arkhipovich Leonov became a hero on this day in 1965 when he took the first space walk. Leonov's space capsule was called *Voskhod 1*. He walked in space for 10 minutes. Leonov was born on May 30, 1934, in the village of Listvyanka in Siberia. Because of a cold, he had failed the centrifuge test and was almost disqualified from the Soviet cosmonaut program. Leonov's friends asked officials if he could take the test again. The officials agreed and Leonov passed the test.

 Write about something your friends did for you that was really terrific. If they haven't done anything for you yet, write about what you'd like them to do.

 Create a space helmet. Use a paper bag as the base. Add straws, wires, empty paper towel rolls, and other important-looking gizmos. Create an oxygen tank from an empty cereal or tissue box. Hold a space helmet contest to decide who has created the silliest, the most realistic, or the most fun helmet.

 This date usually falls during National Wildlife Week. It is sponsored by the National Wildlife Federation. During this week, explore and enjoy wildlife. Take a wildlife hike and look for animals that live in your area.

 For more suggestions on how to observe National Wildlife Week, send a letter to:

National Wildlife Federation
Wildlife Week
1400 16th Street NW
Washington, DC 20036-2266

March 19

Spring is almost here. People in San Juan Capistrano, California, know that spring has arrived when the swallows return. Each year on this day, hundreds of swallows return to the Capistrano Mission from their winter home in Mexico. Since 1776, the swallows have faithfully returned to this same town. According to legend, the swallows have only been late once when a storm at sea delayed their flight.

 Write about a place you wish you could visit every year.

 San Juan Capistrano is in southwestern California about 60 miles south of Los Angeles. The Mission San Juan Capistrano was founded on November 1, 1776. In 1812, an earthquake destroyed the church. The swallows now nest in the church's ruins. Find San Juan Capistrano on a map. How far is Mexico from this town? What flight route do you think the swallows take to get from Mexico to San Juan Capistrano?

 Finches, canaries, parrots, parakeets, and love birds are often kept as pets. To learn more about them, read *Birds as Pets* by Paul Villiard.

 Ornithologists are people who study birds. Become an amateur ornithologist. A bird's beak and its feet are adapted to help the bird find food and shelter. Notice various birds' beaks. Some birds have short, thick beaks. They use them to crack open shells. Notice some bird feet. What kind of feet does a duck have? Why? What kind of feet does a hawk have? Why? A woodpecker has two toes that point backward. Try to figure out why.

RESOURCE

Birds as Pets by Paul Villiard (New York: Doubleday, 1974).

March 20

Spring usually arrives on March 20 or 21. This day marks the first day of spring in the northern hemisphere. In the southern hemisphere, it marks the beginning of autumn. Today is the Vernal Equinox. It's called an equinox because the hours of day and night are equal (we'll have 12 hours of light and 12 hours of darkness). Many countries all over the world celebrate spring. The celebration is often called a rite of spring.

 Write about something you can do to celebrate spring.

 In Israel, Tu Bi-Shebat, the New Year of the Trees, is celebrated at springtime. In the Jewish culture, a tree symbolizes a good and noble life. Israelis use this day to plant trees. If you could be a tree, what kind would you be? Draw a picture of yourself. Do you hold a bird's nest, or tree house, or part of a hammock? Are you a tall, old tree? Are you a young tree just beginning to grow?

 The word "spring" names the season between winter and summer. What other meanings for the word spring can you find?

 Take a walk outside and look for signs of spring. *Examples*: Look for green grass, small plants, and robins. Take a deep breath and use your nose to find other signs of spring.

MarcH 21

Debi Thomas became the first African-American athlete to win a women's world figure skating championship. She did so on this day in 1986. Thomas grew up in a poor family. As a child, she wore secondhand skates. Her mother sewed her costumes. Thomas loved to skate and kept practicing. In 1988, she became the first African-American to win an Olympic medal in figure skating. After the Olympics, Thomas decided not to compete anymore. She went to college to study medicine.

 What type of skating is your favorite to watch or participate in? Ice skating? Roller skating? In-line skating? Skateboarding? Write about why you like it.

 Iranians celebrate Noruz about this time every year. Noruz marks the beginning of the Iranian new year and the arrival of spring. The celebration lasts 12 days. Just before Noruz, people thoroughly clean their houses. The cleaning is called khaneh takani.

Iranians have other rituals to celebrate this day. Children go door to door and collect small gifts. On the last Wednesday of the year, every family member jumps over a small bonfire. This symbolizes leaving behind the sadness of the old year. Another ritual is to put a colored egg on a mirror. As the New Year begins, Iranians believe that the renewed earth trembles and so does the egg. With your class, talk about how you can create a similar ritual that celebrates spring.

 In 1843, thousands of people in America panicked. They thought that on March 21, 1843, the world would end. William Miller, a preacher from Massachusetts, predicted it would happen.

Predict something you think will occur in the next year. Write down your prediction and put it in a safe place. Remember to look at it a year from now. See if your prediction came true.

 If you have seen the Walt Disney movie *Fantasia*, you have heard the work of Johann Sebastian Bach. An orchestra played Bach's "Toccata and Fugue in D Minor" in the movie. Bach was born on this day in 1685, in Eisenach, Germany. To celebrate this composer's birthday, listen to some of his music. You can find a selection in the recording *Bach's Greatest Hits*.

R E S O U R C E

Bach's Greatest Hits recording (CBS Masterworks, 1984).

March 22

French painter and sculptor Rosa Bonheur was born on this day in 1822. She was best known for her accurate pictures of animals. In 1841, she exhibited her work for the first time at the Paris Salon. She became one of the most successful painters of the 1800s. Her most famous work is titled *The Horse Fair*.

 Would you want to own a horse? Why or why not?

 On this day in 1990, President George Bush said he wouldn't eat broccoli. After hearing Bush's statement, the California Broccoli Shippers Association sent the president a truckload—10 tons—of broccoli. Bush donated most of the load to places that feed the homeless.

Here are some broccoli facts: Broccoli is part of a genus (or family) of plants. The genus of broccoli is called Brassica. Other members of the Brassica family include cabbage and cauliflower. The part of broccoli that's eaten is actually the plant's flowers. If you've eaten broccoli, cabbage, or cauliflower, describe what they taste like to your classmates. What other kinds of vegetables have you eaten?

 Today is Marcel Marceau's birthday. He was born in Strasbourg, France, in 1923. Marceau was a pantomimist; he used only movements, facial expressions, and gestures to tell a story. Marceau created a character he called Bip. When he played Bip, he wore white face makeup. Today, mime artists usually wear white makeup. They accent their eyes and mouth to make facial expressions clear.

Try some pantomime of your own. Express these emotions in pantomime: anger, happiness, relief, fright, and exhaustion. Think of another emotion and pantomime it. See if others can guess what you're showing.

 Have everyone in your classroom write down a situation to pantomime. *Examples:* reading a scary book, eating a piece of chewy candy, using the telephone, or playing an instrument. Fold up the pieces of paper and put them all on a desk. Take turns choosing a piece of paper and acting out the situation. Can your classmates guess what the pantomimist is doing?

March 23

On this date in 1857, cooking expert Fannie Merritt Farmer was born in Boston, Massachusetts. She wrote the *Boston Cooking School Cook Book*, which was published in 1896. Her book was the first cookbook to include standard level measurements. Before Farmer's book, written recipes told cooks to add a "pinch" of this or a "dash" of that. Many times, cooks didn't know how big a pinch or a dash should be. As the "Mother of the Level Measurement," Farmer helped cooks make great dishes with fewer mistakes.

 Write about something you made—or helped make— by following a recipe. If you haven't cooked anything yet, write about something you'd like to make.

Most recipes have two parts: a list of ingredients (and how much of each ingredient is needed) and directions on how to put the ingredients together. Look through a cookbook—*Betty Crocker's New Boys and Girls Cookbook* is a fun one. Find a recipe you'd like to make someday.

 In 1857 on this day, the first modern safety elevator was installed in Haughwout Department Store, New York City. Haughwout was the first store to use an elevator. Customers could ride from the first floor to the fifth floor in less than a minute. Elisha Graves Otis, an American engineer, invented the elevator.

Time how long it takes you to walk five flights of stairs. You may not have five flights in a row so use the same one over and over. Today's elevators can travel over 100 floors in less than a minute.

 Locate David Macaulay's book *The Way Things Work*. Can you find the purpose of the first elevator built in 1743? What brave thing did Elisha Otis do to demonstrate the safety of his design? Can you explain to someone how an elevator works?

RESOURCES

Betty Crocker's New Boys and Girls Cookbook (Prentice Hall, 1990).

The Way Things Work by David Macaulay (Boston: Houghton Mifflin, 1988).

 **March 24**

John Wesley Powell, an American geologist, was born on this day in March 1834. In the Battle of Shiloh during the Civil War, Powell lost his right arm. But he didn't let his disability stop him from becoming a college professor. In 1867, he took a group of students and amateur scientists to Colorado. While he was there, he came up with the idea of traveling down the Colorado River through the Grand Canyon. Two years later, Powell and his crew braved the rapids and were the first people to explore this twisting, turning river.

 Describe the Grand Canyon. If you haven't seen it in person, look at a picture of it and then describe what you see.

 The annual Iditarod race begins around this date in Anchorage, Alaska. The Iditarod is a grueling dogsled race. Hundreds of racers and dogs leave the starting line in Anchorage and spend 11 to 30 days racing toward the finish line in Nome. Find Anchorage (in southern Alaska) and Nome (along the western coast). Try to figure out how many miles the dogsled racers travel to finish the Iditarod.

 Create a diorama that represents the scenery Iditarod racers see. To create a diorama, you'll need a box about the size of a shoe box, magazines, plastic wrap, and glue. Cut out pictures from the magazines that show dogs, snowy trees, and people wrapped in warm coats (if you can't find any pictures, draw some). Bend back the bottoms of your pictures to make them stand. Put the shoe box on its longer side and decorate the inside with snow scenes. Glue the cut-out pictures onto the shoe box base. After you've created the scene, seal up your diorama by wrapping plastic wrap around the box.

 Have everyone in your class list all the ways that people can travel. Use a time limit of three minutes. How many different ways did people think of?

March 25

On this day in 1871, Gutzon Borglum, an American sculptor, was born in Bear Lake, Idaho. You've probably seen pictures of his most important work. You may even have visited the real thing. The Mount Rushmore National Memorial in South Dakota was his idea. Borglum decided to carve the faces of George Washington, Thomas Jefferson, Abraham Lincoln, and Theodore Roosevelt into the granite side of Mount Rushmore. He spent 14 years working on the project. Borglum died in Chicago on March 6, 1941. The memorial was finished seven months later.

 Write about a project that took you a long time to finish. Was it completing a homework assignment, cleaning out your closet, or helping someone else complete something?

 The faces that make up the Mount Rushmore National Monument are gigantic. Each face is five stories high from the chin to forehead. Each eye is 11 feet across. Each mouth is 18 feet across. Each nose is 20 feet high. Push your tables or desks together until they measure 11 feet across. Can you imagine an eye this size?

 During the construction of Mount Rushmore, Jefferson's face had to be moved. The workers discovered a defect in the stone where it was originally supposed to go. Draw the faces of four famous people you'd like to see on Mt. Rushmore.

 When sculptors look at a piece of wood or stone, they try to imagine the form they want to sculpt. Use your powers of imagination and create a sculpture. You'll need a piece of soap and a heavy-duty plastic knife.

Study the soap and think about something you'd like to carve, like a face or a funny animal. Now pick up your knife and create your piece of art.

March 26

In 1981, Sandra Day O'Connor became the first woman associate justice of the U.S. Supreme Court. She was born on this date in 1930. Before she was selected for the position, one interviewer asked her, "How do you want to be remembered?" At the time, O'Connor answered, "I hope I am remembered as the first woman who served on the Supreme Court." Twenty days after she made that statement, her nomination was approved.

 Write about how you would like to be remembered.

 According to Gene Roddenberry, who created the *Star Trek* characters, Captain James T. Kirk will be born on this date in 2228. Kirk is the commander of the original starship *Enterprise* that goes where no one has gone before. Captain Kirk's birthplace will be a small town in Iowa.

Leonard Nimoy was born on this date in 1931 in Boston, Massachusetts. He is famous for his role as Mr. Spock in the original *Star Trek* series. Nimoy is also a director and writer. Mr. Spock's character has pointed ears, which makeup artists created to cover Nimoy's ears. Draw your own set of unique ears for a new series of space stories.

 In 1874, Robert Lee Frost, an American poet, was born in San Francisco. Frost didn't attend school until he was 12 years old and he didn't read a book until he was 14. Yet he won four Pulitzer Prizes for poetry. Before he became a famous poet, Frost was a farmer, teacher, shoemaker, and editor. He used his past personal experiences to write poems. Ask someone to read a Frost poem to you. *A Swinger of Birches: Poetry of Robert Frost for Young Readers* has many of his poems. After you've listened to the poem, draw a picture of what Frost wrote about.

 Look up the word "March" in the dictionary. What are its definitions? What are three words you find before the word "March"? What are three words you find after it?

···

RESOURCE

A Swinger of Birches: Poetry of Robert Frost for Young Readers by Robert Frost, illustrated by Peter Koeppen (Owings Mills, Maryland: Stemmer House, 1982).

···

March 27

A small eruption of Mount St. Helens occurred on this day in 1980. The volcano in southwestern Washington state had been dormant for 100 years. Beginning in March, the volcano began to stir with a series of small eruptions that only a few people noticed. On May 18, 1980, the volcano violently erupted and spewed tons of ash and debris 11 miles into the sky.

 Write about a time when something small turned into a big problem for you.

 Wilhelm Konrad Roentgen earned the first Nobel Prize in physics in 1901. He was born on this day in 1845 in Prussia (modern-day Germany). In 1895, Roentgen discovered X-rays. That year, he X-rayed his wife's right hand and discovered that X-rays could penetrate skin and show the bones underneath. With X-rays, doctors could see inside people to find out what was wrong with them. Roentgen died in Munich, Germany, on February 10, 1923.

Draw a person being X-rayed. Show the skeleton bones.

 Easter is celebrated between March 22 and April 25. It's an important holiday in the Christian religion. Christians celebrate their belief that Jesus rose from the dead. To celebrate Easter, some families dress in new spring clothing and prepare special meals. They hide colored eggs and Easter baskets.

The original Easter bunny stories may have begun in Germany. People there tell a story of a poor woman who hid some colored eggs for her children to find. When the children found the eggs, they also noticed a nearby rabbit. The children thought the rabbit had brought the eggs.

Create your own Easter bunny. You'll need construction paper, cotton balls, marker, glue, and scissors. Using the whole sheet of paper, draw a large rabbit. Glue the cotton closely together all over the rabbit's body. The cotton will make the rabbit look furry and fluffy. Use markers or colored paper to add the eyes, nose, mouth, and whiskers.

 What does a rabbit do all day? Imagine that you and your classmates are rabbits. Talk about a rabbit's typical day. Be creative and imaginative.

March 28

Today is Teachers' Day in Czechoslovakia. It celebrates the birthday of Jan Amos Komensky who was born on March 28, 1592. Komensky, a famous educator in Czechoslovakia, was the first person to write a book especially for children. He felt that children could remember words better if there were pictures to go with them. In 1658, his book *Visible World of Pictures* became the first book written just for children.

 Write about your favorite children's book.

 Draw a picture of your teacher. Under your picture, write a sentence about the good things your teacher does for your class.

 With its gusty winds and warm weather, March is a favorite time for flying kites. In China, kite flying is an ancient tradition. Many people believe that kites originated there. Others think that people who lived on the South Sea islands first flew kites to help them fish. To learn more about the history of kites, read *Fishing for Angels: The Magic of Kites* by David Evans.

 Workers began digging America's first subway on this day in 1895. A subway is a railroad that travels underground. The first subway was built in Boston, Massachusetts. Workers needed two years to build the 1 1/2 mile track. Today, many large cities in the world have subways. In Paris, people call the subway the Metro. In London, the subway is known as the Tube. Design some new form of transportation. Describe it to your class.

....

R E S O U R C E

Fishing for Angels: The Magic of Kites by David Evans (Toronto, Canada: Annick Press, 1991).

....

Dr. John Pemberton introduced Coca-Cola on this day in 1886. He called his invention a brain tonic and an intellectual beverage. Today, the formula for making Coca-Cola is a company secret. Only the top two executives know what it is. Company rules say that these two executives must not travel together. If something happened to both executives, the formula would be lost.

 Write about your favorite soft drink.

 Take a poll and find out which soft drinks your classmates like best. Keep track of which soft drink gets the most votes. Ask people why they like their soft drink better than others.

 On this date in 1848, Niagara Falls stopped flowing. For 30 hours an ice jam prevented the water from flowing. Normally, 500,000 tons of water rush over a cliff every minute to form the falls.

Pretend you're a news reporter in 1848. Your editor has sent you to cover the Niagara Falls story. It has been 29 hours and 55 minutes since the falls stopped; the ice jam is just about to break. Write a news story about what you see as the water begins to flow down the side of the cliffs and into the rocks below. Include a flashy headline for your story. *Examples:* "Jammed Falls Breaks Big" or "Niagara Now Flows Freely."

 Niagara Falls is the great waterfall of the Niagara River. It's located on the boundary between the state of New York and the province of Ontario. The falls drop 158 feet on the Canadian side and 167 feet on the

American side. Cave of Winds, Whirlpool Rapids, and Luna Falls are all part of the U.S. Niagara Reservation State Park. The Canadian government maintains Queen Victoria Park. On a map of the United States, find Niagara Falls. Look either in the far western border of New York state or the southeast border of Ontario, Canada.

March 30

Hyman L. Lipman patented the first pencil with an eraser attached to it on this day in 1858. English chemist Joseph Priestly had already invented the eraser in 1770. He had discovered that rubber could wipe out pencil marks. Two hundred years earlier, someone had figured out that graphite could be used for writing. Lipman put these two inventions together to make his writing tool. Lipman's pencil had a groove in one end with a piece of prepared rubber glued to it.

 What do you like to use when you write? a pencil? colored pen? a marker? Write about the writing utensil you use the most.

 List all the writing instruments you can think of. Now think of unusual things to write with. *Examples:* the pointed end of a stick or a leaf.

 Dutch painter Vincent van Gogh was born on this date in 1853 in Zundert, Netherlands. He produced over 800 paintings and hundreds of drawings; he created more than 1,500 works of art. Vincent is famous for using bright colors.

Vincent once said, "There is nothing in the world as interesting as people...one can never study them enough." Using a piece of paper, create as many different people as you can on your page. Give them different eye, skin, and hair colors. Dress them in special costumes. In honor of van Gogh, use bright, brilliant colors.

 Do you agree with Vincent van Gogh that people are the most interesting thing to study? Write about a time you were in a large crowd. What did you notice about the people around you?

March 31

Daylight Savings Time (DST) began today in 1918. People moved their clocks ahead one hour to conserve power and provide more usable daylight hours for afternoon and evening activities.

In the United States, DST begins on the first Sunday in April and ends on the last Sunday in October. The phrase, "Spring forward, fall back" can help you remember which way to set your clock in the spring and fall.

 Write about something that would take you one hour to do.

 Create a poster that reminds people to wake up on time after this shortened weekend. How inventive can you be?

 The Eiffel Tower in Paris, France, was completed in 1889 on this date. Alexandre Gustave Eiffel built this superstructure. When it was complete, the Eiffel Tower was the tallest building in the world. It stands 985 feet high. By 1890, all the building costs had been paid because people were charged to climb the stairs to the top.

Look for a picture of the Eiffel Tower and use it to build your own tower. You'll need toothpicks or Popsicle sticks and glue.

Cesar Estrada Chavez was born on this day in 1927. He was the son of a migrant worker. A migrant worker travels from one city to another working in farmer's fields. In 1962, Chavez organized migrant farm workers to help them gain better working conditions. He died on April 23, 1993. Read more about him and his work in the book *Cesar Chavez* by Ruth Franchere.

R E S O U R C E

Cesar Chavez by Ruth Franchere (New York: Harper & Row Junior Books, 1988).

" **A**pril Fool's!" How many times will you hear that today? Actually, those words were first used almost 500 years ago. Then, the New Year began on March 25, Annunciation Day, not January 1. On Annunciation Day, Christians believe, an angel told Mary of the coming birth of Jesus. The Annunciation was celebrated with an eight-day festival that ended on April 1. As more countries adopted new calendars, people changed New Year's Day to January 1. Some people didn't want to change, though. Those people were called "April Fools."

 Write about how you feel when someone plays a trick on you.

 Have a fool-ish day. Do something silly. Wear your clothing inside out. Wear your shoes on the wrong feet. Eat dessert first and your meal last. Say "good-bye" to friends when you see them. Say "hello" when you leave.

 Set up a "Joke-A-Day" program. Use a class bulletin board. Decorate it with happy faces, question marks, and silly drawings.

Write down jokes and riddles on the front of 3" x 5" cards. Put the answers on the backs. Change the cards daily. A different person could be responsible for a new joke each day.

 On this day in 1957 the British Broadcasting Corporation (BBC) aired a film about spaghetti harvesting. The program showed spaghetti hanging on trees. But spaghetti isn't harvested, it's made of a flour dough. After the TV program, many people called the station to ask where they could buy spaghetti plants. The company aired the film as a harmless April Fool's joke. With your class, talk about the difference between a harmless joke and a harmful one.

Today is International Children's Book Day. It's a day to recognize authors around the world. It's also the birth date of Hans Christian Andersen. Andersen was born in 1805 in Odense, Denmark. He wrote fairy tales. "The Little Match Girl," "The Ugly Duckling," "The Snow Queen," and "The Red Shoes" are some of his stories. Children's Book Day is celebrated in his honor.

 Describe the kind of children's book you would like to illustrate. Would you draw animals, adventure scenes, or a special alphabet book? Tell why you made your choice.

 If you would like more information on how people celebrate International Children's Book Day, write to:

The Children's Book Council
568 Broadway
New York, NY 10012

Every two years, the International Board on Books for Young People sponsors the Hans Christian Andersen Awards. These awards recognize outstanding authors and illustrators of children's books. What are the names of your favorite books? Tell your class about the ones you'd give an award to.

 Before he became a writer, Hans Christian Andersen worked as an actor, singer, and dancer. When he was 30 years old, he began writing—he wrote 168 fairy tales. To find out more about Andersen, read *Hans Christian Andersen: Teller of Tales* by Carol Green.

RESOURCE

Hans Christian Andersen: Teller of Tales by Carol Green (Chicago: Childrens Press, 1986).

Washington Irving was born on this date in 1783 in New York City. He was an American writer and lawyer. In 1820, Irving wrote "Rip Van Winkle," one of his most famous stories. That story is about Rip, a lazy man who wanders into the woods. Rip meets some weird characters and drinks their strange brew. When he lies down for a nap in the forest, he sleeps for 20 years. When Rip awakens, he walks through his village and finds few familiar faces and places.

 Imagine that you've discovered Rip Van Winkle in your backyard. He has just awakened from his long nap. What will you tell him? How will you help him?

 The Pony Express began on this day in 1860. Riders carried mail from St. Joseph, Missouri, to Sacramento, California. Stations were set up about every 10 miles all along the 1,980-mile route. Riders picked up fresh horses at each station to be able to ride faster. At some stations, riders changed places with other riders. One rider might have to travel through 10 of the stations for 100 miles. That rider stopped only to change horses. When the transcontinental telegraph was finished in 1861, the Pony Express was no longer needed. It was shut down only 18 months after it had begun.

On a map of the United States, find St. Joseph (it's in the northwest corner of Missouri) and Sacramento (in the north central part of California). If the Pony Express were to ride today, what states would the riders travel through? What rivers would they cross?

 Set up a relay like the one the Pony Express used. In a large space, like the gym or playground, divide into two teams. You'll need two dice, one for each team. Select a starting and ending point. Each racer carries a die and runs to the ending point, turns around, and runs back to the starting point. There, the racer rolls the die with the next person on the team. If the runner rolls a 1, 3, or 5, he or she hands off the die to the next person and that person runs the course. If the runner rolls a 2, 4, or 6, he or she runs the course again and rolls the die with the next person in line.

 Faziur R. Khan was born in 1929. He was the architect who designed Chicago's Sears Tower. The Sears Tower has 110 stories. It's 1,454 feet high, not including the television antenna on top.

Build a skyscraper using whole dried peas that have been soaked overnight. You'll also need some round or flat toothpicks. Take the peas out of the water and use them to connect the toothpicks. Create a square using four toothpicks and four peas. From this base, create a box. Continue building from this base. As the peas dry, they will shrink and create strong joints.

 ApriL 4

Many authors write about their hopes and dreams. That's what Maya Angelou did in her book *I Know Why the Caged Bird Sings*. Angelou was born on this day in 1928. Her book is about growing up as an African-American girl in the South. Angelou titled her book after reading a poem called "Sympathy." It was written by Paul Laurence Dunbar, an African-American poet. The songbird in Dunbar's poem sings because it wants to be free of its cage.

 Write about how you feel when you see animals in cages.

 On this day in 1802, Dorothea Lynde Dix was born in Hampden, Maine. Dix worked hard for better conditions in prisons. She was especially concerned about people who were poor and mentally disabled. Because of her efforts, laws were passed that said people with mental disabilities should be treated in hospitals, not in prisons. Dix was a quiet, soft-spoken person, but she managed to make some huge changes.

Today, many young people are involved with social problems. They've helped injured animals in New Mexico. They've cleaned up parks in New York. Read *The Kid's Guide to Social Action* by Barbara Lewis. This book tells how you and your friends can help solve some social problems in your neighborhood.

 Social issues—such as homelessness and pollution—affect everyone. Use current newspapers or news magazines to create a collage of social issues. Cut out pictures or words that describe the issues you're concerned about. Glue them onto construction paper. Start thinking about what you can do to help solve these problems in your neighborhood.

On this day in 1614, Pocahontas married John Rolfe. At 11 years of age, this Native American girl saved the life of Englishman and explorer John Smith. Smith had founded Jamestown, Virginia, but had built the town on land Pocahontas' tribe lived on. Pocahontas begged her father to spare Smith's life and her father did. To learn more about Pocahontas, read *The Double Life of Pocahontas* by Jean Fritz.

RESOURCES

The Kid's Guide to Social Action by Barbara Lewis (Minneapolis: Free Spirit Publishing, 1991).

The Double Life of Pocahontas by Jean Fritz (New York: Puffin Books, 1987).

 **ApriL 5**

Dr. Judith A. Resnick was a mission specialist on the first flight of the space shuttle *Discovery*, which left on August 30, 1984. Resnick was an electrical engineer and one of the first six women to be selected for the U.S. Space Shuttle Program. As a mission specialist for the National Aeronautics and Space Administration (NASA), Resnick coordinated all of the shuttle operations. In 1984, she was awarded the NASA Space Flight Medal. She was born in Akron, Ohio, on this day in 1949. Resnick died on the space shuttle *Challenger* when it exploded above Cape Canaveral, Florida, on January 28, 1986.

 Would you want to live and work in space someday? Why or why not?

 Today marks the birth date of Booker T. Washington. He was born near Hale's Ford, Virginia, in 1856. Washington felt that African-Americans should work for equal opportunities in jobs and schools. He thought making gradual changes was better than arguing for civil rights. Washington spent much of his life talking to young African-Americans. He encouraged them to come to school and stay in school. In 1881, he organized what became Tuskegee Institute in Alabama. He headed the school until his death in 1915.

Create a poster or flyer that advertises the good parts of your school. List reasons why students should stay in school.

 Lord Joseph Lister was born on this date in 1827. He studied germs and how they spread diseases. He encouraged people who worked in hospitals to wash their hands more and to use antiseptics. These methods saved the lives of those who had surgery. To find out more about germs, bacteria, and viruses, read *Germs Make Me Sick* by Melvin Berger.

 On this date in 1887, Anne Sullivan made a teaching breakthrough with her student Helen Keller. Helen Keller was blind and deaf. She communicated by spelling words with her fingers. At first, she did not know the meaning of the words she was spelling.

Then, during one session at a water pump, Sullivan put Helen's hands in the water and used her fingers to spell "water." Helen finally made the connection that what her teacher was spelling was the word for water. Helen wrote later, "That living word awakened my soul, gave it light, hope, joy, set it free! It was as if I had come back to life after being dead."

Read a book on sign language. *A Show of Hands* by Mary Beth Sullivan and Linda Bourke is a good choice. Learn to spell your name with your hands.

RESOURCES

Germs Make Me Sick by Melvin Berger (New York: HarperCollins Children's Books, 1985).

A Show of Hands by Mary Beth Sullivan and Linda Bourke (New York: Scholastic, 1980).

APRIL 6

In 1881, ethnologist Alice Fletcher went to live among the Omaha tribe in Nebraska. Ethnologists study the cultural heritage of societies. They study the things that influence growth and change in a group of people. Fletcher was the first and only ethnologist to write a complete description of a Plains Indian ceremony. She included musical information and words that the Native Americans spoke and chanted. She was born in Havana, Cuba, on this day in 1838.

 Write about a ceremony you attended. Why was the ceremony held? Was music a part of the ceremony?

 Lowell Thomas was a reporter, editor, and radio newscaster who traveled around the world. For 51 years he explored remote villages and sought out interesting people. He reported his stories on radio news shows. In the 1950s, he appeared on several TV travel shows. Thomas was one of the first newscasters to report events at the scene, while the events were happening. He usually ended his broadcasts by saying, "So long, until tomorrow." Thomas was born on this day in 1892, in Woodington, Ohio.

Imagine you're a TV reporter. Write about where you would go to find an interesting story. Why would you go to that place?

 What were the headlines on the day you were born? Ask your parents or teachers what news items were happening at that time. Or ask a librarian to help you find a newspaper that was published on your birth date. (You could even find your birthday in this book and see what other events happened on that day.)

 Admiral Robert E. Peary became the first man known to reach the North Pole. After 23 years and many unsuccessful attempts, Peary reached the pole on this date in 1909. Matthew A. Henson, an African-American, and four Eskimos went with him. Some history books say that Henson reached the North Pole 45 minutes before Peary. The group spent 30 hours at the pole. They planted an American flag and then left. For Henson's account of the journey, read his book *Negro Explorer at the North Pole.*

....

R E S O U R C E

Negro Explorer at the North Pole by Matthew A. Henson (Salem, New Hampshire: Ayer Company Publishers, 1969).

....

Today is World Health Day. On April 7, 1948, the United Nations formed the World Health Organization (WHO). This group's main purpose is to provide good health care to every person in the world by the year 2000.

 Write a prescription for good health. What would your directions be to someone who wished to be healthier?

 If you'd like more information about WHO, send a letter to:

Pan American Health Organization
American Association for World Health
Public Information Office
1129 20th Street NW, Suite 400
Washington, DC 20036

 Create a plan to become a healthier person. List the days of the week across the top of a sheet of paper. For each day, write down the healthy foods you will eat at breakfast, lunch, and dinner. Write down when you will exercise. When will you sleep? When will you have time for some daydreaming (mental exercising)? Try to follow your plan for a whole week.

 Draw your favorite way to exercise.

On this date in 1974, baseball's Henry Louis Aaron hit his 715th home run and broke Babe Ruth's record. By the time he retired from baseball, Aaron had hit 755 home runs. Through 25

years of playing baseball, Aaron set records for runs scored, total bases taken, and runs batted in. Aaron was born in Mobile, Alabama, on February 5, 1934.

 Write down your thoughts about baseball. Is this a sport you like to participate in? Why or why not?

 Make a list of sports you like to play. List words that are part of those sports. *Example:* If you like soccer, you might include words such as goal line, corner kick, and dribbling.

 In 1912 on this day, Sonja Henie was born in Oslo, Norway. When she was 15, Henie became a world champion figure skater. She won gold medals in figure skating during the 1928, 1932, and 1936 Olympics. Although Jackson Haines, an Austrian ballet master, had created the sport of figure skating in the 1800s, Henie's performance at the 1936 Olympic games brought international attention to this sport.

Find out about other female figure skaters. Ask your librarians for books about women who have competed in this sport.

 Today is Food Day; it's sponsored by the Center for Science in the Public Interest. The purpose of this day is to remind people to eat healthier foods. Divide a piece of paper into two columns. Label one column "Junk Food." List the junk food that most people eat. Label the second column "Healthy Food." List healthy foods they could eat instead.

Today is Winston Churchill Day. Churchill was the prime minister in England from 1940-1945 and 1951-1953. During World War II, he encouraged people in his country to fight Adolph Hitler. He was made an honorary citizen of the United States on this date in 1963.

 What kind of person is a good leader? Describe the qualities he or she should have.

 Many Eastern countries celebrate Buddha's birthday on or near this date. Siddhartha Gautama, also known as Buddha, was born in 563 B.C. When he was 35 years old, he sat under a Bo tree in the lotus position and meditated. His followers say Buddha gained enlightenment through this meditation. Buddha built his teachings into the faith known as Buddhism. He died at the age of 80. In Japan, this day is called Kambutse or Hana Matsuri. In Hawaii, it's called the Wesak Flower Festival and begins on the first Sunday in April. Many Buddhists call it Vesak and celebrate it on the full-moon day of the month.

Look at a book about yoga, such as *Yoga for Children* by Erene Cheki-Haney and Ruth Richards. Practice sitting in the lotus position. How long do you think you could sit that way? Try out some other yoga positions.

 Today is the birth date of Eadweard Muybridge. He was an English photographer born in 1830. Muybridge was famous for his action photographs. His photos of dancers and racing horses in motion influenced other artists. *Muybridge's Complete Human & Animal Locomotion* shows many of his photos. Draw a picture of something in motion.

On this date in 1882, P. T. Barnum brought a gigantic elephant to the United States. The elephant's name was Jumbo. It was 11 feet high and weighed 7 1/2 tons. Its trunk was 26 feet long. Since that time, the word "jumbo" has been used to describe something very large. List the words you use to describe something large.

RESOURCES

Yoga for Children by Erene Cheki-Haney and Ruth Richards (New York: Macmillan, 1973).

Muybridge's Complete Human & Animal Locomotion: All 781 Plates from 1887 by Eadweard Muybridge (New York: Dover Publications, 1979).

alter Hunt patented the safety pin on this day in 1849. According to one story, Hunt thought up the idea for the safety pin and made a model of it in about three hours. By the time the third hour was over, he had sold all his rights to his invention for $100.

Write about all the uses for the safety pin that you can think of.

The U. S. patent system was established on this date in 1790. It was formed to protect the rights of inventors. When inventors come up with a new idea, they file for patent numbers. Research some patented things that people use every day. Locate the dates they were patented.

Many annual prizes are given in the fields of journalism and literature. Among the most famous and important are the Pulitzer Prizes. The awards are named after Joseph Pulitzer, who was born in Mako, Hungary, on

this date in 1847. He came to the United States when he was 37 years old. During his lifetime he was a reporter, Missouri legislator, and lawyer. He was also a member of the U.S. House of Representatives and a newspaper owner. He founded the Columbia School of Journalism. Pulitzer died in 1911.

If you'd like more information about these prizes, send a letter to:

Pulitzer Prize Board
702 Journalism
Columbia University
New York, NY 10027

The American Society for the Prevention of Cruelty to Animals (ASPCA) was founded on this day in 1866. Today is Humane Day. Ask an expert on animals to come to talk about animal rights. Call or visit the Humane Society in your area to get more information.

oday is Barbershop Quartet Day. On this date in 1938, 26 people in Tulsa, Oklahoma, founded SPEBSQSA. That stands for the "Society for the Preservation and Encouragement of Barbershop Quartet Singing in America." A barbershop quartet is an American singing group. It contains four people. They sing *a cappella*, which means without any musical instruments. Each quartet has a bass, baritone, lead, and tenor. The bass sings the lowest notes. The tenor sings the highest notes. The baritone and lead sing the notes in between. Women who sing in barbershop quartets are called Sweet Adelines.

Describe the kind of music you listen to. Tell why you listen to that type of music.

The theme song of SPEBSQSA is "Keep America Singing." The song encourages people to smile while they're singing. It tells listeners to sing all day long. It also says that a shared song makes everyone feel better about each other. Listen to a recording of a barbershop quartet. Then share a song. Sing with someone.

 Jackie Robinson joined the Brooklyn Dodgers on this date in 1947. He was the first African-American player in the major leagues. In Robinson's honor, play a game of baseball outside or kickball in the gym. Sing "Take Me Out to the Ball Game."

 April is Keep America Beautiful Month. Its purpose is to educate Americans about the problems of littering. During this month, people think about ways to improve the environment. Recycling is one way you can help save natural resources.

If you'd like more information about keeping America beautiful, send a letter to:

Keep America Beautiful, Incorporated
9 West Broad Street
Stamford, CT 06902

Today is the birth date of author Beverly Cleary. She was born in McMinnville, Oregon, in 1916. Cleary is best known for her series of books about two children named Henry Huggins and Ramona Quimby.

 Invent a character you could write books about. Describe your character. Give your character a name.

 Ask someone to read part of a Henry Huggins or Ramona Quimby book. Sit back and enjoy the crazy and funny situations that these characters sometimes get into.

 In 1981 on this day, the United States launched the first reusable spacecraft, the space shuttle *Columbia*. Astronauts John Young and Robert Crippen piloted the craft. *Columbia* and its crew completed the mission two days later by landing safely on a special runway.

Look up the words "space exploration," "rocket," and "space shuttle" in an encyclopedia. List the differences between the early rocket ships and the modern-day space shuttles.

 Marietta Peabody Tree was born in Lawrence, Massachusetts, on this day in 1917. In 1961, she became the first woman to serve as chief U.S. delegate to the United Nations. Three years later, she became the first woman to be a U.S. representative with the rank of ambassador.

Ambassadors work to keep good relations between their country and another country. They often frequently visit or live in the country that they work with. Write about the country you'd want to be an ambassador for.

RESOURCES

Some books by Beverly Cleary:

Henry Huggins, Henry and the Clubhouse, Ramona the Pest, Beezus and Ramona (New York: Morrow).

On this date in 1796, Jacob Crowninshield brought the first elephant to America. The two-year-old elephant was from Bengal, India. It measured 6 1/2 feet tall. Many Americans had never seen such a huge animal.

 Write about the largest animal you've ever seen.

 "The Blind Men and the Elephant" is a folktale. It's about six blind men who meet an elephant for the first time. The first blind man touches the elephant's skin. He thinks, "An elephant must be like a wall!" The second blind man touches a tusk. He says, "An elephant must be like a spear!" The third blind man feels the trunk. He thinks, "An elephant must be like a snake!" The fourth blind man feels a knee. He decides that an elephant must be like a tree. The fifth touches an ear. He says, "An elephant is like a fan." Finally, the sixth blind man feels the elephant's tail and thinks, "It's like a rope."

As you can see, none of these men accurately described an elephant. Write what might happen if these same men touched a bicycle for the first time.

 Communication is an important skill. You communicate when you talk on the phone and laugh out loud. In the game of charades, however, you communicate without talking or making noises. To play charades, have your classmates write words on small pieces of paper. Combine all the slips. Everyone takes turns picking a word and acting it out. Use hand gestures, smiles, and shrugs. But no talking!

 From 1896 to 1940, Annie Jump Cannon was an astronomer at the Harvard College Observatory in Cambridge, Massachusetts. She was the first person to classify everything that appears in the sky from the North to the South Pole. She recorded the existence of more stars during her lifetime than any other person ever had. She put more than 350,000 stars in groups according to

their temperatures. Cannon was born in Dover, Delaware, on December 11, 1863. She died on this day in 1941.

Why do we need astronomers? With your class, talk about why we need people to study the stars.

 In 1828, the first edition of Noah Webster's *American Dictionary of the English Language* was published. Webster and his staff worked for more than 20 years on the book. It introduced 12,000 words that had never been included in any other dictionary. Since that first edition, many more words have been added to the dictionary.

 Create a new word. Write a definition and pronunciation for it. Use it in a sentence.

 Gather together several dictionaries. *Examples: The American Heritage* or *Webster's New World.* Look up the same word in each dictionary. Compare the definitions. Does each dictionary spell the word the same way? Look for an unusual word. Share the word and its meaning with the class.

 To learn more about Noah Webster, read *What Do You Mean? A Story about Noah Webster* by Jeri Ferris.

On this day in 1910, President William Howard Taft started a baseball tradition. He threw out the first ball of the baseball season. Since that first throw, many presidents have begun the baseball season this way.

Baseball is played on a diamond-shaped area. Each side of the diamond is 90 feet long. The distance from the pitcher's mound to home plate is 60 feet 6 inches. How far can you throw a baseball? Measure out 60 feet. See if you can throw the ball that far.

R E S O U R C E

What Do You Mean? A Story about Noah Webster by Jeri Ferris (Minneapolis: Carolrhoda Books, 1988).

Leonardo da Vinci was born on this date in 1452. He was a painter, sculptor, architect, engineer, and scientist. Leonardo foresaw many discoveries. He made accurate drawings and notes about the circulation of the blood, the function of muscles, and the workings of the brain. He made these notes and drawings long before anyone else. His notes also included ideas for an airplane, armored tank, submarine, and cannon. He included many details that the eventual inventions actually had.

 Write about an idea you have for a new invention.

 Leonardo painted the *Last Supper* and the *Mona Lisa*, two of the most famous pieces of art ever created. The *Mona Lisa* shows a woman with a famous mysterious smile. To learn more about Leonardo's art and his inventions, read the book *Leonardo da Vinci: Art for Children* by Ernest Raboff.

 Draw a woman or man with a mysterious look on her or his face.

 Just before midnight on April 14, 1912, the *Titanic*, a huge cruise ship, struck an iceberg. It sank at 2:27 a.m. on April 15. About 2,200 people were on board. More than

1,500 died. The ship *Carpathia* reached the scene of the sinking at 3 a.m. The crew rescued about 700 people from the cold water.

Because the *Titanic* sank in such deep water, no one was able to find it for many years. Then in July 1986, Dr. Robert Ballard led an expedition that located the sunken ship. Two memorial plaques were left on the deck. Look through *Exploring the Titanic* by Ballard to find out more about this treasure hunt.

R E S O U R C E S

Leonardo da Vinci: Art for Children by Ernest Raboff (New York: HarperCollins Children's Books, 1987).

Exploring the Titanic by Dr. Robert Ballard (New York: Scholastic, 1988).

In 1783, the Revolutionary War ended. Because of the war, the British government began to pay Molly Brant an annual pension. The British were rewarding this Canadian citizen for spying on the Patriots. During the war, Brant told the British the location and plans of the Patriot soldiers. Brant was born in 1736. She died on this day in 1796.

 Have you ever spied on anyone? Has anyone ever spied on you? Write about how you felt.

 On this day in 1988, the residents of Fort Madison, Iowa, raised money for a playground. They raised $12,383.06 in pennies. Draw your ideal playground. Where would your playground be located?

 Charles Spencer Chaplin—also known as Charlie Chaplin—was born in London, England, on this day in 1889. He was a comedian who made his film debut in a silent movie in 1914. His most famous character

was the "Little Tramp." For this character, Chaplin put on a little mustache, carried a cane, and walked with a shuffle. Chaplin was knighted by England's Queen Elizabeth in 1975. He died in Switzerland on December 25, 1977.

Pick a story. Pretend that you're an actor in a silent movie. Act out the plot without talking out loud.

 National Library Week begins on the third Sunday of April. Have a Library Scavenger Hunt. Make a list of items to locate in the library. *Examples:* Look for books by certain authors or illustrators. Locate the card catalog or a computer. Find a partner, set a time limit, and see which teams can find all the items on the list.

Thornton Niven Wilder was born on this day in 1897 in Madison, Wisconsin. Wilder was an author and a playwright. He was famous for expressing his ideas simply. He wrote the play *Our Town*, which takes place in a small American town. By the end of his career, Wilder had won three Pulitzer Prizes for his work.

 As simply as you can, describe your town or city. Tell where it's located. Write about some of the people who live there.

 Playwrights not only write a story. They also describe the scenes so actors can play out the story on stage. Playwrights write down where the play takes place and when the scenes change. They tell the characters where to sit, when to laugh, and when to leave the stage. Stage directions usually appear in brackets within the text. As the characters talk to one another and themselves, they reveal the story line, or plot.

Look through a play. Write down some stage directions. *Examples:* He walks to the left. She kisses her mother. They sit on the couch. Write down some stage directions you would use if you were writing a play.

 Members of the Boston Athletic Association went to the first modern Olympics games in Athens, Greece, in 1896. When they returned to the United States, they organized the Boston Marathon. It was first run on this day in 1897. The Boston Marathon is held every year on the Monday closest to April 18.

The marathon begins in Hopkinton, Massachusetts. The runners travel through eight towns before reaching the finish line in downtown Boston—a distance of 26 miles, 385 yards. If you'd like more information about this marathon, send a letter to:

Boston Athletic Association
Boston Marathon
P.O. Box 19__ (fill in the year; for example in 1995, you'd write P.O. Box 1995)
Hopkinton, MA 01748

 Plan your own marathon. In the playground or gym, map out a running course. For your marathon, tell your runners that they need to run around the course a certain number of times to complete the race.

On this day in 1775, Paul Revere rode through the night warning the Patriots that British soldiers were about to attack. In the mid-1800s, Henry Wadsworth Longfellow wrote a poem titled "Paul Revere's Ride." In it, Longfellow writes, "Listen, my children, and you shall hear of the midnight ride of Paul Revere." Actually, Revere started his ride at about 10 p.m. Longfellow didn't use the correct facts. His poem could be called historical fiction.

 Create your own historical fiction scene. Pretend you've been awakened by Paul Revere as he rides by your house yelling, "The British are coming!" Write about who you are and what you'll do next.

 When authors write historical fiction, they use names of real people along with made-up characters and situations. You may have read a book called *Ben and Me*. In the story, Amos, the mouse, and Ben Franklin are the main characters. The story is written as though Amos is telling it. The book contains some interesting true facts. Of course, there wasn't really a talking mouse.

Pick an event in history. *Examples:* The first flight to the moon. The tearing down of the Berlin Wall. Then pretend you're an animal. From your new point of view, write about what you'd see.

 According to the book *I Love Paul Revere Whether He Rode or Not* by Richard Shenkman, Paul Revere didn't really finish his ride. A British guard stopped and arrested Revere. Many people don't believe that story. They feel that he and William Dawes rode to carry the warning like all the stories say.

What do you think really happened? Debate the issue with members of your class. Divide into two teams. One team takes Paul Revere's side and argues that he completed his ride. The other team takes the side of the British and argues that a guard captured Revere before he completed his ride.

 On this day in 1906, a powerful earthquake hit San Francisco, California, at 5:15 a.m.

Half of the city was destroyed and more than 500 people were killed. There was $350 million in damages. Find out three more facts about this earthquake and its aftermath. Share the facts with your class.

RESOURCES

Ben and Me by Robert Lawson (New York: Dell Publishing Company, 1973).

I Love Paul Revere Whether He Rode or Not by Richard Shenkman (New York: HarperCollins Publishers, 1991).

The biggest gum bubble on record was 22 inches wide. That's wider than some school desks! It was blown on this day in 1985 by a young girl named Susan Montgomery Williams.

 Create a new bubble gum flavor. Describe and name your new creation. How about Pepperoni Pizza Pizzazz? Or Strawberry Ice Cream Surprise?

 Have a class bubble blowing contest. Don't use bubble gum, use soap bubbles. You'll need some dish washing liquid soap, a shallow pan, water, and a coat hanger.

Create your own wand by bending the coat hanger into an unusual shape. Pour some of the dish washing liquid into the shallow pan and add an equal amount of water. Dip your wand into the solution. Carefully swish it back and forth in the air. Try to make a small bubble. Now try a colorful one. Create an unusually shaped bubble.

 On April 19, 1775, Captain John Parker gave a famous order to his troops of minutemen. "Stand your ground," he told his men. "Don't fire unless fired upon: but if they mean to have a war, let it begin here." The soldiers were fighting near the Massachusetts villages of Lexington and Concord. This battle began the Revolutionary War. For eight years the minutemen battled the British soldiers for American independence.

Pretend that you must ask men and women to join the minutemen. Design a poster to encourage people to join. Use Captain Parker's quotation as part of your poster.

 On a map of Massachusetts, locate Lexington and Concord. Research Paul Revere's route to Lexington and note it on the map.

In late April, you can celebrate Egg Salad Week. This week is dedicated to all the ways to use those cooked and colored Easter eggs. Even people who don't color Easter eggs can enjoy this week by eating eggs.

 Write your special recipe for egg salad. Start out with plain, hard-cooked eggs. What ingredients would you add to make an eggstra-special sandwich?

 Would you like to know more about eggs? For more information, send a letter to:

The American Egg Board
1460 Renaissance Drive, Suite 301
Park Ridge, IL 60068

 You can fool your friends with the help of two eggs. You will need one egg that's hard boiled and one that's uncooked. Tell your friends that you can guess which of the two eggs is the hard-boiled one. Give the eggs to a friend and ask that person to switch them around a few times while your back is turned. Turn around, take the first egg and

hold it pointy side down on a flat surface. Spin it. If it spins easily, it's hard boiled. If it won't spin on its top at all, it's raw. You may want to practice this to make sure it works for you.

 Try some eggshell art! You'll need eggshells, hot water, vinegar, food coloring, small containers, measuring cup, teaspoon, paper towels, cotton swabs, construction paper, and glue.

First, wash and dry the egg shells and crush them into small pieces. Next, fill the small containers with about 1/2 cup of hot water. Into each container, add a teaspoon of vinegar and a few drops of food coloring. Drop some of the crushed shells into the water. They will need to soak up the color for a few minutes. Remove the shells from the water. Spread them out on the paper towels to dry.

Using a cotton swab, paint a design on the construction paper with the glue. Sprinkle the colored eggshells onto the glue. After the glue dries, shake off any extra shells.

John Muir was born on this day in 1838. He was an American explorer, conservationist, and author. He was also a naturalist who became famous for his efforts to preserve the environment. When he was 29 years old, Muir walked from Indiana to the Gulf of Mexico. He wrote about the plants he saw and published his findings in a book. A year later, he went to California's Yosemite Valley. Later, he helped to establish Yosemite and Sequoia national parks.

 Describe the most beautiful place you've ever seen. This place could be one you've been to or one you've seen pictures of in a magazine or book.

 Tell your classmates about any national parks, forest preserves, or town or city parks that you've visited. Tell them what you liked about the places visited. Would you want to go back?

 Friedrich Froebel was a German educator and author who was born on this day in 1782. Froebel believed that toys and music were important to a child's education. He thought playing was as important to learning as homework. Froebel started the first kindergarten in 1837.

Froebel also invented a series of toys that he felt would make learning easier. His toys were made of different shapes and colors. His simplest toys were wooden blocks. Draw something you could build out of blocks.

 Design your own educational toy or game. Keep in mind that it should be fun to play with yet teach a skill. *Examples:* Design a toy that would help young kids learn their colors. Think of a toy that would help them tell the time. Create a game that would help them with counting.

April 22

Today is Earth Day. The first Earth Day was observed in 1970. Millions of Americans came together to protest pollution. In 1990, people around the world celebrated the 20th Earth Day. Concerts and festivals helped people celebrate the Earth and its resources. Exhibits showed ways to recycle and listed endangered animals. This day was designed to promote ecological awareness.

 In your opinion, can you help to save the Earth? Tell what you can do to make a difference.

 If you would like more information about Earth Day, send a letter to Renew America. This group also can tell you about kids who have made a difference in their community. The address is:

Renew America
1460 Renaissance Drive, Suite 301
Park Ridge, IL 60068

 Read *50 Simple Things Kids Can Do to Save the Earth* by John Javna. This book is full of activities and ideas that show things you can do. You can "Be a Bottle Bandit" or "Stamp Out Styrofoam." You can "Adopt a Piece of the Earth" and "Teach Your Parents Well." There are many more suggestions on what you can do to save the Earth.

 Have you noticed litter around your school? Why not clean it up? Organize your class and collect the litter in plastic bags. Wear gloves to protect your hands from the trash. Make your school grounds beautiful again.

··

R E S O U R C E

50 Simple Things Kids Can Do to Save the Earth by John Javna (Kansas City: Andrews & McMeel, 1990).

··

April 23

On this day in 1928, movie star Shirley Temple was born in Santa Monica, California. When she was six years old, she won a special award for being "the outstanding personality of 1934." Between 1935 and 1938, Temple was one of the most popular movie stars. She stopped making movies when she was 21 and began to work in politics. She was the U.S. ambassador to Ghana in the mid-1970s and the ambassador to Czechoslovakia from 1989 to 1992.

 What would you rather do—act in movies and TV shows or travel the world meeting people? Why?

 William Shakespeare was born in Stratford-on-Avon, England, on April 23, 1564. He died at the age of 52, on this same day in 1616. Shakespeare was the author of over 150 sonnets (poems) and 36 plays. His wrote *Romeo and Juliet* and *Hamlet*. His birthday is a festival day in Stratford-on-Avon. Shakespeare lovers in many nations around the world observe this day by reading his works.

"Good night, Good night! Parting is such sweet sorrow." This is a quote from Shakespeare's play *Romeo and Juliet*. Have you ever been sad to leave someone? Write about why you didn't want to leave.

 Look at a model or picture of Shakespeare's Globe Theater. Shakespeare helped to build this theater in 1598. During the first performance of the play *Henry VIII* in 1613, the actors shot a cannon for a royal salute in Act I. The cannon set fire to the theater. It burned to the ground. The Globe was rebuilt in 1614, but was permanently closed in 1644.

 In honor of Shakespeare's birthday, write a poem. A poem can be as simple as putting a few words together. To get started, write down the words you think of when you hear the phrase "warm weather." Use your words to write a poem.

Congress approved the creation of the Library of Congress on this day in 1800. The library is housed in Washington, D.C. It has more than 81 million books, magazines, brochures, and other items. It takes 535 *miles* of shelves to house all of these things. It would be impossible to see the entire collection, even if you looked at one item per minute for 150 years. The library contains the oldest example of printing, which dates back to A.D. 770.

 Describe something of yours that you'd add to the Library of Congress collection. Why is that item important to you? Why would you want that item in the library?

 Consumer Protection Week begins on or near this date each year. Its purpose is to warn people that some companies may lie to get customers to buy their products. Some companies use false advertising. They say a product is better than it really is or that it can do something that it really can't. If you'd like more information about Consumer Protection Week, send a letter to:

The U.S. Postal Service
Communications Department
475 L'Enfant Plaza SW, Suite 4485 E
Washington, DC 20260-6757

 This is Reading Is Fun Week. It's also National Humor Month. Celebrate by reading a funny book. Try the *World's Wackiest Riddle Book* by Evelyn Jones or *Laughing Together: Giggles and Grins from around the Globe*, compiled by Barbara K. Walker.

 On or near this day, the Rattlesnake Derby in Mangum, Oklahoma, takes place. Hunters compete to bring in the most rattlesnakes or the longest ones. People sell snake skins and snake meat. You might even find a herpetologist there. Can you guess what a herpetologist does? Find the word in a dictionary.

RESOURCES

World's Wackiest Riddle Book by Evelyn Jones (New York: Sterling Publishing Company, 1987).

Laughing Together: Giggles and Grins from around the Globe, compiled by Barbara K. Walker (Minneapolis: Free Spirit Publishing, 1992).

April 25

Edward Roscoe Murrow was born on this date in 1908. He was born in Greensboro, North Carolina. Murrow became one of the world's most noted reporters. He produced a TV program called "See It Now." He also interviewed people in their homes in the show "Person to Person." Both of his shows started a new style of on-the-scene reporting. Murrow was director of the U.S. Information Agency from 1961 to 1964. He died in 1965.

 Pretend you're an on-the-scene reporter for your school. Write about something you'd like to report on.

 Today begins the Tin Hau Festival in Hong Kong. This is the festival of the heavenly queen. Fishermen decorate their boats and worship the Goddess of Fishermen. Chinese fishermen ask for good catches in the coming year. If you'd like more information about this festival, send a letter to:

Hong Kong Tourist Association
590 Fifth Avenue, Fifth Floor
New York, NY 10036-4706

 New York became the first state to require license plates for cars on this day in 1901.

Only 954 cars registered. Each license plate showed the initials of the car's owner.

Design your own personalized license plate. *Examples*: 10SNE1 (tennis anyone?). SAY AH (for a doctor). Use the color and style of your state's license plates. Read *CDC?* or *CDB!* by William Steig to get some ideas about playing with words, letters, and their sounds.

 What slogan appears on the license plates in your state? Why do you think people chose that saying? Create an original slogan for yourself or your state.

RESOURCES

CDC? by William Steig (New York: Farrar, Straus & Giroux, 1986).

CDB! by William Steig (New York: Simon & Schuster, 1987).

April 26

On this date in 1785 John James Audubon was born. He was an ornithologist and artist. He painted all the species of birds in the United States that were known in the early 1800s. In 1826, his paintings were published in *The Birds of America* series. Audubon became a great success and wrote *A Synopsis of the Birds of North America*. Today, Audubon's paintings are still popular and respected for their beauty and accuracy.

 Write a detailed description of your favorite bird. Include its size, color, and what it eats.

 Although some of Audubon's books are no longer in print, a reproduction of an 1840 edition of *The Birds of America* is still available. *Audubon's Birding Guide*, edited by

John Farrand also includes examples of Audubon's work. If you can't find a book that includes Audubon's bird pictures, locate and enjoy any other books that have pictures or photographs of birds.

 Take a walk outside. Carry a sketch pad with you. Draw the birds that you see along the way.

 Paul Revere was not the only one to warn the American colonists about the British. On this night in 1777, Sybil Ludington rode through Connecticut. She was 16 years old and the daughter of an army colonel. She warned 400 of her father's men that British soldiers were approaching. Find the names of other women who played a role in history. Share their accomplishments with your classmates.

R E S O U R C E S

The Birds of America by John James Audubon (Magnolia, Massachusetts: Peter Smith Publisher, reproduction of 1840 edition).

Audubon's Birding Guide, edited by John Farrand (New York: Knopf, 1987).

On this day in 1900 Walter Lantz was born. He was the creator of the cartoon character Woody Woodpecker. More than 200 species of woodpecker exist in the world today. They are found on every continent except Australia.

 In his cartoons, Woody Woodpecker is always getting himself into trouble. Write a paragraph about Woody or a real woodpecker.

 Today is the birth date of Ludwig Bemelmans. He was born in 1898 in Meran, Austria. In 1939, he wrote a book about a little French girl and titled it *Madeline*. In that first book, Madeline has her appendix taken out. Bemelmans continued the story of Madeline and her friends in *Madeline's Rescue*, *Madeline and the Bad Hat*, and other books. Read a Madeline book today.

 Hugh Moore was born on this day in 1887. The disposable paper cup is his claim to fame. He invented the cup in 1908. Experiment, play, figure, test, or just amaze your friends with a paper cup. You'll find some great activities in the book *Boiling Water in a Paper Cup and Other Unbelievables* by Jerome S. Meyer. Discover the fascinating things you can do with Moore's invention.

 Save some disposable cups and use them again for a fun activity. Wash them and have a cup stacking contest. For one contest you'll need a set of 15 cups for each person or team. Have each person create a pyramid of cups. Starting with five cups in a line, place four cups between and on top of those five. Place three cups on top of the four. Two cups balance on the three. End with one cup on the top of the pyramid. See who can stack the cups the fastest. Take turns stacking the cup while blindfolded. Stack the cups using the hand you don't normally use. Think of other variations to challenge yourself.

R E S O U R C E S

Some books by Ludwig Bemelmans:

Madeline, Madeline's Rescue, Madeline and the Gypsies (New York: Viking Children's Books).

Madeline and the Bad Hat, Madeline in London (New York: Puffin Books).

Boiling Water in a Paper Cup and Other Unbelievables by Jerome S. Meyer (New York: Scholastic, 1972).

April 26

A man named J. Sterling Morton said, "Other holidays repose upon the past; Arbor Day proposes for the future." Morton founded Arbor Day on this date in 1872. He encouraged people to plant trees. He wanted people to protect and appreciate them. To celebrate the first National Arbor Day, 1 million trees were planted in Nebraska in 1872.

 Write a tribute to your favorite tree. Describe its color and location. Does it hold a tree house? Is it an old tree that you can hardly put your arms around? Is your favorite tree a young one that's easy to hug?

 Thor Heyerdahl is a Norwegian explorer and anthropologist. He tried to prove that people from ancient cultures traveled across oceans. He also wanted to prove that these travelers started new cultures. Heyerdahl built a raft using the same materials and techniques of the ancient people. He named his raft the *Kon Tiki*.

On this day in 1947, Heyerdahl set sail from Callao, Peru. He landed on the Marquesas Islands in French Polynesia. He proved that ancient people could have traveled from the Americas to the South Pacific. The book about his adventure was titled *Kon Tiki* after the raft. Find Callao, Peru, on a map (it's near Lima). Now find the Marquesas Islands in the South Pacific Ocean. Try to figure out how far Heyerdahl traveled.

 Ask someone to read part of Heyerdahl's book *Kon Tiki* to you. In chapter 4, he describes some of the fascinating sea life that he saw.

 Sham al-Nessum takes place today in Egypt. Sham al-Nessum means "Smell the Spring Day." This celebration has been around since ancient times. It's the only holiday that is observed by all religious groups in Egypt. Families go on picnics and bring brightly colored eggs. They wear new clothes and spend the day celebrating spring. List all the smells and tastes you think of when you think of spring.

RESOURCE

Kon Tiki by Thor Heyerdahl (New York: Simon & Schuster, 1987).

April 29

Today is the birthday of Andre Agassi, a professional tennis player. He was born in Las Vegas, Nevada, in 1970. Agassi has his own way of playing tennis—and his own style of dressing. He wears his hair long and often has a scruffy beard.

 Write about something you do or something you wear that shows your personal style.

 Send Andre Agassi a note or a birthday card. Address the envelope to:

Andre Agassi
International Management Group
One Erieview Plaza
Cleveland, OH 44114

 Gideon Sundback patented a "separable fastener" on this date in 1913. His invention is now known as the zipper. Sundback was an employee of Hook and Eye Company in Hoboken, New Jersey. The name "zipper" comes from the sound it makes. It is an onomatopoeia.

Come up with a new way to fasten your clothes. *Examples*: use bubble gum, staples, paper clips. What's the most outrageous way you can think of to fasten your clothes?

 Today is Lei Day in Hawaii. A lei (pronounced lay) is a garland or necklace of flowers worn around the neck. Have a Lei Day festival with your own flower leis. You'll need a large needle (it doesn't have to be sharp), some string or fish line, and a roll of brightly colored crepe paper.

Take the string and make a large loop. Make sure the loop is large enough to fit easily over your head. Cut the string and thread it through the needle. Tie a tight knot in one end. Put the needle and string through one end of the crepe paper and pull the needle through until the knot reaches the paper. Put the needle back into the crepe paper a few inches away and pull the string all the way through again. Continue sewing through the crepe paper. When your string is covered in paper, tie the two ends of the string together. Place your garland around your neck and celebrate.

April 30

On this day in 1939, music composer Ellen Taafe Zwilich was born in Miami, Florida. In 1975, she became the first woman to receive her doctorate in composition from The Juilliard School of Music. Orchestras all over the United States have performed her work. In 1983, one of her symphonies won the Pulitzer Prize for music. She was the first woman to receive the prize in that category.

 Have you ever attended a concert? If you have, write about the sights and sounds you saw and heard. If you haven't been to a concert yet, would you like to someday? Why or why not?

 Franklin Delano Roosevelt became the first U.S. president to appear on television on this date in 1939. The first regularly scheduled television broadcasting also began today. The first TV show was a three-hour program about the New York World's Fair. What's your favorite TV show? Write about why you like that show.

 Johann Karl Friedrich Gauss was born on this day in 1777. He was a German mathematician and physicist. He loved math. When he was young, his teacher asked his class to add all the numbers from 1 to 100 together. Gauss had the correct answer—5,050—quickly. His classmates worked for more than an hour and still didn't get the answer. Gauss was only ten years old but he saw that each pair of numbers added up to 101. That is: $1+100= 101$, $2+99=101$, $3+98=101$, $4+97=101$, and so on. The total of the 50 pairs would be 50×101 or 5,050.

Since April is Math in Education Month and this is Gauss Day, stump your classmates with a complicated problem. There are some figuring-fun problems, with the answers, in *Funny Number Tricks* by Rose Wyler.

 On this day in 1904 the first burger was cooked. This event took place at the World's Fair in St. Louis, Missouri. Where is your favorite place to eat a hamburger? Is it at a local restaurant? At home? Or in the school cafeteria? Draw a picture of your favorite place to eat a hamburger. Include yourself in the picture eating a burger. Show what you put on a burger by the dribbles on your shirt.

RESOURCE

Funny Number Tricks by Rose Wyler (New York: Parents Magazine Press, 1976).

May 1

On this day in 1955, explorer Ann Bancroft was born in St. Paul, Minnesota. In 1986, Bancroft became the first woman to walk to the North Pole. She was part of the eight-member Will Steger International Polar Expedition team. The group walked from Ward Hunt Island, Canada, to the North Pole, covering 1,000 miles in 55 days. For most of the trek, the temperature was minus 70 degrees Fahrenheit.

 Describe a time you were very cold. What did you do to keep warm?

 May Day is a celebration that takes place on this day. Some people believe the celebration of May Day began when the ancient Romans honored Flora, the goddess of flowers, with outdoor festivals. Others believe that May Day celebrations began with the ancient Egyptians. May 1 marked the beginning of a welcomed season in which flowers bloomed and crops grew.

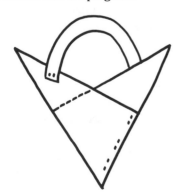

In honor of May Day, make a May Day basket. You'll need two square pieces of paper, one long strip of paper, and a stapler or glue. Fold each paper into a triangle. Hold each triangle by its folded edge and slip one triangle into the other until the bottom tips of the triangles meet. Staple or glue the edges together. To make a handle, staple or glue the long strip of paper onto the basket. Put flowers or candy in your May Day basket and give it to someone special.

 Have a quick contest to see who can create the longest list of words that rhyme with May. Use your list of words to write a May poem.

 On May 1, 1931, the Empire State Building was completed in New York City. For many years, the 102-story building was the tallest structure in the world. For more information about tall buildings, read the book *Up Goes the Skyscraper* by Gail Gibbons.

RESOURCE

Up Goes the Skyscraper by Gail Gibbons (New York: Macmillan Children's Book Group, 1990).

May 2

On May 2, 1927, Benny Benson, a seventh grader, won a competition. He entered his design for a new flag for Alaska and his design won. Maybe Benson was interested in becoming a vexillologist. A vexillologist is a person who studies the history, uses, and types of flags.

 Write about why you think countries and states have flags.

Design a flag for your school or classroom. Your flag could be square, rectangular, triangular, or any shape you want. Include symbols of things that represent your school. *Examples:* textbooks, faces of teachers and students, swings or jungle gyms, pencils, computers. Does your school have special school colors? If it does, include those on your flag. Show your flag to your class and explain why you made your flag the way you did.

In 1927, when Benny Benson designed his flag, Alaska was not part of the United States. The people who lived there held the flag competition because they wanted a flag to represent their area. For 42 years, the people of the Alaska Territory struggled to become a state. Look up the word "Alaska" in the encyclopedia or in another reference book. Find out when this territory finally became a state.

On May 2, 1837, Henry Martyn Robert was born. He was an American army officer and military engineer. In 1876, he wrote *Robert's Rules of Order*. This book tells people how they should act during meetings. Robert based his rules on the way the British Parliament ran its meetings. The book tells how people in a meeting should bring up new ideas, vote, and speak out. Robert's rules help keep meetings organized and orderly.

Discuss the rules of order for your classroom. Talk about how people will be called on to speak. Who will call on people to speak? Talk about how you can avoid interrupting someone.

Today is the birth date of Golda Meir. She was born in Kiev, Russia, in 1898. When she was eight years old, Meir and her family moved to Milwaukee, Wisconsin. After attending college in Wisconsin, she emigrated to Palestine. In 1969, Meir became the prime minister of Israel. She worked hard for better conditions in Israel and better communication between Israel and the Arabs. When war broke out between Israel and the Arabs in 1973, Meir resigned as prime minister.

Write about a time you found it hard to talk to someone. What could you say to that person to make it easier to talk to him or her next time?

To find out more about Golda Meir, read *Our Golda: The Story of Golda Meir* by David A. Adler.

The World's Colombian Exposition opened in Chicago on this day in 1893. Part of the Exposition was the Palace of Fine Arts Building. Today, that building is the Museum of Science and Industry. Another part of the exposition was the largest Ferris wheel ever built. The wheel was 250 feet in diameter and had 36 enclosed cars. Each car could hold 60 people each. More than 2,000 people could ride on it at the same time. George Washington Gale Ferris, an American engineer, invented the ride just for the exposition.

Write about a time you rode on a Ferris wheel. If you haven't ridden on one, write about how you think it would feel to ride high in the air on a Ferris wheel car.

Today, Ferris wheels are popular rides at carnivals, amusement parks, and fairs. Most Ferris wheels are about 50 feet in diameter. Many can be put up and taken down in only a few hours. The largest Ferris wheel was put up in London in 1894. It was 328 feet high and had 40 cars. Draw a picture of a Ferris wheel.

R E S O U R C E

Our Golda: The Story of Golda Meir by David A. Adler (New York: Puffin Books, 1986).

In 1780, Englishmen Edward Smith Stanley, 12th Earl of Derby, and his friend Sir Charles Bunbury established a race for three-year-old thoroughbred horses. But they couldn't decide who to name the race after. The two men flipped a coin and it landed in the earl's favor. The two men decided to call their race the Derby.

 Write about an event you'd like to have named after you.

 The Belmont Stakes, Preakness, and Kentucky Derby are three important horse races in the United States. A horse that wins all three of these races wins the Triple Crown. Some horses that have won the Triple Crown are Gallant Fox, Whirlaway, Seattle Slew, and Affirmed. Needles, Majestic Prince, and Dust Commander are the names of other winning horses. If you had a race horse, what one-of-a-kind name would you choose for it?

 National Sleep Month occurs in May. Some people require more sleep than others. We all sleep for different amounts of time. We also enjoy sleeping in different places: on a regular bed, on a waterbed, in a sleeping bag on the ground, and on the top or bottom bunk of bunk beds.

When someone has trouble sleeping, that person has insomnia. Some people drink warm milk or take a warm bath when they can't get to sleep. Make a list of your suggestions for curing insomnia.

 In 1776 on this day, Silas Deane arrived in France from the American colonies. He wanted to purchase military supplies for the colonists who were fighting the Revolutionary War. Deane helped set up an alliance between France and the struggling new country, but he worried that the British might capture him. Because he didn't want the British to know what was going on, he wrote all of his instructions in invisible ink.

You can create your own invisible ink. You'll need a paint brush, paper, small bowl, sugar, and water. In the bowl, mix together a teaspoon of sugar and a small amount of water to make a thin syrupy mixture. Dip the paintbrush in the solution and write your message on the paper. Let the message dry. To see what you wrote, hold the paper over a light bulb. The sugar and water mixture will make the paper turn brown and you'll be able to read your message. You can also use lemon juice or milk to write invisible messages.

After writing a letter to the *Pittsburgh Dispatch* in 1885, Elizabeth Cochrane Seaman got her first newspaper job. She wrote the letter to oppose the paper's stand against women's suffrage. During her reporting career, Seaman used the pen name "Nellie Bly." She became famous when she exposed the harsh conditions at an asylum. Bly had pretended she needed treatment and made notes on how the staff treated her while she was in the hospital. Nellie Bly was born in Cochrane's Mills, Pennsylvania, on this day in 1865.

 Write about something you'd like to be famous for.

 On May 5, 1862, 4,000 untrained Mexican soldiers defeated 10,000 well-trained French soldiers in four hours of fighting at the Battle of Puebla. General Zaragoza was the leader of the Mexican army. His battle cry of "No Pasaran!" ("They shall not pass!") inspired the Mexican soldiers. They forced the French Army to retreat.

Today, Mexicans remember this victory in the Cinco de Mayo celebrations. In Mexico City, the president reviews the troops. People decorate the streets with banners and flags and listen to bands play. Families and their friends enjoy a celebration dinner. Some people attend a ball where everyone dances until morning. In the United States, Cinco de Mayo is also an important holiday. Mexican-Americans put on parades, dance, wear colorful costumes, and eat ethnic foods.

Draw a picture of a Cinco de Mayo celebration—or of any other colorful celebration.

 You can celebrate Cinco de Mayo by creating a papier-mâché piñata. You'll need a balloon, newspaper cut into long strips, and papier-mâché solution.

Blow up the balloon and tie it shut. Dip the newspaper strips into the papier-mâché solution and lay the wet strips over the balloon. Cover the entire balloon, but leave a small hole in the bottom of the balloon

near the stem. After the papier mâché dries, pop the balloon and paint the piñata with bright colors.

Fill your piñata with candy, small gifts, or pieces of paper with special messages and hang it from the ceiling. Ask people to take turns hitting the piñata with a stick while they're blindfolded. When someone hits the piñata, it will burst and spill out the contents.

 In Japan, people celebrate Feast of Flags Day on the fifth day of the fifth month every year. Young people across the country are wished happiness and health. For each of their children, families fly special paper kite-flags shaped like carp, a type of fish. The Japanese feel carp show strength and courage because once a year these fish make a difficult journey upstream to find their mates. Families encourage their children to have the same determination.

To celebrate your own Feast of Flags Day, think of an animal and write about the qualities you admire in that animal.

In 1929 on this date, the Academy of Motion Picture Arts and Sciences awarded the first Academy Awards. The award was a statue of a man stabbing a film reel with a sword. The silent movie *Wings* won for best picture. Each year since then, actors, directors, movies, and technicians are honored for the best contributions to the movie industry.

 Write about the last movie you saw and why you liked or disliked it.

 Besides best picture awards, the Academy of Motion Picture honors the best actor, actress, special effects, music, and costumes. Write down the movies you've seen lately. If you held an award ceremony, which one would win the best picture award? Who would win the best actor and actress? Which movie would win the best special effects? Think of other awards for your movies.

 If your school has a video camera you can use, make a short movie. With your class, write a script and determine who in your class will play the different parts. Rehearse your movie, then videotape it.

 Sir Roger Gilbert Bannister became part of history on this date in 1954. A British athlete, he became the first person to run the mile in under 4 minutes. His time was 3 minutes, 59.4 seconds. He broke the record in Oxford, England.

Measure 1/20 of a mile on your playground or in your gym (1/20 of a mile is 264 feet). If you were to run back and forth 20 times, you would have run a mile. Time yourself and see how long it takes to run a mile.

Some fascinating photographs from the planet Neptune arrived from outer space on this day in 1989. *Voyager 2*, a tiny star ship, took the photos from an onboard camera. The star ship had traveled 12 years and 4.43 billion miles to reach the far-away planet. Scientists studied the photos and discovered six new moons and several unusual rings around Neptune. After taking its photos, *Voyager 2* continued its journey through the Milky Way.

 Pretend you're outside on a clear night. You lie back, look up into the stars, and then....Write about what you'd see or hope to see.

 Astronomy Day is observed on the Saturday nearest to the first quarter moon between mid-April and mid-May. Today could be Astronomy Day. If you'd like more information on this day or on the field of astronomy, write to:

Amateur Astronomers Association
1010 Park Avenue
New York, NY 10028

 Astronomers constantly search the sky for new stars, moons, and planets. Some astronomers also hope to find other life forms in the universe. Many people claim to have seen beings from other worlds. Their stories of UFOs—Unidentified Flying Objects—are well known. Do you think there are other creatures living in space? Why or why not? Talk with your class about what you think.

 If you want to look at color photographs of Neptune and the other planets, find *Journey to the Planets* by Patricia Lauber. For information on meteors, stars, moons, and other astronomy-related topics, read *The Children's Space Atlas* by Robin Kerrod.

RESOURCES

Journey to the Planets by Patricia Lauber (New York: Crown Publishers, 1993).

The Children's Space Atlas by Robin Kerrod (Brookfield, Connecticut: Millbrook Press, 1991).

May 8

Jean Henri Dunant was born in Geneva, Switzerland, on May 8, 1828. In 1862, Dunant published an article about the sufferings of people during war. He wrote that an organization should be formed to help those who were hurt or who had lost their homes. After he wrote the article, he founded the Red Cross. In 1901, Dunant was awarded the Nobel Peace Prize for his work with victims of war.

 Write about problems or concerns in your neighborhood or city. What can you do to help solve these problems?

 Clara Barton, an American, heard about the Red Cross while she was in Europe in 1870. When she returned home, she helped the soldiers who had been wounded during the Civil War. The soldiers nicknamed her "The Angel of the Battlefield." In 1881, Barton and her friends formed the American Association of the Red Cross. A year later, Barton convinced President Chester A. Arthur to join other countries and sign the Geneva Convention for the care of men and women wounded in war.

To learn more about Clara Barton and why she felt so strongly about caring for others, read *The Story of Clara Barton* by Zachary Kent.

 Both Henri Dunant and Clara Barton were humanitarians. Humanitarians work to improve people's lives. They help people find food and shelter. They ask government and businesses to treat minorities fairly. They constantly work to make a difference in their neighborhoods and cities. Make a list of people you know who are trying to make a difference in your school, neighborhood, or city.

 For more information about the services of the American Red Cross, write to:

The American Red Cross
431 18th Street NW
Washington, DC 20006

RESOURCE

The Story of Clara Barton by Zachary Kent (Chicago: Childrens Press, 1987).

May 9

On this day in 1944, the first eye bank was started. An eye bank keeps track of people who need a cornea transplant. (The cornea is the see-through structure that lies directly over the pupil of your eye.) When a donated cornea becomes available, the eye bank helps to get the organ to the hospital for the transplant. Thousands of people who are visually impaired have been helped through cornea transplant surgery.

 Close your eyes and keep them closed while you count to 50. Write a description of the first thing you see when you open your eyes.

 Today, doctors can save lives by transplanting kidneys, livers, even hearts and lungs. Start a class collection of newspaper and magazine clippings about people who have had organ transplants. Perhaps people in your city have had this operation. Watch for any news of their recovery.

 In 1988, firefighters in Warren, Michigan, had an unusual task. The firefighters were called to rescue ducklings. Someone had witnessed 14 ducklings fall through a sewer grate. The fire department arrived and promptly reunited mother and ducklings. Draw a picture of a firefighter during a rescue—or draw some ducklings.

 The book *Make Way for Ducklings* is about a duck family walking through the city streets. Read all about their adventures in the book by Robert McCloskey.

....

R E S O U R C E

Make Way for Ducklings by Robert McCloskey (New York: Viking Children's Books, 1941.)

....

On this day in 1908, Mother's Day became a public holiday in Philadelphia, Pennsylvania. Julia Ward Howe and Anne Jarvis wanted people all over the United States to recognize and honor mothers. On May 9, 1914, President Woodrow Wilson issued a proclamation making the second Sunday in May Mother's Day in the United States. On Mother's Day, millions of greeting cards, flowers, and other gifts are given to mothers all over America.

 Write about your mother, stepmother, grandmother, or another woman who is important in your life.

 Draw a picture of someone special to you. Your special someone could be a parent, grandparent, neighbor, or anyone else who loves you. All around the picture, write words that describe your someone.

 Make a medal for someone who has taken care of you. You'll need the plastic top from a coffee can or other container, yarn, glue, a marker, and scissors. Glue yarn around the edges to decorate your medal. In the center, write a slogan or some words of love with the

marker. With some scissors, make a small hole in the top of your medal. Cut a piece of yarn about 30 inches long and thread it through the hole. Tie the ends of the yarn together and your medal is complete.

 Read more about Mothers and Mother's Day in *Mother's Day* by Mary K. Phelan or *Mothers Can Do Anything* by Joe Lasker.

....

R E S O U R C E S

Mother's Day by Mary K. Phelan (New York: HarperCollins Children's Books, 1965).

Mothers Can Do Anything by Joe Lasker (Morton Grove, Illinois: Albert Whitman & Company, 1972).

....

Minnesota, the 32nd state, was admitted to the United States on this day in 1858. One of Minnesota's nicknames is "Land of 10,000 Lakes." Some estimates, however, say the total number of lakes in the state is as high as 22,000! If all of the lakes were put together, they'd take up more than 4,750 square miles. Lake Itasca is one of Minnesota's most famous lakes. It's where the Mississippi River begins.

 Write about the lakes in your state, if there are any. Or write about a time you went to a lake.

 Read more about the midwestern state of Minnesota in the books by Kathleen Thompson and R. Conrad Stein or look up "Minnesota" in the encyclopedia.

 Glacier National Park was established on this day in 1910. It's located on 1 million acres in the northwestern corner of Montana. A million years ago, as glaciers formed and moved in this area, they gouged out the park's deep valleys. Today, visitors can still see about 50 glaciers. To find out more about this national park, write to:

National Park Service
Rocky Mountain Region
P.O. Box 25287
Denver, CO 80225-2500

 On this date in 1888, songwriter Irving Berlin was born. In his musical *Annie Get Your Gun*, Berlin wrote a song called "Anything You Can Do I Can Do Better!" It's an argument between two people about who's better at doing things.

Hold a debate between celebrities or other famous people. Divide your class into two teams. Have each team pretend to represent a famous person. *Examples:* Teams could represent movie stars, singers, inventors, sports players, or authors. Using what you know about those famous people, carry on an argument about the things one person can do better than the other.

RESOURCES

Minnesota by Kathleen Thompson (Milwaukee, Wisconsin: Raintree Publishers, 1988).

Minnesota by R. Conrad Stein (Chicago: Childrens Press, 1990).

Today in Belgium the Cat Festival begins. According to a legend, the festival began in A.D. 962. Once a year, Baudouin III, the Count of Flanders, threw cats out of his castle's tower to prove he wasn't superstitious. For centuries, Belgians continued the custom. In 1938, toy cats replaced the real ones. On this day in Ypres, Belgium, people dress up as all kinds of cats.

 Write about what you think of cats. Do you have a special one? If not, would you like a cat as a pet?

 House cats have been around for centuries. In ancient Egypt, people worshipped cats and thought that they had special powers. Bast, the Egyptian goddess of life, had the head of a cat and the body of a woman. In one hand, Bast held a metal noisemaker. In the other hand she carried a shield. A basket was over one arm. Every year in ancient times, nearly a million Egyptians traveled to her shrine. Draw a picture of what you think Bast looked like.

 Dogs, birds, gerbils, tarantulas, turtles, rabbits, cats—these are just some of the pets people have. Write a paragraph about your pet. Tell what it likes to eat, where it sleeps, how you take care of it, and the reason you got your pet.

If you don't have a pet, write about the kind of pet you'd like to have someday. Would you like to have an unusual one?

 Edward Lear was born on this day in 1812. He was an English poet who wrote limericks. Here's one of them:

There was an old man with a beard,
Who said, "It is just as I feared—
Two owls and a hen,
Four larks and a wren
Have all built their nests in my beard."

In honor of Lear, today is Limerick Day. A limerick is a poem with five lines. The first two lines and the last line rhyme with each other and have eight syllables each. The third and fourth lines rhyme and have five syllables each. With your class, work together to write a limerick. Use your fingers to count out the syllables. Make your limerick as silly as you can.

MAY 13

Stevland Morris was born on this date in 1950 in Saginaw, Michigan. When he was 12 years old, he recorded "Fingertips," his first song. Today, Morris is known as Stevie Wonder. He's a musician who sings, plays keyboards, and composes blues and rock songs.

 Write about a special talent you have.

 Perhaps you've heard some of Stevie Wonder's songs. "You Are the Sunshine of My Life" and "Ebony and Ivory" are two of his popular tunes. In 1982, he was inducted into the Songwriters' Hall of Fame. In 1986, Wonder and other celebrities got together to record "That's What Friends Are For." To learn more about Stevie Wonder, read *Stevie Wonder* by Carl Green and William Sanford.

 "Every man's got to figure to get beat sometime," said Joe Louis. Joseph Louis Barrow, an American boxer, was born on this day in 1914. His nickname was the Brown Bomber. From 1937 to 1949, Louis was the World Heavyweight Champion. He defended his title 25 times. Of the 25 times he boxed, he knocked out his opponent 21 times.

What do you think about boxing and all-star wrestling? Do you enjoy watching these sports? Why or why not? Discuss this issue with your class. Find out what other people think of these sports.

 Do you have triskaidekaphobia? The word comes from the Greek words meaning "three-and-ten fear." Triskaidekaphobia is a fear of the number 13—today's date. Have some fun with this number. Find a word in the dictionary that has 13 letters. Look up something interesting in Volume 13 of the encyclopedia. Find out who was the 13th president. Estimate the weight of 13 people. Can you find some more information on 13?

RESOURCE

Stevie Wonder by Carl Green and William Sanford (New York: Macmillan Children's Book Group, 1990).

MAY 14

George Lucas, Jr., a motion picture director, writer, and producer, was born on this day in 1944 in Modesto, California. In 1977, Lucas directed the movie *Star Wars*. His space fantasy became one of the most popular films in history. Lucas also directed the movie's sequels *The Empire Strikes Back* in 1980 and *The Return of the Jedi* in 1983. Many people enjoy his movies because of their creative special effects.

 Write about the strange characters and unusual machines you think should be included in a space fantasy story.

 Directors use special effects to create illusions. Special effects can make a 10-foot monster walk, a dog talk, or a planet explode. Directors use makeup on the actors and small models to create their special effects.

Think about your favorite movie. Can you remember a part of the movie that may have used a special effect? Write about it. Try and figure out how that special effect was created.

 Did you ever think about the behind-the-scenes people needed to make a movie? Here's a list of some of them:

Producer
Scriptwriter
Animal Trainer
Prop Person
Songwriter
Manager
Makeup Artist

Set Director
Director
Costume Designer
Camera Operator
Sound Effects
Wardrobe Manager

If you were asked to work on a movie, which job would you choose? Tell the class your reasons for choosing that job.

 For more information on special effects, read *Special Effects: A Look Behind the Scenes at Tricks of the Movie Trade* by Rick Clise. You can find out how to make special effects in your own productions in the book *Make Your Own Animated Movies and Videotapes* by Yvonne Andersen.

···

R ESOURCES

Special Effects: A Look Behind the Scenes at Tricks of the Movie Trade by Rick Clise (New York: Viking Kestrel, 1986).

Make Your Own Animated Movies and Videotapes by Yvonne Andersen (Boston: Little, Brown, 1991).

···

 In *The Wonderful Wizard of Oz*, the good witch gives Dorothy a magical pair of ruby red slippers that will grant wishes. Pretend you have a chance to borrow the famous shoes. In one sentence, write what you'd wish for.

 Peace Officers' Memorial Day is today. People honor all the law-enforcement personnel who have lost their lives in the line of duty. The week surrounding this day is called Police Officers' Week. If you'd like more information about Peace Officers' Memorial Day and Police Officers' Week, write to:

International Association of Chiefs of Police
1110 North Glebe Road, Suite 200
Arlington, VA 22201

 More and more police departments have juvenile officers. Juvenile officers work only with young people. These officers help kids work through their problems. Discuss with your class why you think juvenile officers are needed more today than ever before.

May 15

Lyman Frank Baum was born on this day in 1856. He was a newspaper reporter who became a children's book writer. In 1900, he wrote his most famous book—*The Wonderful Wizard of Oz*. To create the name of this enchanted land, Baum looked around his office. He spotted his filing drawers that were labeled A-N and O-Z. By seeing the letters on the second filing drawer, Baum was inspired to name his fantasy world.

 Write about a time you came up with a sudden, bright idea.

May 16

On this day in 1957, long-distance runner Joan Benoit Samuelson was born in Cape Elizabeth, Maine. Samuelson began running in 1973 because she wanted to rebuild her muscles after a skiing accident. When the 1984 Olympic committee included a women's marathon event, Samuelson decided to compete. After the first 14 minutes of the race, she ran ahead of the other runners—and stayed in the lead for the rest of the marathon. She won the 26-mile race in 2 hours, 24 minutes, and 52 seconds.

Write about a time when you had to run for a long distance.

 George A. Wyman left San Francisco on this date in 1903. He headed east on his motorcycle. Wyman became the first person to cross the United States on a motorcycle. Write about how you'd like to see the United States. Would you ride a motorcycle? Or would you rather ride in a car, train, or bus?

 Gottlieb Daimler, a German engineer, invented the first motorcycle in 1885. Daimler was really trying to invent a more powerful engine. He tested his engines by mounting them on two wheels and came up with a new way to travel. Today, companies around the world create motorcycles ranging from small mopeds to racing motorcycles.

Before they drive a motorcycle on public streets, motorcyclists take a special driving test. They learn the proper way to drive in traffic and the right way to make a turn. Do you think people who ride motorcycles should wear helmets? Talk about the need for helmets with your class.

 Jim Henson, creator of Kermit the Frog and other muppets, died of pneumonia on this day in 1990. Kermit, Henson's favorite muppet creation, started as a worn-out green overcoat that belonged to Henson's mother. Henson used two Ping-Pong balls for eyes. He named his frog puppet after Kermit Scott, a schoolmate from Mississippi.

Create your own puppet. You could use an old sock or a paper lunch bag. Be creative with the items you use for facial features and hair. *Examples:* buttons, yarn, ribbon, and fabric scraps. After your puppet is finished, create a story where it's the lead character.

MAY 17

In Norway, today is a holiday called Syttende Mai (pronounced Soot-en-da My). On this day in 1814, Norway's leaders established a national government and declared Norway's independence from Sweden. Norwegians celebrate their independence with parades and dinners with friends and family. Many Norwegian-Americans also celebrate this day.

 Create your own ethnic celebration. Write about the food you'd serve and the activities you'd do.

 Syttende Mai is a favorite day for Norwegian celebration. St. Patrick's Day is a favorite day for Irish celebration. Does your family celebrate a favorite day that has something to do with your background? Maybe you have a yearly family reunion or potluck dinner. Maybe your family gets together during the holidays in December. Tell the class about your favorite family celebration day.

 On this day in 1620, the first merry-go-round was introduced in Turkey. Today, you can find merry-go-rounds in amusement parks and some shopping malls. Draw a picture of a colorful merry-go-round.

 Racial discrimination means to deny rights, privileges, and opportunities to a person or group because of race. In the United States, racial discrimination has been outlawed by amending the Constitution and by decisions from the Supreme Court. In 1954 on this day, the Supreme Court ruled on a case called *Brown vs. Board of Education of Topeka*. This ruling said that the separation of races in public schools was against the law.

Have you ever been discriminated against? Tell the class about your experiences. What can you do to make sure that discrimination doesn't happen?

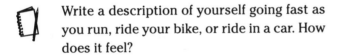

May 18

Pilot Jacqueline Cochran took her first flying lesson in 1932 when she was 22 years old. During World War II, she organized the Women's Air Force Service Pilots, a group of 1,000 female pilots who flew transport planes. On this day in 1953, Cochran became the first woman to break the sound barrier. While flying a Canadian Sabre jet, she flew faster than Mach I, the speed of sound. In her lifetime, she set over 200 flying records. She retired from the U.S. Air Force Reserve in 1970.

Write a description of yourself going fast as you run, ride your bike, or ride in a car. How does it feel?

On this day in 1852, the first law about attending school was passed in Massachusetts. The new law said that all children between the ages of 8 and 14 years had to go to school for 12 weeks a year. Six of those 12 weeks had to be in a row.

In recent years, some school districts have decided to start the school year on the Tuesday after Labor Day. Some still start their classes in August. Most schools begin summer vacation in late May or the first part of June. Get a copy of your school calendar. Add up how many days during the year you attend school. Now calculate how many days you have off (be sure to include Saturdays, Sundays, summer vacation, Thanksgiving vacation, and other holidays). Do your results surprise you?

 Many school districts would like their students to attend school all year round. You'd have the same amount of time off as you do now, but your vacation would occur at different times of the year.

Talk about an all-year school with your classmates. What would be some disadvantages? What would be some advantages? What's your opinion about going to school in June, July, and August?

On May 18, 1980, Mount St. Helens, in Washington state, sent smoke, steam, and ash more than 11 miles into the sky. When the volcano's eruption was over, 1,300 feet of the mountaintop were gone, leaving a crater nearly one mile wide. After the explosion, winds carried and spread the volcanic debris over three states. The eruption caused more than $1.6 billion in damage. It was the mightiest volcanic eruption in U.S. territory. Within a few months after the eruption, small flowers and grass began to grow up through the gray-black volcanic ash.

To see some pictures of the destruction Mount St. Helens caused and to find out more about volcanoes, read *Why Mount St. Helens Blew Its Top* by Kathryn A. Goldner and Carole G. Vogel.

RESOURCE

Why Mount St. Helens Blew Its Top by Kathryn A. Goldner and Carole G. Vogel (New York: Dillon Press, 1981).

May 19

On this date in 1925, Malcolm Little, known as Malcolm X, was born in Omaha, Nebraska. When he was young, Malcolm was arrested and jailed for burglary. While in prison, he learned about the Nation of Islam and became a minister. Malcolm became known as a person who said what he thought. He spoke out against white people but he also urged all people to be more caring toward each other. In the mid-1960s, Malcolm changed his views about whites and thought that blacks and whites could learn to live together. In February 1965, he was assassinated.

 Write about something you feel strongly about.

 People have many different opinions about Malcolm X. Some say he used violence to get what he wanted. Others say he helped African-Americans realize that they should help each other. Read more about this leader in *Malcolm X* by Arnold Adoff or *Malcolm X and Black Pride* by Robert Cwiklik.

 Today is Youth and Sports Day, a public holiday in Turkey. On this day, people celebrate Turkey's independence movement. Mustafa Kemal, who was later known as Ataturk, led the movement that began in 1919. Turkey wanted to be independent from Greece. Ataturk became the Turkish Republic's first president on October 29, 1923.

Some schools have outdoor sports days at the end of the school year. Some schools hold relay races, kickball tournaments, or a sports practice day. If you were in charge of a sports day at your school, what activities would you include? Write about how you'd organize the event.

 On this day in 1911, a man named Caesar Cella was convicted of burglary. The evidence against him included a new identifying technique called fingerprinting.

Using an inked stamp pad, create drawings using your thumb print. You'll also need paper and some pens or markers. Place the pad of your thumb on the ink pad. Then press your thumb onto a piece of paper. Add eyes, feet, or arms to create a thumb person. Create a whole thumb person village.

RESOURCES

Malcolm X by Arnold Adoff (New York: HarperCollins Children's Books, 1985).

Malcolm X and Black Pride by Robert Cwiklik (Brookfield, Connecticut: Millbrook Press, 1991).

May 20

Dolley Payne Madison as born on this day in 1768. She was the wife of James Madison, the fourth president of the United States. During her time as first lady, Madison saved the portrait of George Washington when the British burned the capital in 1812. She became known for her charm, grace, and talent for entertaining. Madison began the Easter egg rolling custom, which is still done yearly on the White House lawn.

 Write about why you think Dolley Madison saved the portrait of George Washington.

 To learn more about Dolley Madison, read *Dolley Madison: Famous First Lady* by Mary R. Davidson.

 Find out who is the first lady of the United States today. With your class, look through newspapers and magazines to find information about her.

 Today is Cher's birthday. She was born Cherilyn La Pierre on this day in 1946. In the 1960s, Cher and her husband Sonny Bono became a popular singing duo. Since the 1970s, however, Cher has been a solo singer and has acted in movies. In 1988 she won an Oscar for Best Actress. If you'd like to send Cher a birthday card or note, write to:

Cher
Creative Artists Agency
9830 Wilshire Boulevard
Beverly Hills, CA 90201

RESOURCE

Dolley Madison: Famous First Lady by Mary R. Davidson (New York: Chelsea House Publishers, 1992).

On this day in 1819, the first bicycles were imported from England to the United States. In New York City, a law was passed prohibiting people from riding bicycles on the sidewalk.

 Write about the first time you rode a bike.

 When they were first introduced in New York, bicycles were called velocipedes. To learn more about bicycles, read *Bicycles Are Fun to Ride* by Dorothy Chiad or *Bicycle Safety* by Cynthia Lingel.

 Learn to ride a bike safely. Here are some things to remember the next time you're riding your bike:

- Use hand motions to signal your turn. (To turn left, straighten your left arm and point it in the direction you want to turn. To turn right, bend up your left arm at the elbow.)

- Wear shoes.

- If you ride on the street, stay close to the curb.

- Keep your hands on the handlebars.

- Wear a bike helmet.

- Remember, most bikes are made for only one rider.

What other bike safety rules can you think of?

 Draw the bike of your dreams. *Examples:* Would you like a bicycle equipped with a radio? How about one with an umbrella to shade you on a hot summer days? Would you like a bike with four, five, or six seats? Would you want an enclosed bike or a bike with four wheels?

RESOURCES

Bicycles Are Fun to Ride by Dorothy Chiad (Chicago: Childrens Press, 1984).

Bicycle Safety by Cynthia Lingel (Mankato, Minnesota: Creative Education, 1986).

The frog-jumping contest in Angels Camp, California, begins on or near this day. Every year, more than 3,000 frogs participate. People from as far away as South America, Australia, and Sweden travel to this town with their frogs. Contestants put their frogs down on the starting line and coax them into jumping three times. Judges measure the distance from the starting line to the frog's last jump. The frog that jumps the farthest wins.

 Write about the strangest or funniest contest you've ever seen—or write about a contest you'd like to see someday.

 The Angels Camp frog-jumping contest was started because of a story by Mark Twain published in New York's *Saturday Press* on

November 18, 1865. Twain's story was called "The Celebrated Jumping Frog of Calaveras County." The story's main characters are a man named Jim Smiley and a frog named Daniel Webster. Smiley claimed that Daniel could out-jump any other frog around.

Have someone read "The Celebrated Jumping Frog of Calaveras County" to you.

 If you'd like more information about the frog-jumping contests at Angels Camp, write to:

Calaveras County Visitors Center
P.O. Box 637
1301 South Main Street
Angels Camp, CA 95222

 Here are some frog facts: Tree frogs cling to leaves and branches with sucker disks at the ends of their toes. Burrowing frogs have shovel-like feet and pointed snouts. The North American cricket frog is so small that it could fit on your fingernail. The Colombian giant toad towers over mice. Look in an encyclopedia or other reference book for more information on frogs. Share your frog facts with your class.

....
R E S O U R C E
"The Celebrated Jumping Frog of Calaveras County" in the *Classic Short Story Series* by Mark Twain (Mankato, Minnesota: Creative Education, 1990).
....

Margaret Wise Brown started writing children's books in the 1930s. By the 1950s, she had written over 100 stories. Brown cared about young readers and wrote about feelings that were important to them. She wrote books about feeling lonely, getting lost, and being shy. She published some of her books under the pen names Golden MacDonald, Timothy Hay, and Juniper Sage. Brown was born on May 23, 1910, in Brooklyn, New York. She died in 1952.

 Write about a feeling that's important to you.

 If you worry sometimes about getting lost and being alone, read *Young Kangaroo* by Margaret Wise Brown.

 Junko Tabei, a 35-year-old Japanese mother, became the first woman to reach the top of Mount Everest on this day. She made the climb in 1975 with 14 other women from Japan. Tabei's expedition took the same route other climbers used in the first successful ascent in 1953. Draw a picture of Junko Tabei standing at the top of Mount Everest.

 Mount Everest, the highest mountain in the world, is located in southern Asia in the Himalayas. The mountain is on the border between the countries Nepal and Tibet. Locate Mount Everest on a map. Find out its elevation. What are some other facts you can find about Mount Everest?

....
R E S O U R C E
Young Kangaroo by Margaret Wise Brown (New York: Kingswood, Surrey, World's Work, 1959).
....

As the mother of 12 children, Lillian M. Gilbreth was a busy person. She was also an engineer who, along with her husband, pioneered the idea of time-motion study. That's the study of the fastest and easiest ways to complete a task. Today, industries use time-motion study to improve the way they create products. Gilbreth was born on this day in 1878.

 Write about the times when you're busiest. Are you busiest in the morning when you get ready for school? At night when you're doing your homework? Or at some other time?

 Pick a task. Describe the fastest and easiest way to complete the task successfully. *Examples*: What's the fastest way to make your bed? Set the table? Mow the lawn?

 The first American bicycle race was held on this date in 1878. The winner took 12 minutes, 27 seconds to cover the three-mile course. Make a list of all the things you can do in 12 minutes or less.

 On this date in 1935, the Philadelphia Phillies played the Cincinnati Reds in the first major league baseball game played at night. The Reds defeated the Phillies by a score of 2 to 1. More than 20,000 fans enjoyed that first night game at Crosley Field in Cincinnati, Ohio.

Divide a piece of paper into two columns. Label one column "Night Game." List all the things you need for a night game. Label another column "Day Game." In that column, list all the things needed for a day game. How do the items on the two lists compare? How do they differ?

May 25

On this date in 1986, more than 6 million people held hands. They participated in "Hands Across America." From the Pacific Coast to the Atlantic Coast, people gathered together for this transcontinental event. The people who organized the event hoped to raise funds for— and let people know about— America's homeless people.

 What do you know about homelessness in America? Write about what you know and how you feel about this subject.

 With all the members of your class, hold hands. Measure the distance between the outstretched hands of the two people at the ends. How many of your classmates would it take to reach from one end of your school to the other?

 Igor Ivan Sikorsky was born in Kiev, Russia, on this day in 1889. Sikorsky's mother was a medical school graduate and his father was a university professor. When he was young, his parents helped him develop an interest in science. Sikorsky grew up to be an aeronautical engineer and designer. In 1913, he built the first airplane that had four engines. In 1939, he built and flew the first successful helicopter. Sikorsky became a U.S. citizen in 1928. He died in Easton, Connecticut, in 1972.

Write about something your parents have helped you to do or get interested in. Do they take you to music or dance lessons? Attend special functions for you? Read to you? Talk to you? Do things with you?

 Igor Sikorsky was especially interested in Leonardo da Vinci's drawings of a helicopter-like machine. Some of the popular names given to the helicopter include "whirlybird," "whirligig," "egg beater," and "chopper." Create more names for the helicopter.

May 26

In 1951, Sally Kirsten Ride was born on this day in Encino, California. In 1978, Ride earned her Ph.D. in physics. That same year, she read a newspaper ad announcing that the National Aeronautics and Space Administration (NASA) was looking for young scientists. Ride applied for and got the job. On June 18, 1983, at the age of 32, she became a mission specialist on the seventh flight of the space shuttle. Ride became the first American woman to fly in space.

 Write a newspaper ad for a job you're interested in. Explain why you're interested in that job.

 When Sally Ride attended Westlake School for Girls, she met Elizabeth Mommaerts, a physiology teacher. The teacher encouraged Ride to study—and enjoy—science classes. Write about a teacher you like. Why do you like that teacher?

 Marion Michael Morrison, better known as John Wayne, was born on this day in 1907 in Winterset, Iowa. Wayne starred in many movies about the Old West. In 1969, he won an Oscar for his performance in the movie *True Grit.* Wayne died on June 11, 1979.

Draw a picture of a cowhand on horseback.

 When someone asked John Wayne's advice on acting, he told them, "Talk low, talk slow, and don't say much." Practice reading a paragraph from a book the way John Wayne might have read it. If you've seen a John Wayne movie, can you imitate his voice?

May 27

This is the birth date of Julia Ward Howe. She was born in New York City in 1819. During the Civil War while visiting some soldiers, Howe wrote the "Battle Hymn of the Republic." The first stanza of the song is:

"Mine eyes have seen the glory of the coming of the Lord, He is trampling out the vintage where the grapes of wrath are stored; He hath loosed the fateful lightning of His terrible swift sword; His truth is marching on."

 Many people think that this song is inspiring. Write about a song that you find inspiring.

 Amelia Jenks Bloomer was born in Homer, New York, on this day in 1818. She was the founder and editor of the *Lily*, the first women's rights newspaper. In the winter of 1850-1851, Elizabeth Smith Miller visited Bloomer. Miller wore Turkish pantaloons, or pants, under a short skirt. Bloomer liked the outfit and began to promote it in her newspaper. Other newspapers began to give Bloomer credit for the outfit and called it the "Bloomer Costume."

Amelia Bloomer helped to promote a new fashion for women. Write about the kind of fashion you'd like to promote for you and your friends.

 Vincent Price, born on this day in 1911, spent much of his life scaring people. He starred in many movies—most of them were horror films. Some of his movies were *The Fly*, *The Pit and the Pendulum*, and *The Raven*. Price also recorded the scary laugh you hear on Michael Jackson's song "Thriller."

Make a list of words that you could use someday to write a scary story. Here's a few words to start you off: groan, shriek, spooky, haunted house, boo, poltergeist, vampire, ghoul, eerie.

 The Golden Gate Bridge in San Francisco, California, opened on this date in 1937. Joseph Strauss spent 13 years planning the bridge and four years building it. He designed a huge net that stretched on a steel frame below the construction area. The net saved 19 workers from falling into the deep water.

The Golden Gate Bridge is one of the largest suspension bridges in the world. It's called a suspension bridge because it's suspended from steel cables attached to high towers on each bank. There are other types of bridges: truss, beam, arch, pontoon, and cantilever. Find out about one of these types of bridges and then draw a picture of it.

The Great and Little St. Bernard Passes are named after Bernard of Montjoux. In the 11th century, he ministered to people who lived in the Swiss Alps. During the 18th century, monks who lived in the Hospice of the St. Bernard Pass bred a special dog called a St. Bernard to help with rescue and guide work. A St. Bernard is a large, furry working dog that can weigh up to 170 pounds.

 Would you like to have a dog as a pet? Why or why not? If you have a dog, write about the things you like to do with your pet.

 James "Jim" Francis Thorpe was born on this day in 1888. He was a Native American,

born in Bright Path near Prague, Oklahoma. In the 1912 Olympics, Thorpe won both the pentathlon and decathlon. A year later, however, he was forced to give up his medals because the judges discovered he had played semi-professional baseball. In 1973, the Amateur Athletic Union voted to restore his Olympic records and medals.

Read more about Jim Thorpe in *Jim Thorpe* by Thomas Fall or *Jim Thorpe (Story of an American Indian)* by Robert Reising.

 The first surviving quintuplets were born in a farmhouse near Callander, Ontario, Canada, on this day in 1934. The babies were so small that when they were born their mother's wedding ring fit over their hands. Marie, Cecile, Yvonne, Emilie, and Annette were born to Oliva and Elzire Dionne. The Dionnes already had six other children. Draw a picture of five small babies in their bonnets.

 Ian Lancaster Fleming was born on this day in 1908 in London, England. He wrote many books about a spy named James Bond. Bond is Agent 007 of Her Majesty's Secret Service. The first James Bond book Fleming wrote is titled *Casino Royale*.

Spies who appear in books often have dangerous assignments. List all the words you can think of that have something to do with spies and undercover work.

R E S O U R C E S

Jim Thorpe by Thomas Fall (New York: Harper & Row, 1970).

Jim Thorpe (Story of an American Indian) by Robert Reising (New York: Dillon Press, 1974).

May 29

On May 29, 1917, John Fitzgerald Kennedy was born in Brookline, Massachusetts. He was the 35th president of the United States. In 1961, Kennedy said, "Ask not what your country can do for you; ask what you can do for your country."

 Write about what you can do for your country.

 Sir Edmund Hillary and Tenzing Norkay reached the top of Mount Everest on this day in 1953. They were the first men ever to climb the mountain. Hillary was born in New Zealand, Norkay was born in Nepal, and Colonel John Hunt, the officer in charge of the expedition, was from India. Norkay carried four flags with him to the mountaintop. One flag each from Great Britain, Nepal, India, and the United Nations (to represent international peace) was wrapped around his ice ax handle.

What supplies do you think mountain climbers need to help them reach the top of a summit? With your class, talk about the supplies—including climbing gear and warm clothes—climbers need to complete their tasks.

 On this day in 1987, Mathias Rust, a 19-year-old resident of Hamburg, West Germany, made history. He flew a single-engine Cessna plane from Helsinki, Finland, across 400 miles of air space over what was then known as the Soviet Union. Rust landed his plane in Moscow's Red Square just a few feet from the Kremlin wall. He talked to the people who gathered around his plane before soldiers arrested him.

Rust's flight embarrassed Soviet officials and caused problems for the Soviet Air Defenses. The Defense Minister Marshal Sergei Sokolov and the Commander in Chief of Air Defense Marshal Aleksandr Koldunov were fired. Soviet officials thought that Rust's plane should have been detected on radar and stopped. Find Helsinki, Finland, on a world map. Trace Rust's trip southeast to Moscow.

 On this date in 1939, Al Unser was born in Albuquerque, New Mexico. Unser is a race car driver who won the Indianapolis 500 in 1970, 1971, 1978, and 1987.

Each year at the end of May, 100,000 spectators travel to Indianapolis, Indiana, to watch this race. Racers and their cars from all over the world compete for the first-prize trophy. To find out more about this 500-mile race, look up "Indianapolis 500" or "automobile racing" in an encyclopedia.

May 30

On this day in 1968, President Lyndon Johnson signed a bill that officially made Memorial Day a legal holiday. By law, it is to be observed each year on the last Monday in May. Memorial Day is a time to remember the men and women who have died as a result of war.

 Memorial Day is a sad day for many people. Should we have sad holidays? Why or why not?

 Make a Memorial Day mural. On a large sheet of paper, draw or paint scenes of how to observe this day. *Examples*: attend a parade, display the American flag.

Memorial Day is also a time to think about peace. Make a class book called "How I Would Stop War and Create Peace." Ask everyone in your class to draw a picture of how they could create peace in school, the neighborhood, or the city. Staple all the pictures together to create a book for your class library.

 Melvin Blanc was born on this date in 1908 in San Francisco, California. His name may not be familiar to you, but his voice is. Blanc was the voice of Bugs Bunny, Porky Pig, Barnie Rubble, and many other cartoon characters. Through his ability to mimic sounds, he created the voices of nearly 400 characters. Lines like "Th-th-that's all folks!" and "I tawt I taw a puddy tat" are his originals.

Blanc could make many sounds with his mouth, including a rusty hinge or a person chomping a piece of celery. Try mimicking a sound. Start out with an easy sound like a train whistle. Next try to mimic the sound of a creaky door hinge and the sounds people make when they eat spaghetti or chew gum. Can others guess the sound you're mimicking?

MAY 31

The first copyright law was passed on May 31, 1790. The law said that printed materials belong to their authors; no one can copy them without permission. Short stories, poems, music, and maps are just some of the things that people have copyrighted. A notice somewhere on the material lets people know the name of the person or company who owns the copyright. The notice also states the year the material was copyrighted.

 Write about how you'd feel if someone copied your homework or your answers on a test.

 A copyright notice includes the word "Copyright," the copyright symbol ©, the date, and the name of the copyright holder.

Look through the first pages of one of your books for its copyright information. Who holds the copyright to the book? In what year was the book published?

 If you were in New York City in 1906, it would have been impossible to get a cab. That's because the taximeter cabs didn't arrive until this day in 1907. The new cabs arrived from Paris, France, and were the first taxis to be seen in any American city. Draw a picture of a taxi cab.

 Tetsuya Theodore Fujita—known as Mr. Tornado—is a professor of geophysical science at the University of Chicago. He started studying violent storms in his native country of Japan. He came to the United States because more tornadoes occur here than anywhere else on Earth.

Find out about other places on Earth where tornadoes might occur. What are some safety rules you should follow if you find yourself near a tornado?

JUNE 1

In 1937, the dairy industry began saluting American dairy producers during the month of June. Since then, June has been National Dairy Month. Dairy products are those made from milk. They include ice cream, yogurt, milk, cheese, butter, and cottage cheese.

 Write about your favorite dairy product.

 If you'd like more information about dairy products or Dairy Month, send a letter to:

American Dairy Association
Director of Food Publicity
6300 North River Road
Rosemount, IL 60018

 Turn a milk carton into a bird feeder. You'll need a half-gallon cardboard milk container, glue, scissors, and string.

Rinse out the milk carton with water and glue the top shut. With an adult's help, cut an opening almost as large as the side of the carton. But only cut the opening on three sides. Leave the bottom of the opening uncut. Fold the opening out to make a perch for the birds.

With the tip of the scissors, make a small hole in the carton's top and thread the string through it. Tie the string together to make a large loop. Fill your bird feeder with bird seed and hang it from a high tree.

 Archaeologists found ancient pictures that show people in India raised cattle for dairy products in 6000 B.C. The first cheese factory in the United States was started in 1851. Learn more about cows and the dairy industry by reading *Cows* by Tessa Potter or *Dairy Cows* by Kathy Henderson.

RESOURCES

Cows by Tessa Potter (Austin, Texas: Steck-Vaughn Company, 1990).

Dairy Cows by Kathy Henderson (Chicago: Childrens Press, 1988).

JUNE 2

Martha Dandridge Custis Washington was born on this day in 1731. When she was 28 years old, she married George Washington. In 1886, a one-dollar silver certificate was issued with a picture of Martha Washington. She became the first woman to have her portrait appear on U.S. paper currency. In 1902, an eight-cent stamp was issued with her picture on it; she became the first women to have her portrait on a postage stamp.

 Would you like to have your face on a coin, paper money, or stamp? Why or why not?

 Henry Louis Gehrig died on this day in 1941. Gehrig played first base for the New York Yankees from 1925 to 1939. During those 14 years, he played in seven World Series. From June 1, 1925, until May 2, 1939, Gehrig played in every Yankees game. Because he played those 2,130 games, his teammates called him the "Iron Horse." In 1939, he was elected to the Baseball Hall of Fame. Gehrig contracted a terminal illness called Amyotrophic Lateral Sclerosis. He died of the disease in New York. Read more about Gehrig's life in *Lou Gehrig: Iron Man of Baseball* by Willard and Celia Luce.

Lou Gehrig was 38 years old when he died. His death saddened many people. When a famous person dies, reporters write newspaper articles describing the person's life. TV reporters talk to people who knew the deceased person. When a not-so-famous person dies, his or her family must remember the person.

Think about all the ways to remember someone who has died. You can look at photographs and sing his or her favorite song. You can also sit back, close your eyes, and picture that person in your mind. Make a list of the ways you remember someone who has died.

On this day in 1953, Queen Elizabeth II was crowned queen in Westminster Abbey in London. The 27-year-old princess became queen after her father, George VI, died. Hundreds of guests filled the pews of Westminster for the coronation. Elizabeth solemnly knelt in front of the archbishop of Canterbury as he placed the crown on her head. During the ceremony, Elizabeth was named queen of the United Kingdom of Great Britain and Northern Ireland, head of the Commonwealth, and defender of the faith.

Use your imagination and draw a picture of an archbishop crowning a queen. What would the queen wear? What kinds of decorations would be on the walls and pews?

RESOURCE
Lou Gehrig: Iron Man of Baseball by Willard and Celia Luce (Champaign, Illinois: Garrard Publishers, 1970).

JUNE 3

In ancient Rome, people married in June because that month was dedicated to Juno, the queen of heaven. Today, people still like to be married during this month. Brides and grooms enjoy the warm weather, bright summer colors, and flowers that can be used for their celebration.

Write about a wedding you've attended. If you've never been to a wedding, write about what you think happens at a wedding.

The custom of throwing rice at a wedding began because of a superstition. In medieval Europe, people thought that evil spirits were waiting to ruin a couple's wedding day. People also thought that the evil spirits were hungry. As the couple left the church, guests threw food to distract the spirits and allow the couple to escape. Today, this custom is continued as guests throw rice, confetti, and even bird seed at a newly married couple. Read more about wedding superstitions in the book *Superstitions* by Suzanne Lord or look up the word "superstition" in an encyclopedia.

People believe all kinds of superstitions. Some people won't walk under a ladder because they think they'll have bad luck. Some sports players wear a certain piece of clothing for good luck. Do you wear a certain piece of clothing or carry something in your pocket for good luck? If so, you might have some superstitions of your own. Make a list of your superstitions. Ask your family and friends about their superstitions.

On June 3, 1888, a funny poem appeared in the *San Francisco Examiner*. The poem was about a self-assured baseball player who had some problems in the ninth inning. The poem was called "Casey at the Bat." It begins, "The outlook wasn't brilliant for the Mudville nine that day; the score stood four to two with but one inning more to play." Ask someone to read the rest of this poem to you and find out what happens to Casey and the Mudville baseball team. You can find the poem in the book *Casey at the Bat* by Paul Frame.

....

RESOURCES

Superstitions by Suzanne Lord (New York: Macmillan, 1990).
Casey at the Bat by Paul Frame (New York: Prentice Hall, 1964).

....

JUNE 4

On this day in 1896, Henry Ford completed his first car, a quadricycle. The quadricycle had four bicycle tires and a long steering stick instead of a steering wheel. When Ford tried to drive the car out of his shed, he found that the car was wider than the door. After cutting away the door, Ford drove his quadricycle out of the brick shed at 58 Bagley Avenue in Detroit, Michigan.

Pretend it's June 4, 1896, and you live on Bagley Avenue. You've never seen a car before. All of a sudden you hear strange wheezes, chugs, and honks. Write about what you see and hear.

Today, designers think about what the car of the future will look like. Some think future cars will have built-in maps. Drivers would program their destinations into the car and it would drive itself.

What kind of car would you like to drive when you're older? Will your car have a phone or TV inside it? When you get a flat tire, will your car replace the old tire with a new one? How many wheels will your car have? On a large sheet of paper, design the most wild and creative car you can think of.

John Adams was the first president to live in the White House in Washington, D.C. John and his wife Abigail moved into the White House on this day in 1800.

What's the name of the president living in the White House today? Would you like to tell the president something? You could tell the president about a problem in your neighborhood. Or you could ask a question. Send a letter to the president at this address:

The White House
1600 Pennsylvania Avenue
Washington, DC 20500

On this day in 1989, the Chinese government ordered its troops to open fire on unarmed protesters in Tiananmen Square. The demonstrators had come together on April 18. Several thousand students marched to mourn the death of Hu Yaobang, a leader in the Chinese government. But officials banned the marches. In the dark morning hours on June 4, the troops opened fire on the crowds. They drove armored vehicles into the square and crushed many students as they slept. The government claimed that only a few people died in the attack. Witnesses say thousands of people died.

Should people be allowed to hold marches and demonstrations? Why or why not? Talk about this with your friends or family.

juNe 5

The International Centennial Exposition was the first world's fair. It was held in the United States from May to November 1876. The exposition covered 450 acres in Philadelphia, Pennsylvania. It took $11 million to build the fair's buildings, booths, and walkways. Vendors at the Philadelphia Centennial Exhibition sold a new delicacy on this day in 1876. It was called a banana.

 Write about your favorite way to eat a banana. Do you like banana Popsicles, banana cream pie, banana gum, dried banana chips, or a banana split?

 The first Conference on Human Development was held on this day in 1972 in Stockholm, Sweden. People from 114 countries talked about the future of the environment. As a result of the conference, the countries formed the United Nations Environment Program. In honor of the meeting, today is World Environment Day. If you'd like more information about what you can do for the environment, write to:

The Sierra Club
Public Information
730 Polk Street
San Francisco, CA 94109

 Make a rubbing of some of the things you find outside. You'll need a piece of paper and a pencil or crayon. Look around outside for things with texture. Rocks, tree bark, and leaves have special textures. Place the paper over one of these objects. While holding onto the piece of paper, gently rub your pencil or crayon over the paper. The texture of your object will show through on the paper.

 The first piloted hot-air balloon made its ascent into the air on this day in 1783. If you'd like more information on ballooning, read *Hot-Air Ballooning* by Charles Ira Coombs.

Draw a large hot air balloon on a piece of paper. Inside the balloon write all the words you can think of that might describe a hot-air balloon. *Examples:* colorful, airy, fun, huge.

RESOURCE

Hot-Air Ballooning by Charles Ira Coombs (New York: Morrow, 1981).

juNe 6

Nathan Hale was born on this day in 1755. He was an American Revolutionary War officer. He graduated from Yale University and taught school before joining the Continental Army in 1775. He volunteered to go behind British lines on Long Island, New York, to gain military secrets. He was captured on September 21, 1776. The British hanged him the next day. Hale's last words were, "I regret that I have but one life to lose for my country."

 Patriotism means to love and support your country. Write about what you can do to show love and support for your country.

 To find out more about Nathan Hale, read *The Spy Who Never Was and Other True Spy Stories* by David C. Knight.

 Diego Rodríguez de Silva y Velázquez was born on this day in 1599. He was a Spanish painter in the seventeenth century. He became court painter to King Philip IV. Throughout his career, Velázquez painted many royal portraits. (A portrait is a picture of a person.) Velázquez influenced artists, and many people still consider him one of the finest of all portrait painters. Pick a famous person and draw a portrait of him or her.

 Edward Vincent Sullivan was a radio and television star. From 1948 to 1970, Sullivan hosted TV's leading variety show called "Toast of the Town" (which was retitled "The Ed Sullivan Show"). On this date in 1956, one of Sullivan's most famous guests, Elvis Presley, appeared on his show for the first time.

With your friends or by yourself, create a variety show act. You could sing, dance, tell jokes, or do tricks. Put some acts together and create your own "Toast of the Town" show. Ask someone to be the emcee and announce the acts.

··

RESOURCE

The Spy Who Never Was and Other True Spy Stories by David C. Knight (New York: Doubleday, 1978).

··

JUNE 7

Gwendolyn Brooks was born on this day in 1917 in Topeka, Kansas. She was the first African-American to win a Pulitzer Prize. She won the award for poetry in 1950 for a poem called "Annie Allen." Brooks writes about living in the poor areas of the North. She once wrote a poem about her special hiding place. She wrote, "My secret place, it seems to me, is quite the only place to be."

 Write about your secret place. What makes it special?

 Gwendolyn Brooks also said, "Collect words. Read your dictionary every day.

Circle exciting words. The more words you know, the better you will be able to express yourself, your thoughts." Take her advice. Start a list of interesting words you hear and read. Keep it in your notebook.

 To create some privacy—or a secret place—for yourself, make a doorknob hanger to announce that a room is yours for a short time. You'll need a sheet of tagboard, scissors, and crayons or markers.

Cut a rectangle out of the tagboard. At the top of the rectangle, cut a hole large enough to fit over a doorknob. Decorate the tagboard with a message. *Examples:* "Do Not Disturb," "Genius at Work," "Quiet Time Is Needed," or "Homework Is in Progress." The next time you need a little privacy, hang your sign outside the door.

 George Bryan Brummell was born on this day in 1778, in London, England. George's friends nicknamed him Beau Brummell because they thought George dressed perfectly. They considered Brummell a "dandy" and a fashion leader in the early 1800s. (A dandy is a person who tries to look perfect and in fashion all the time.) Even though he was a good dresser, Brummell was not a polite person. He insulted many people. He lost all of his money and had few friends when he died in Caen, France, on March 30, 1840.

What fashions do you and your friends wear today? Do you wear baggy pants and high tops? Jeans and T-shirts? Colorful pants and shirts? Draw a picture of what a fashion leader would look like today.

juNe 8

June is National Tennis Month. Tennis can be played outdoors or indoors by two or four players. In 1873, Major Walter C. Wingfield invented the game of tennis, which has become one of the most popular international sporting events.

 What do you think is the most popular sport? Write about why you think that sport is so popular.

 Think about how many games—besides tennis—you can play with a tennis ball.

 Today is Architects' Day in honor of Frank Lloyd Wright, who was born on this day in 1867. Wright's mother wanted her son to be an architect even before he was born. She decorated his bedroom walls with pictures of cathedrals. She gave him blocks and other toys that could be arranged into furniture or buildings. Throughout his career, Wright designed many homes and over 700 buildings. He died in 1959.

Would you want to be an architect? Look up the word "architect" in the dictionary to find out what it means.

 Be an architect for a day. Design a fantasy room with book shelves, toy boxes, and windows. Or design a clubhouse with comfortable chairs for you and your friends.

Start with a blank sheet of paper. Draw a large shape on that paper (triangle, circle, rectangle). Pretend you are looking down into your room. Think about where the door

will be and draw that in. Where will the windows be? What other things could you include in your room. *Examples:* A refrigerator and sink, cozy furniture, tables, rugs.

juNe 9

Today is Donald Duck's birthday. Walt Disney created the funny duck wearing the blue sailor suit in the 1930s. In 1934, Disney showed the movie *The Wise Little Hen* starring Donald Duck. After that first movie, Disney created Daisy, Donald's girlfriend, and Donald's nephews Huey, Dewey, and Louie.

 Cartoon characters are often able to do things that real animals or people can't do. Write about what you'd be able to do if you were a cartoon character.

 Create your own animal cartoon character. Just follow these steps:

■ Draw an animal. Use colors to decorate its eyes, nose, feet, and hands.

■ Draw some clothes on your character, perhaps some funny shoes, a goofy hat, gloves, tie, or jewelry.

■ Draw your character doing something. Does it play the banjo? Hit home runs? Sing the latest songs? Jump over tall buildings in a single bound?

■ Think of a name and print it under your character's picture.

 On this date in 1978, one of 21 known copies of the Gutenberg Bible was sold in London for $2.4 million. It was the highest price ever paid for a printed book. Johann Gutenberg, a German goldsmith and printer, printed the first Bible in about 1455.

You may know of some other sacred texts besides the Bible. Jewish people study two books. One is the Torah, part of the Hebrew Bible. The other is the Talmud, which provides directions in correct Jewish life. Mormons study the Book of Mormon. Muslims read the Koran. Hindus read the Veda.

If one of your friends has a different religion than you, look through your friend's religious books. How are your friend's books different from yours? How are they similar?

 Cole Porter was born on this day in Peru, Indiana, in 1893. Porter wrote musical comedies, including *Anything Goes* and *Leave It To Me!* In 1937, he fell and hurt himself, but he continued to compose songs even though he had to be in a wheelchair.

People make music all over the world. *Examples*: The orchestra is a large group; sometimes over 100 musicians play in one orchestra. Japanese music is called gagaku; the musicians play many of the instruments while sitting on the floor. The sitar is a large instrument used in India. Play and listen to some music from other parts of the world. Or listen to some Cole Porter songs.

JUNE 10

On this day in 1926, Maude B. Campbell paid $180 to fly from Salt Lake City, Utah, to Los Angeles, California. She was the only passenger in the open cockpit, two-seater biplane. As a precaution, the pilot gave her a parachute and told her that in an emergency she should "jump, count to ten, and pull the rip cord." The flight took about seven hours. According to airline records, Campbell was the first woman to fly on a commercial airline as a paying customer.

 Write about how you think it feels to fly in an open cockpit.

 Maurice Sendak was born on this date in 1928. Although he didn't like going to school, he loved books, comics, movies, and folktales. When he grew up, Sendak designed displays for windows. In one window he displayed children's books and began to study the pictures. Sendak decided to draw his own picture book. He wrote and illustrated *Where the Wild Things Are*, *Outside Over There*, and other books. In 1964, Sendak won the Caldecott Medal for *Where the Wild Things Are*. Many of his books contain strange and wonderful monsters and creatures.

To celebrate Maurice Sendak's birthday, read *Where the Wild Things Are*.

 Construct a critter cage to temporarily house your own wild things—like insects or small reptiles. You'll need a half-gallon cardboard milk carton, one knee-high stocking or one leg from a pair of old hosiery (nylons), scissors, some grass, small sticks, and a rubber band. Rinse the milk carton with water. Cut a large panel out of one side of the milk carton. Cut another panel out of the opposite side. Put the grass and sticks in the carton. Slip the carton into a hose leg but keep the top of the carton open.

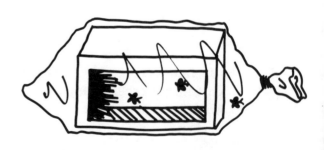

Catch an insect and place it inside your cage through the top. Pull the stocking up over the top and secure the stocking with a rubber band. Look at your insect closely. How many legs does it have? Where's the head, thorax (middle part of the body), and abdomen (the bottom part of the body)? Look carefully at your insect and draw a picture of it. Release the insect outside when you're through.

 Frances Ethel Gumm was born on June 10, 1922, in Grand Rapids, Minnesota. She sang "Jingle Bells" in her first public performance when she was 2 1/2 years old. When she was four years old, her family moved to California. Frances changed her name to Judy Garland and began her film career at 13. Four years later, in 1939, she starred in *The Wizard of Oz*. The song "Over the Rainbow" from that movie became her trademark song.

Red, **O**range, **Y**ellow, **G**reen, **B**lue, **I**ndigo, and **V**iolet are the colors that make up a rainbow. (Remembering the name Roy G. Biv will help you to remember these colors.) They are also the colors in the light spectrum. Draw a rainbow with the colors in the right order. Then draw one with the colors in any order you choose. Which do you like best?

··

R E S O U R C E

Where the Wild Things Are by Maurice Sendak (New York: Harper Children's Books, 1988).

··

JUNe II

Jacques Yves Cousteau was born on this day in 1910. He is a French author and oceanographer. With Emile Gagnan, he invented the Aqua-Lung in 1943. The Aqua-Lung is also called the **S**elf-**C**ontained

Underwater **B**reathing **A**pparatus or SCUBA. It's a diving unit with a tank of air that's strapped to a diver's back. Cousteau also invented a TV camera that works under water. Since 1950, Cousteau and his crew have traveled the seas aboard the research ship *Calypso*.

 Pretend you're traveling with Jacques Cousteau on *Calypso*. You've come to study the sea. Write a short description of where you are, what you've come to study, and why.

 National Geographic magazine contains many of Jacques Cousteau's underwater photographs. Take a trip to the library and look in the magazine section for *National Geographic*. Collect some of the magazines, sit in a comfortable chair, and see if you can locate his pictures. (The photographer's name is usually written on the side or bottom of photos.)

 On this day in 1988, Adragon Eastwood DeMelio became the youngest college graduate. He received a Bachelor of Arts Degree in Mathematics from the University of California. He was 11 years and 8 months old.

Make a timeline of your life. Draw a straight line across a sheet of paper. At the left end of the line, make a small mark. Below the mark, write the date you were born. Fill in other dates. Make a mark a little to the right of your first mark and put down the date of your first birthday. A little further down the timeline add a mark and write the date of your fourth birthday. Do you remember that day? Add the date your sister or brother was born. Or the date you got a pet. Add the date you started kindergarten and the date you began second grade. What other dates can you add to your timeline?

 Theodore Geisel received his Doctor of Fine Arts Degree from Princeton University on

this day in 1985. You probably know him as Dr. Seuss. When he was asked how he draws the pictures for his books, Dr. Seuss said, "I may doodle a couple of animals. If they bite each other, it's going to be a good book. If you doodle enough, the characters begin to take over."

To doodle means to draw or scribble while you're thinking about something else or not really concentrating. Do some doodling. Do you create animals?

june 12

Today marks the birthday of Swiss writer Johanna Spyri, who was born in 1827. Her father was a country doctor and Spyri was one of six children. Spyri wrote short stories about her childhood. Her most famous book, *Heidi*, was published in 1881. Many people like reading Spyri's books because she describes thoughts and emotions that young people often experience.

 Think of an emotion (like happiness or excitement) and write a short paragraph describing that emotion.

 Heidi is about a girl who lives with her grandfather in the Swiss Alps. But relatives take Heidi away from her grandfather because they think Heidi should live in the city. Heidi misses her grandfather and the beautiful mountains. To find out what happens, read *Heidi* by Johanna Spyri.

 Yodeling is a type of singing that is often done in mountain areas. Yodelers stand at the edge of a cliff, cup their hands around their mouth, and yell "Yodel-ay-he-ho." They stop and listen as the echoes bounce off the mountainsides. Have a yodeling contest. See who can make the longest or quietest yodel.

 The Baseball Hall of Fame opened in Cooperstown, New York, on this day in 1939. Since its opening, over 200 officials, managers, umpires, and players have been honored. Plaques in the Hall of Fame Gallery represent each person who has been inducted. In addition to the plaques, visitors can look at rare baseball cards, uniforms, equipment from old games, photographs, and relics from ballparks that have been torn down.

What words do you think of when someone says "Baseball"? Write a list of baseball words.

RESOURCE

Heidi by Johanna Spyri (New York: Scholastic, 1989).

june 13

On this day in 1967, President Lyndon Johnson nominated Thurgood Marshall as an associate justice of the U.S. Supreme Court. Marshall had worked as a lawyer for the National Association for the Advancement of Colored People (NAACP). He believed that schools should not be segregated, or separated, by race. In 1954, he argued his case before the Supreme Court and won. Marshall became the first African-American to be appointed to the position of associate justice. He served until his retirement in 1991. He died on January 24, 1993.

 Would you want to be a lawyer and fight for the rights of others? Why or why not?

To learn more about Thurgood Marshall and his career, read the *Book of Black Heroes from A to Z: An Introduction to Important Black Achievers for Young Readers* by Wade Hudson.

 On this day in 1927, 4 million people welcomed aviator Charles Lindbergh. He had completed the first solo flight from New York to France. New Yorkers participated in a ticker-tape parade for Lindbergh. Ticker tape is a long strip of paper that stock brokers used to keep up with changing company prices on the stock market. During a ticker-tape parade, office workers throw these strips of paper out of windows like streamers.

New Yorkers have given ticker-tape parades to all kinds of famous people. Make a list of people you feel deserve a ticker-tape parade. *Examples:* your parents, a teacher, a close friend, a personal hero or heroine.

 "You have the right to remain silent. Anything you say can and will be used against you in a court of law." This statement is part of a person's Miranda rights. On this date in 1966, the U.S. Supreme Court made a decision on a case called *Miranda vs. Arizona.*

A man named Ernesto Miranda had been imprisoned for confessing to a crime. But he had not been told that he could have a lawyer present while he was answering questions. The Supreme Court's decision provided a strict code for police conduct. The court said that officers have to inform accused people of their rights before they ask questions. Officers also have to allow accused people to contact lawyers. Many officers now carry Miranda cards, which they read aloud to suspects.

Talk with your friends or family about why it's important for accused people to have rights.

RESOURCE

Book of Black Heroes from A to Z: An Introduction to Important Black Achievers for Young Readers by Wade Hudson (Orange, New Jersey: Just Us Books, 1988).

juNe 14

Harriet Beecher Stowe was born on this day in Litchfield, Connecticut, in 1811. In 1848 she wrote a novel about people who were forced into slavery. *Uncle Tom's Cabin* became one of the most widely circulated books in history. The book is about Tom, a slave, who is sold to Simon Legree, a brutal plantation owner. In the North, the novel made more people aware of the horrors of slavery. In the South at the time, people considered the book inaccurate.

 Write about a book character that seemed real to you. Why did you think that character was so real?

 On June 14, 1777, John Adams introduced a statement to the Continental Congress in Philadelphia, Pennsylvania. It said: "Resolved, that the flag of the thirteen United States shall be thirteen stripes, alternate red and white; that the union be thirteen stars, white in a blue field, representing a new constellation."

Using only the words of John Adams's resolution, design your own flag. Try to make it different from the flag we now know, but follow the directions given above.

 In honor of John Adams' proposal, today is Flag Day. In 1916, President Woodrow Wilson made this day a holiday. All over the United States, people fly their flags. To help you celebrate Flag Day, here are some traditional flag rules:

- The flag must not touch the ground.

- When the American flag is flown with other flags, the American flag must be higher than all other ones.

- When saying the Pledge of Allegiance, salute the flag by placing your right hand over your heart.

- When an important American dies, the flag is flown at half mast, meaning halfway down the pole.

 On June 14 at 7 p.m. Eastern Standard Time, many Americans pause and say the Pledge of Allegiance. Tonight, ask your family and friends to say the pledge:

"I pledge allegiance to the flag of the United States of America and to the republic for which it stands, one nation under God, indivisible, with liberty and justice for all."

JUNE 15

On this day in 1215, the barons of the court of King John of England insisted that the king sign a document called the Magna Carta. John had made many demands on the church and his subjects and they wanted more civil rights. The 63 clauses in the Magna Carta protected the rights of the church and the subjects of the king. It also put limits on the behavior of royal officials saying what they could and could not do. Although it is over 800 years old, four original copies of the Magna Carta still exist today.

 Write about the oldest thing you own. Is it one of your baby blankets or something your grandmother gave to you?

 On June 15, 1752, Ben Franklin made a kite out of silk handkerchiefs. On the end of the kite's string, he attached a metal key and then flew his kite in a thunderstorm. When lightning struck his kite, the electrical charge traveled down the string. Franklin collected the charge in a special device called a Leyden jar. With this experiment, Franklin showed the electrical nature of lightning and that lightning is a form of electricity.

Make a list of things at your school and in your home that use electricity.

 Electricity occurs naturally, as when lightning strikes and creates an electric charge. It also can be generated. Across the country, power stations generate enough electric current to light hundreds of millions of light bulbs. To find out more about electricity, read the book *Sparks to Power Stations* by Kathryn Whyman.

 El Cid Campeador is a national hero of Spain. His name is Spanish for "the lord champion." El Cid made himself famous in wars against the Moors. On this day in 1094, he conquered the cities of Valencia and Murcia in Spain and rescued the people from the Moors. He ruled these cities until his death in 1099. To learn more about this warrior hero, read *Great Warriors: True Stories of Outstanding Leaders* by Kenneth Allen.

RESOURCES

Sparks to Power Stations by Kathryn Whyman (New York: Gloucester Press, 1989).

Great Warriors: True Stories of Outstanding Leaders by Kenneth Allen (Englewood Cliffs, New Jersey: Silver Burdett, 1980).

JUNE 16

In 1984, Bernhard Goetz was riding the subway in New York when four young men approached him. Goetz shot all four of them because he thought they were going to rob him. On this day in 1987, Goetz was found not guilty of attempted murder. During the trial, the young men had said they weren't going to rob Goetz. Some people think that Goetz (who is white) shot the young men (who are African-American) because he became scared when he saw people who were different from him.

 Write about how you feel when you see someone different from you. Describe your feelings.

 Valentina Vladimirovna Tereshkova-Nikolayeva of the Soviet Union became the first woman to orbit Earth on this day in 1963. She spent three days aboard *Vostok VI* and orbited Earth 49 times. Draw Earth as though you are Nikolayeva looking out a window in her space ship.

 A dusky seaside sparrow died on this day in 1987; it was the last of its kind. It died in a cage at Walt Disney World. There are no more of these birds alive today; the species is now extinct. Dusky seaside sparrows were known to live only in a small part of Florida near Cape Canaveral. Scientists hope that one day they might be able to bring a species back from extinction by duplicating cells. They froze the bird's heart and lungs to preserve the cells as much as possible.

With your friends or family, talk about why it matters when a species becomes extinct.

 Using a bird identification book, draw your version of a dusky seaside sparrow. You could use *A Field Guide to the Birds East of the Rockies* by Roger Tory Peterson as a reference. The author wrote this book before the dusky seaside sparrow became extinct.

R E S O U R C E

A Field Guide to the Birds East of the Rockies by Roger Tory Peterson (Boston: Houghton Mifflin, 1980).

JUNE 17

The Battle of Bunker Hill took place on June 17, 1775, on Boston's Charlestown Peninsula. It was the first major battle of the Revolutionary War. Over 3,000 British soldiers fought 1,000 American patriots. The Americans lost this first battle, but they caused many British casualties. Just before the battle, Israel Putnam said to the patriots, "Men, you are all marksmen...don't one of you fire until you see the whites of their eyes." One hundred years later, in 1825, the cornerstone was laid for the Bunker Hill Monument.

 Pretend you're at the Battle of Bunker Hill in 1775. Write a journal entry about what you see.

 Research the battles that occurred during the Revolutionary War. On a map of the United States, label where the battles were fought.

 On this day in 1955, Disneyland opened in Anaheim, California. Walt Disney wanted to create the best family amusement park. He wanted all the park rides, shops, and games to be part of a theme. He borrowed ideas from his movies and TV shows to create small worlds within the park. Visitors to Disneyland walk through Adventureland, Frontierland, Fantasyland, Tomorrowland, and Main Street, U.S.A.

Today, visitors can also shake hands with Disney characters who walk around the park. List as many Disney characters as you can. Here are a few to start your list: Mickey Mouse, Goofy, Chip and Dale.

 On this date in 1898, Maurits Corneille Escher was born in the Netherlands. He was a Dutch graphic artist who drew pictures that are fun to study. His works are called visual riddles that fool the eye. Look at Escher's puzzles. You can find some in *The Infinite World of M. C. Escher* by Maurits Corneille Escher.

RESOURCE

The Infinite World of M. C. Escher by Maurits Corneille Escher (New York: Abrams, 1984).

juNe 18

Paul McCartney was born on this day in 1942. He is a British musician, bass guitarist, vocalist, and songwriter. His fame began when he formed the Beatles with John Lennon, George Harrison, and Ringo Starr. Between 1962 and 1971, the Beatles were one of the most popular rock and roll groups. After the Beatles broke up, McCartney formed a new band called Wings. Since then, he has continued to write and sing rock and roll songs.

 If you were going to form a musical group, what would you call the group? Write about the kind of music you'd play.

 The term "rock and roll" was first used in the mid-1950s by a broadcaster in Cleveland, Ohio. But rock and roll isn't the only type of music. There's country, heavy metal, rap, classical, jazz, and blues, to name a few.

Pick a type of music that you don't usually listen to and find a recording of that music in the library. Listen to the recording just for fun.

 June is Zoo and Aquarium Month—a month when zoos encourage people to learn more about all animals. To learn more about zoos and aquariums, write a letter to:

American Association of Zoological Parks and Aquariums
Public Relations/Development Office
7970-D Old Georgetown Road
Bethesda, MD 20814

Author/illustrator Chris Van Allsburg was born on this day in 1949. When he was in elementary school, he loved art class. Once, he felt ill before school but didn't tell his mother because he didn't want to miss art class. Later that morning, the art teacher sent him home. Look through Van Allsburg's books to find Fritz. Fritz is a bull terrier that appears somewhere in each of Van Allsburg's books. Read *Ben's Dream*, *The Garden of Abdul Gasazi*, or *The Mysteries of Harris Burdick*. See if you can find Fritz.

RESOURCES

Some books by Chris Van Allsburg:

Ben's Dream, *The Garden of Abdul Gasazi*, and *The Mysteries of Harris Burdick* (New York: Houghton Mifflin).

JUNE 19

The first Father's Day was celebrated on this date in 1910. Sonora Louise Smart Dodd was the first to suggest this day. After the death of her mother, Dodd's father raised her and her brothers. Dodd felt that her father deserved to be honored for all he had done for her family. In 1924, President Calvin Coolidge made Father's Day an official holiday. Each year, on the third Sunday in June, Americans and Canadians honor fathers.

 Write about your father, grandfather, or another man who is important in your life.

 Create an acrostic poem to honor your father or other adult. Write a word on a sheet of paper so that the letters are under each other. Think of words describing that word, which begin with each of those letters. *Examples*: Write the word "Father" or "Friend" to come up with these words.

Fair	**F**aithful
Active	**R**espectful
Tender	**I**nquisitive
Happy	**E**njoyable
Eager	**N**ice
Responsible	**D**edicated

 Make a custom-made card for your father or other adult you admire. Cut out pictures from magazines of things that person likes to do. Decorate the card with the pictures. Draw a picture of your special person or glue the person's photograph in the middle of your card.

 On this date in 1978, Garfield the cartoon cat appeared for the first time. Garfield is a funny feline. He's a lasagna-loving character that's lazy and always hungry. Read more about

Garfield in *Garfield A to Z Zoo*, *Garfield at Large*, or *Garfield Treasury*, all by Jim Davis.

RESOURCES

Some books by Jim Davis:

Garfield A to Z Zoo (New York: Random House, 1984).

Garfield at Large and *Garfield Treasury* (New York: Ballantine Books, 1982).

JUNE 20

The Great Seal of the United States was adopted on this date in 1782. Charles Thomson, the first official U.S. record keeper, designed the Great Seal. The motto on the seal is "E Pluribus Unum," which means "One out of many" in Latin. The motto refers to working together to make one nation out of many states. U.S. officials use the seal on important documents. You can also find the seal on the one dollar bill.

 People working together can accomplish tasks that a person working alone cannot. Write about a time when teamwork was important to you.

 Create your own seal. You'll need some construction paper, scissors, glue, and pens, crayons, or paints. Cut out a large shape (circle, triangle, rectangle). Think of things that you like to do (*Examples*: ballet, soccer, read, paint) and things that are part of your life (*Examples*: your family, friends, relatives, brothers or sisters, pets). Now think of symbols that represent these things (*Examples:* ballet shoes, soccer ball, books, crayons, people's faces). Draw these symbols on other pieces of construction paper. Cut them out and glue them to the larger sheet of construction paper.

 The Great Seal shows a bald eagle with wings spread. In one claw, the eagle holds arrows, which represent national defense. In the other claw, the eagle holds an olive branch, which represents peace. The bald eagle is the national bird of the United States. Officials chose this bird because it is a symbol of power, courage, and freedom. If you could pick a new national bird, what would you choose? Would you choose a robin, which is seen all over the United States? Or a dove, which is a symbol of peace? Write about your choice.

 Walter Farley, author of the "Black Stallion" books, was born in 1915. As a child, Farley wanted a horse, but his family lived in the city, and he couldn't convince his parents to let him keep a horse in the garage. His uncle, who was a horse trainer, encouraged Farley to visit stables. He told Farley to write down his experiences with horses. Farley took his uncle's advice and used his notes years later when he wrote his first book *The Black Stallion*.

Keep notes about your family pet. If you don't have a pet, write notes about a neighbor's pet or about a squirrel or bird in your yard. Later, use your notes to create a story.

june 21

Today—or, depending on the year, tomorrow—marks the summer solstice. The summer solstice is the day summer begins in the Northern Hemisphere and winter begins in the Southern Hemisphere. The sun is now brighter than at any other time of the year. On this day, in some parts of Sweden, Norway, Denmark, and other areas in the Arctic Circle, the sun won't set at all.

 Write about what you'll do with the extra daylight time.

 You should never look directly at the sun, but there is a safe way to see the sun's light. You'll need two index cards and scissors. Poke a small hole in one index card so that sunlight can shine through it. Hold another card below the hole so that the sunlight shines on it.

 With summer comes hot weather. The hottest place—for the longest time on record—is Marble Bar, Australia. For 162 consecutive days during 1923 and 1924, the temperature there soared over 100 degrees Fahrenheit. At one time during that hot spell, the temperature in Marble Bar reached 121 degrees Fahrenheit. Design an invention that will keep you cool.

 Cut bookmarks out of paper in the shape of things that remind you of summer. You'll need scissors, some paper, and crayons or markers. On the paper, draw something that reminds you of hot, summer days. *Examples*: an inner tube, a baseball hat, a watermelon, or an ear of corn. Cut out the shape. Now you can start your summer reading and have a cool bookmark to keep your place.

juNe 22

Anne Morrow Lindbergh was born on this day in 1907 in Englewood, New Jersey. She was an author and aviator. In 1929, she married Charles Lindbergh. Lindbergh and her husband developed air routes to China and India and flew on many flights together. She wrote *Listen! The Wind* in 1938. That book recorded her traveling experiences.

 Write about what you hear when you listen to the wind. Be creative and use your imagination.

 Keep your own travel journal to record your travels on vacation or around your neighborhood this summer. Before you go to bed each night, write one or two sentences about who you saw or where you went. At the end of the summer, you can look back at all the things you did.

 On this day in 1922, Bill Blass was born in Fort Wayne, Indiana. He is a famous American fashion designer. He has designed furs, swimsuits, jewelry, and other fashion items. His advice, when asked how to decide what to wear, was, "When in doubt, wear red."

Write about a red clothing item you like to wear. If you don't have anything red, write about a red item someone else wears.

 Try designing clothes with your own paper figures. You'll need some paper, scissors, tape, and crayons, markers, or pens.

Draw a figure—a boy or a girl— on a sheet of paper and cut it out. On the other sheets of paper, create clothes for your person. Draw a bright sweater or a black pair of jeans. Cut out the clothes and attach them to your figure with tape. If you don't like those clothes, draw new ones. How about dressing your person in a striped hat or blue and red shoes? Pretend your person is a water skier and design a swimsuit that's bright and colorful.

juNe 23

On this day in 1940, Wilma Rudolph was born in St. Bethlehem, Tennessee. When she was four years old, polio crippled her left leg. Her family learned to massage the leg and the treatment worked. Rudolph was able to remove her leg brace and special shoe and walk normally. After she was cured, Rudolph became interested in running. She practiced and ran in races whenever she could. In the 1960 Olympics she won three gold medals— for the 100- and 200-meter runs, and for the 400-meter relay.

 Write about why you think it's important to hear stories about people who have overcome great obstacles to complete a task.

 Wilma Rudolph wasn't the only person to overcome polio. Tenley Albright was a figure skater who contracted polio when she was young. For six years she battled the illness as she continued to skate. Her hard work helped her win the 1953 world figure-skating championship. She was the first American to win the contest. Find out about other people who have not given up in spite of a disabling illness.

 Polio, or poliomyelitis, is a disease of the central nervous system. In the early 1900s, thousands of children died or were paralyzed after contracting polio. In 1952, Dr.

Jonas Salk, a medical research scientist, successfully tested the first vaccine against polio. Today, doctors protect their patients against the polio virus with this vaccine. Ask your parents or other care provider when you received the polio vaccine.

 When a doctor gives you a vaccine, your body forms antibodies against the organism that causes the disease. The antibodies destroy or inactivate the harmful organisms. Many infants receive vaccines to prevent the diseases of measles, mumps, and diptheria. Find out the vaccines you've received.

juNe 24

John Ciardi was born on this day in 1916 in Boston, Massachusetts. Ciardi writes poems for adults and children. Many people consider him one of America's best poets. Ciardi often makes fun of things that other people take seriously. In 1982, he received the National Council of Teachers of English Award for Excellence in Poetry.

 Do you like poetry? Why or why not? Write your opinion of poetry. Give a reason for your opinion.

 Enjoy some of John Ciardi's poetry. Read *I Met a Man*, *The Hopeful Trout and Other Limericks*, or *You Read to Me, I'll Read to You*.

 On this day in 1497, John Cabot landed at Cape Breton Island in Newfoundland. King Henry VII had hired Cabot to find a western route from Great Britain to India. Cabot knew that five years earlier Christopher Columbus had traveled southwest from Spain. Cabot decided to travel northwest.

From Bristol, England, Cabot sailed to the northeast tip of North America. On his second voyage in 1498, he reached Greenland and sailed down to Chesapeake Bay, which is in present-day Virginia. Because of Cabot's travels, the English claimed North America as their own.

Using a map, trace Cabot's travels from Bristol, England, to Cape Breton and from Bristol to Greenland to Chesapeake Bay.

 On this date in 1938, Congress passed the Food, Drug and Cosmetic Act. This law said that manufacturers must print all ingredients on the product's label.

Collect some cereal boxes. Compare the ingredient labels on the side or back panels. How are the ingredients in the cereal different? How are they similar? Which cereal has the healthiest ingredients?

....

RESOURCES

Some books by John Ciardi:

I Met a Man and *The Hopeful Trout and Other Limericks* (New York: Houghton Mifflin).

You Read to Me, I'll Read to You (Philadelphia: Lippincott).

....

juNe 25

On this date in 1798, a nineteen-year-old earned his medical degree from the University of Edinburgh. His name was Peter Mark Roget (pronounced Row-zhay). Besides being a doctor, Roget was a lexicographer who put together a dictionary. He titled his dictionary Roget's *Thesaurus of English Words and Phrases*. His son and grandson continue editing and updating his work.

Write about a dictionary you use. Is it easy to use? Does it have pictures in it?

 A thesaurus is a book of information about words or concepts. Most often, a thesaurus is a book of synonyms. Synonyms are words that have the same meaning. *Example:* pleasing, agreeable, and enjoyable are all synonyms for the word nice.

Describe something hot. Write down as many synonyms for the word hot as you can. Think of the words yourself or use a thesaurus.

 Governor John Winthrop brought the first fork to America on this date in 1630. He had left England to become the Massachusetts colony's first governor. For a while, Winthrop had the only fork in the New World.

What utensils do people throughout the world use? Create an eating-utensils-around-the-world poster. Show chopsticks, forks, or hands to indicate how people eat in different places.

 On this day in 1950, North Korean troops crossed the 38th parallel into South Korea. That move began the Korean War, which lasted from 1950 to 1953. North Korea's communist forces fought against South Korea's noncommunist forces. United Nations forces supported South Koreans and many U.S. troops traveled to Korea to fight.

On a map, find Korea. Look at the degree signs on the latitude lines (the lines that run from left to right across the map). Notice that the 38th parallel comes right in the middle of Korea and separates it into two separate countries.

juNe 26

Pearl Sydenstricker Buck was born on this day in 1892 in Hillsboro, West Virginia. She was an author, educator, and expert on China and Chinese culture. Buck's parents were missionaries and she moved to China with them when she was young. That country became the setting for many of her novels. In 1931, Buck published *The Good Earth*, a book about Chinese peasants.

 Write about a subject you'd like to be an expert in. Why are you so interested in this subject?

 In honor of Pearl S. Buck, practice writing some Chinese characters. You could use the book *Long Is a Dragon: Chinese Writing for Children* by Peggy Goldstein as a reference. Write a sentence using the characters you've read about. On the back of your paper, write the translation.

 Bicyclist Greg LeMond was born on this day in 1961. In 1986, he became the first American to win the Tour de France, a bicycle race held in France. The Tour de France takes 23 days to complete. Bicyclists start in Paris and bike 2,025 miles. The race course loops through the French countryside and the racers end up back in Paris for the finish line.

Draw a map showing a bicycle course around your neighborhood.

On this date in 1945, 50 nations signed an important charter that created the United Nations. From April through June, representatives from countries around the world met in San Francisco for a conference on International Organization. By June 26, the group had drawn up a charter establishing the United Nations. The original signers included China, Cuba, Egypt, South Africa, the United States, and 40 more countries. Today, the United Nations has more than 159 member nations.

Read *United Nations* by Casrold Greene to learn more about this organization.

RESOURCES

Long Is a Dragon: Chinese Writing for Children by Peggy Goldstein (New York: Scholastic, 1991).

United Nations by Casrold Greene (Chicago: Childrens Press, 1983).

juNe 27

Mildred "Babe" Didrikson Zaharias was born on this day in 1914 in Port Arthur, Texas. In the 1932 Olympics, she won gold medals for the javelin throw and the 80-meter hurdles. In 1934, she turned her attention to golf. Thirteen years later, she became the first American to win the British amateur golf title. Besides track and golf, Zaharias also excelled in basketball, softball, and discus throwing.

 Write about someone you know who is good at many things.

 On this date, in 1984, the Motion Picture Association of America introduced a new movie rating of PG-13. Many people had complained that PG-rated movies were too violent. They wanted to add a stricter rating. The association created PG-13 to warn parents that a movie shouldn't be seen by children under 13 without an adult's knowledge.

Write about your opinion on rating the movies. Should you be stopped from seeing certain types of movies? Why or why not?

 The Motion Picture Association rates movies according to the violence and amount of adult themes in a picture. The association's ratings range from G to NC-17.

- G General Audiences; this movie is suitable for children.
- PG Parental Guidance Suggested; some material in this movie may not be suitable for children.
- PG-13 Parents Strongly Cautioned; some material in this movie may not be appropriate for children under 13.
- R Restricted; children under 17 must see this movie with a parent or other adult.
- NC-17 (X) No children under 17 years of age are admitted to this movie.

Look through the movie ads in your newspaper and find the ratings for each movie. Are there many PG-13 movies? How many PG movies can you find? How about G movies?

 Look up the words "censor" and "censorship" in a dictionary or encyclopedia. Find out the definition and the history behind censorship. Discuss the good and bad points of censoring movies, books, and songs.

juNe 28

World War I began on this date in 1914 when Archduke Francis Ferdinand, who was to be the next King of Austria, and his wife were assassinated. Gavrilo Princip, a student, killed the royal couple while they were visiting

Sarajevo, Bosnia. Princip was a member of The Black Hand, a Serbian terrorist group. Four years later, on November 11, 1918, the war ended.

 Why do you think terrorists take part in violent acts against people? Write about how you feel when you hear about terrorist activities.

 Do you know why so many national holidays in the United States fall on Mondays? On this date in 1968, President Lyndon Johnson signed a law that said Americans could have more three-day weekends. By January 1, 1971, George Washington's and Abraham Lincoln's birthdays (which used to be two separate holidays) had been combined into one holiday, President's Day. President's Day is always celebrated on a Monday. Memorial Day, Labor Day, and Columbus Day are celebrated on Mondays, also. Thanks to the 1968 law, Americans enjoy at least four three-day weekends every year.

Can you think of other three-day weekends? Perhaps during the school year your school has special days off for Martin Luther King Day or for teacher workshop days.

 Mary Hays helped the gun crew at the Battle of Monmouth on this day in 1778. The artillery soldiers nicknamed her Molly Pitcher because she carried pitchers of water from a nearby spring to the soldiers in the field. When one of the soldiers collapsed at his battle station, Molly took over his position. She grabbed a gun swab and continued to load the cannon.

Find out more about Molly Pitcher and other women who helped fight in the Revolutionary War by reading *Heroines of '76* by Elizabeth Anticaglia.

 Richard Charles Rodgers was born on this date in 1902 in New York City. He was famous as the composer of Broadway musicals. He teamed first with Lorenz Hart and then with Oscar Hammerstein II in many successful musicals. *Oklahoma!*, *Carousel*, *South Pacific*, *The King and I*, and *The Sound of Music* are just some of the musical theater shows he helped to create. Rodgers died on December 30, 1979. Listen to some music from one of Rodgers' musicals.

RESOURCE

Heroines of '76 by Elizabeth Anticaglia (New York: Walker and Company, 1975).

JUNE 29

Antoine de Saint-Exupery was a French aviator and novelist born on this day in 1900. Saint-Ex, as he is known in France, loved to fly and flew mail planes across the Mediterranean Sea. In 1935, he had to force a landing in the Libyan desert and almost died in the crash. From his experience in the desert, Saint-Ex wrote *The Little Prince*. The story tells how people should appreciate simple things. In 1944 during World War II, Saint-Ex and his plane disappeared while he was flying a mission.

 Write about the simplest, best things in your life. *Examples:* a warm hug, a favorite book or toy, a pretty sunset.

 Ask someone to read part of *The Little Prince* by Antoine de Saint-Exupery to you. It's translated from French into English by Katherine Woods.

 In 1956 on this date, Charles Dumas became the first person to high jump over 7 feet.

Using a yard stick, measure 7 feet high. Can you jump and reach that height? Have a friend hold a yard stick upright and measure how high you can jump.

On this day in 1577, Flemish painter and engraver Peter Paul Rubens was born in Seigen, Germany. When he painted, Rubens paid close attention to every detail. He liked to create muscular figures in action and use bright colors. He created many decorative pieces for churches and palaces between 1620 and 1630.

Draw a picture using bright colors and detail. *Example:* Draw a picture of a house and use a bright color for the roof. Add windows with curtains, a front door with a doorknob, a doorbell, and a mailbox. Can you include some action in your drawing?

· ·

R E S O U R C E

The Little Prince by Antoine de Saint-Exupery, translated by Katherine Woods (New York: Harcourt Brace Jovanovich, 1982).

· ·

jUNe 30

Over 25,000 people watched a man walk 160 feet above them on this date in 1859. They were watching Charles Emile Blondin, a French acrobat and aerialist, cross Niagara Falls on a tightrope. The tightrope cable was 1,100 feet long and stretched from one bank to the other over the roaring water. Blondin's walk took him five minutes.

Imagine that you're Blondin crossing Niagara Falls. Write about how you feel as you look down on the rushing water below.

Lena Horne was born in Brooklyn, New York, on this day in 1917. She was a pop singer and actress and the first widely recognized African-American female vocalist. She was the first African-American woman to receive a long-term Hollywood contract. She starred in *Lena Horne: The Lady and Her Music* in 1981, on Broadway. She won a Grammy Award for her performance the following year. Check an almanac to find out other singers who have won Grammy Awards.

If you were in Darwin, Minnesota, on this date in 1991, you may have seen an unusual sight. According to the *Guiness Book of World Records*, the citizens of Darwin own the largest ball of string on record. The ball of string measures 12 feet, 9 inches in diameter. It measures 40 feet around the outside. Francis A. Johnson, who lived in Darwin, began saving the twine in 1950. He collected the string and wrapped it around the ball until his death in 1989. The citizens of Darwin prepared a place beneath the water tower for the ball of string. With the help of heavy construction equipment, workers moved the ball from Johnson's front yard to its new home.

Measure a length of string 3 yards long. Roll it in a tight ball. Now measure the ball with a tape measure. How large a ball did you get? How much string do you suppose is in Mr. Johnson's string ball?

On June 30, 1971, eighteen-year-old men and women gained the right to vote in local, state, and federal elections. The 26th Amendment to the Constitution was ratified, or made into law. When the amendment passed, 11 million people between the ages of 18 and 21 could now vote.

Write about why you think it's important to vote.

S oap opera writer Irna Phillips was born on this day in 1901. In the 1930s, she was working for a radio station in Chicago when the first soap opera was performed. In 1937 she cowrote "The Guiding Light," which became a TV show in 1952—it's still a popular soap opera today. Phillips was the first to use a tease ending in her shows. She would write a dramatic scene and then cut it short before the main action happened. That way, audiences would want to tune in the next day to find out what happened.

 Create a story with a tease ending. Make your reader want to know what happens next. Continue your scene if you like.

 On this day in 1847, the post office issued the first U.S. postage stamps. The Benjamin Franklin stamp cost five cents. The George Washington stamp was ten cents. In honor of these first stamps, today is American Stamp Day.

Philately is collecting and studying postage stamps. If you'd like to know more about stamp collecting, read the book *Getting Started in Stamp Collecting* by Burton Hobson.

 Imagine that the post office has just hired you to invent a stamp-licking machine. Draw your invention.

 In Canada, today is Dominion Day. Quebec, Nova Scotia, New Brunswick, and Ontario were the four original provinces of Canada. On this day in 1867, those four provinces formed a dominion. Other provinces joined them and took the first step toward Canadian independence. Today, Canada has ten provinces and two territories. On a map of Canada, locate all the provinces and the two territories.

R E S O U R C E

Getting Started in Stamp Collecting by Burton Hobson (New York: Sterling Publishing, 1970).

A t noon today, the year is exactly half over. (If this is a leap year, the halfway point was at midnight on July 1.) Have you ever eaten half of a sandwich or left at half past three? Have you seen a halfback or eaten something half cooked? Have you felt half awake or half human? Have you been called a half-pint or felt halfhearted?

 Write at least a half page using the word *half* as many times as you can.

 July is National Ice Cream Month. This tasty treat has been around since 1295 when Marco Polo told his friends about the flavored ice food that he had tasted in the Far East. It wasn't until 1851, however, that ice cream was first manufactured in the United States. If you'd like more information about ice cream, send a letter to:

International Ice Cream Association
888 Sixteenth Street NW
Washington, DC 20006

In July of 1784, Thomas Jefferson traveled to France. He brought back one of the first recipes for ice cream. His recipe needed two bottles of good cream, five egg yolks, and one-half cup of sugar. Read more about ice cream's history in the book *Scoop after Scoop: A History of Ice Cream* by Steven Krensky.

On this day in 1937, Amelia Earhart and Fred Noonan vanished. The two pilots were attempting to fly around the world. They disappeared between New Guinea and Howland Island in the Pacific Ocean. Earhart was the first woman to fly across the Atlantic and the first person to fly solo from Hawaii to California. In 1992, a woman's shoe, a pillbox, and scraps of metal were found on an island in the Pacific Ocean. Some people thought the items belonged to Earhart. Many experts, however, are still searching for clues to the disappearance. On a large map of the world, locate the place where the pilots supposedly went down.

RESOURCE

Scoop after Scoop: A History of Ice Cream by Steven Krensky (New York: Atheneum, 1986).

JULY 3

On this date in 1890, Idaho became the forty-third state. It's located in the northwestern United States and is a state with one of the smallest populations. Much of Idaho is mountainous and forested. The state's major agricultural product is potatoes.

 Write about your favorite way to eat a potato.

 In honor of Idaho, do some potato printing. You'll need a potato, knife, paper, and some finger paints. Cut the potato in half. On the cut end, carve out a shape, such as a triangle or circle. Dip that end of the potato into the finger paint and press the potato down onto some paper. Once you get used to carving shapes in potatoes, try carving more elaborate designs such as a house, car, or face.

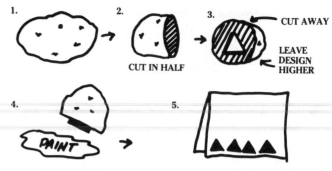

1. 2. 3. CUT AWAY / LEAVE DESIGN HIGHER
CUT IN HALF
4. DIP IN PAINT
5. PRESS ON PAPER TO MAKE DESIGNS

 For more art ideas using potatoes, read *Potato Printing* by Helen Haddad.

 July is National Peach Month. Here are some peachy facts: The Latin name for a peach tree is *Prunus persica*. Before peach trees produce their fruit, they blossom with pink flowers. Most peaches have fuzzy skins, but scientists are developing new peaches with smooth skins. If you'd like more information about peaches, send a letter to:

The National Peach Council
P.O. Box 11280
Columbia, SC 29211

RESOURCE

Potato Printing by Helen Haddad (New York: Crowell Company, 1981).

JULY 4

Happy Fourth of July! All over the United States today, people celebrate the signing of the Declaration of Independence. The warm July weather is a perfect time to watch a parade, eat some summer fruit, and relax while watching fireworks.

 In the year 2076, the United States will celebrate its 300th birthday. Write about how you think people will celebrate this tricentennial. Remember to imagine the future.

Thomas Jefferson wrote the Declaration of Independence to defy King George III. King George had told the colonists that they would die if they continued to work for independence. Read more about America's birthday in *The Fourth of July Story* by Alice Dalgliesh.

 "Oh, beautiful for spacious skies, for amber waves of grain...." Those words to the song "America the Beautiful" were first published on this day in 1895. Some people believe that it should be the United States' National Anthem. An anthem is a song of gladness, praise, or patriotism. With your friends, think of some songs you know and decide if they'd make good national anthems.

 In the United States today, firecrackers will pop and sparklers will hiss. "Pop" and "hiss" are onomatopoeias. This term means that the words make the sound they describe. List some other onomatopoeias that will be heard today.

RESOURCE

The Fourth of July Story by Alice Dalgliesh (New York: Scribner, 1956).

On this day in 1810, Phineas Taylor Barnum was born in Bethel, Connecticut. He established New York City's American Museum in 1842. In 1871, he opened his circus, billed as "The Greatest Show on Earth." Ten years later, he became partners with J. A. Bailey and formed the Barnum and Bailey Circus.

 Write about an act you'd like to be in if you joined the circus. Why would you want to be in that act?

 The running of the bulls takes place around this date each year. It's part of a special eight-day festival in Pamplona, Spain. The bulls are turned loose on certain streets and run to the bullring. Read about a gentle bull in *The Story of Ferdinand the Bull* by Monro Leaf.

 On this day in 1865, William Booth founded the Salvation Army, an organization that helps others. The Salvation Army in the United States began in 1880. The international headquarters are in London. Read more about this organization in *A Gentle War: The Story of the Salvation Army* by Lawrence Fellows.

 On this day in 1709, Etienne de Silhouette was born in France. As a hobby, Silhouette cut out flat, one-color outlines of objects. He attached the outlines to white paper for a dramatic effect.

To create your own silhouette, you'll need a sheet of dark paper and a sheet of light-colored paper, a bright light, scissors, a pencil, and tape. Tape the black paper to a wall and shine the bright light onto it. Put a subject (such as a person or a flower) between the light and the black paper so it casts a shadow onto the paper. Trace the outline of the subject onto the paper. Remove the paper from the wall and cut out the outline. Center the outline on the white paper and tape into place.

RESOURCES

The Story of Ferdinand the Bull by Monro Leaf (New York: Viking Press, 1936).

A Gentle War: The Story of the Salvation Army by Lawrence Fellows (New York: Macmillan, 1979).

JULY 6

On this day in 1957, Althea Gibson became the first African-American to win the women's tennis singles title at Wimbledon. Gibson was born in 1927 in Silver, South Carolina. As a young girl, her family was so poor that they couldn't afford to give Gibson the one thing she had always wanted—a tennis racket. By the time she was 21, however, she had won the first of ten national championships. In 1980, Gibson was one of the first six women to be elected to the Women's Sports Hall of Fame.

 Write about something you've always wanted.

 On this day in 1933, the first All-Star Game was held at Comiskey Park in Chicago. The American League defeated the National League by a score of four to two. Babe Ruth was a member of the American League team and he hit a home run during the game. Every year since then, the best baseball players gather together to make up the All-Star teams. Write down your own All-Star Team. Your team doesn't have to be made up of baseball players. How about creating a team of All-Star friends or pets?

 The month of July is National Hot Dog Month. If you'd like to learn how to prepare hot dogs, send a letter to:

The National Live Stock and Meat Board
444 North Michigan Avenue
Chicago, IL 60611

 In 1935, the fourteenth Dalai Lama was born. A Dalai Lama is the spiritual leader of Tibet and a member of a religious order. Since the eighth century, these orders have been the center of Tibetan religion and society. To learn more about the Dalai Lama, read *Dalai*

Lama: The Leader of the Exiled People of Tibet by Christopher Gibb. It's part of the People Who Have Helped the World series.

RESOURCE

Dalai Lama: The Leader of the Exiled People of Tibet by Christopher Gibb (Milwaukee, Wisconsin: Gareth Stevens, 1990).

JULY 7

On this day in 1880, the story of Pinocchio began appearing in the *Children's Journal of Rome*. Each week, a new portion of the story was printed. Carlo Collodi wrote the story of the puppet who wanted to become a boy.

 In one part of the story, Pinocchio's nose begins to grow when he tells a lie. Write about what happens to you when you tell a lie. If you've never told a lie, write about what you think would happen if you did.

 At the beginning of his story, Pinocchio is a marionette. A marionette is a puppet with strings attached to its arms and legs. A puppeteer stands above the puppet stage and moves the strings up and down to make the marionette move.

Imagine that there are strings attached to your wrists and knees like a marionette. Stand up with your hands at your side. Pretend a puppeteer has just pulled up on the strings attached to your wrists. What would happen if the puppeteer moved the strings very fast or very slow?

 If you'd like to read the story of Pinocchio, look in your library for the book *Pinocchio: Fairy Tales* written by Carlo Collodi and edited by Tony Tallarico.

On this day in 1887, artist Marc Chagall was born in a village near Vitebsk, Russia. When he was 20 years old, Chagall left home to attend the Imperial School of Fine Arts in Leningrad. He didn't have much money and often went without eating and slept on park benches so he could pay for art lessons. Chagall traveled around the world painting and designing stained-glass windows. Many of his paintings look like pictures of a dream. Think about a dream you've had and draw a picture of it.

R E S O U R C E

Pinocchio: Fairy Tales by Carlo Collodi, edited by Tony Tallarico (Harrison, New York: Tuffy Books, 1987).

On this day in 1776, the American colonists read the Declaration of Independence as a bell ringer rang the Liberty Bell for the first time. In 1777, the colonists hid the Liberty Bell under the floorboards of the Zion Reformed Church so the British soldiers couldn't find it. On July 8, 1835, the Liberty Bell cracked as it tolled during the funeral of Chief Justice John Marshal. Today, you can see the Liberty Bell at the Independence National Historical Park in Philadelphia, Pennsylvania.

Write about a time you heard bells ring.

The last time someone rang the Liberty Bell was in 1846 in honor of George Washington's birthday. On June 6, 1944, the day the Allies invaded France, an official tapped the Liberty Bell and its sound was broadcast over the radio to the entire country. To learn more about the Liberty Bell and its history, read *The Story of the Liberty Bell* by Natalie Miller.

On this day in 1838, Count Ferdinand von Zeppelin was born in Konstanz, Germany. When Zeppelin retired from the German Army in 1891, he began to build dirigible balloons (dirigibles are also called airships because a pilot steers them). In 1900, he flew his first airship for 20 minutes. By 1914, people began calling the dirigibles zeppelins in his honor. In the early battles of World War I, German soldiers used zeppelins to bomb England. To learn more about this aircraft, look up "zeppelin" in an encyclopedia.

On this day in 1796, the first recorded U.S. passport was issued. A passport is an official document that travelers carry with them. When travelers visit another country, they show their passport to prove that they're U.S. citizens.

Create your own passport. You'll need a heavy piece of paper that measures 6" x 5". Fold the paper in half so that it measures 3" x 5". On the inside of the booklet, to the left of the fold line, place a photograph of yourself. If you don't have a spare photo, draw a picture of yourself. On the right side of the fold, write down your birth date and place of birth.

R E S O U R C E

The Story of the Liberty Bell by Natalie Miller (San Francisco, California: Children's Book Press, 1965).

On this day in 1819, Elias Howe was born in Spencer, Massachusetts. In 1846, he patented the sewing machine, his newest invention. It wasn't until 1854, however, that Howe became wealthy from his invention. During the Civil War, he served as a private and used his own money to support his regiment.

 Write about how your life would be different if there were no sewing machines.

 Today, a home sewing machine can make up to 1,500 stitches per minute. Industrial sewing machines can sew 5,000 stitches per minute. These large machines mass produce many items, including clothing, shoes, luggage, purses, and baseball gloves.

List all the things you're wearing that were sewn.

 On this day in 1979, the *Voyager 2* spacecraft passed Jupiter on its journey through the Milky Way. Through the photographs sent from *Voyager 2*, astronomers discovered that Jupiter had at least three more moons than they had originally thought. If you'd like to learn more about the fifth planet from the sun, read *Jupiter* by Elaine Landru.

 Using a resource book or encyclopedia, draw a picture of Jupiter with all of its moons.

RESOURCE
Jupiter by Elaine Landru (New York: Franklin Watts, 1991).

On this day in 1875, Mary McLeod Bethune was born in Mayesville, South Carolina. She was the 15th of 17 children. In 1895, she began teaching and nine years later she founded the Daytona Normal and Industrial Institute for Negro Girls in Florida. In 1944, Bethune became director of Negro affairs in the National Youth Administration. She once said, "I have unselfishly given my best, and thank God I have lived long enough to see the fruits of it."

 Write about a time when you did your best.

 President Franklin D. Roosevelt frequently asked Mary McLeod Bethune to advise him on minority affairs. Read more about this remarkable woman in *Mary McLeod Bethune: A Girl Devoted to Her People* by Olive W. Burt.

 On this day in 1834, artist James Abbott McNeill Whistler was born in Lowell, Massachusetts. His best-known work is a portrait of his mother titled *Arrangement in Gray and Black, No. 1: The Artist's Mother*. The painting shows a side view of a woman in a long black dress sitting in a chair.

In honor of Whistler's birthday, draw a portrait of one of your friends sitting in a chair.

 On April 23, 1985, the Coca-Cola Company announced that it was going to offer a new formula for their soft drink and that they would discontinue their old formula. Thousands of Coca-Cola fans were upset because they liked the old formula. Because of the complaints, the company began to produce and market the old formula again. On this day in 1985, Coca-Cola Classic was put back on the soda market.

If you have an opinion about a Coca-Cola project, write to the company at:

The Coca-Cola Company
One Coca-Cola Plaza Northwest
Atlanta, GA 30313

RESOURCE
Mary McLeod Bethune: A Girl Devoted to Her People by Olive W. Burt (New York: Bobbs-Merrill, 1970).

JULY 11

On this day in 1819, children's author Susan Warner was born in New York City. She wrote her first book, *The Wide, Wide World*, in 1851 under the pen name Elizabeth Wetherell. The novel became so popular throughout the world that it sold over 1 million copies. She became the first person to write a book that sold that many copies. After that first book, Warner wrote at least one book a year for the next 30 years.

 If you were to write a book titled *The Wide, Wide World*, what people, places, and things would you include in your book?

 On this day in 1899, Elwyn Brooks White was born in Mt. Vernon, New York. He wrote *Stuart Little*, a book about the adventures of a young mouse. White also wrote *Charlotte's Web*. It's the story of a pig named Wilbur and a spider named Charlotte. Charlotte weaves messages in her webs that say, "Some Pig," "Terrific," and "Radiant." These words inspire Wilbur to do some things he wasn't sure he could do.

If you haven't read *Charlotte's Web* by E. B. White, find a copy at your library and enjoy this story. If you've already read the book, it's worth reading again. *Stuart Little* is also a good book to read on a relaxing summer day.

 E. B. White's first story was published when he was 11 years old. It won a silver medal for excellence and was published in *St. Nicholas* magazine. When he was 14 years old, White won a gold medal for his story about a dog. Draw your favorite dog.

 The *Skylab* space station was part of the U.S. program to put orbiting laboratories in space. In the mid-1970s, three crews of three

men spent 655 days living and working in Skylab before returning to Earth. Scientists planned more activities for the Skylab in the 1980s. But in 1979, Skylab fell to Earth. Western Australia and the Indian Ocean were showered with parts of the space lab.

If you were to live in space for 655 days, what kinds of things would you bring to the space station? Make a list of the toys, books, and food you'd include with your suitcase.

RESOURCES
Some books by E. B. White:
Charlotte's Web and *Stuart Little* (New York: Harper & Row).

JULY 12

On this date in 1984, Democratic presidential candidate Walter Mondale announced that he would nominate Geraldine Ferraro as his running mate. If Mondale had won the 1984 election, Ferraro would have been the vice president of the United States. At the time, Ferraro was a Democratic member of Congress. With this nomination, she became the first woman vice presidential candidate of a major party.

 Would you want to be a vice president? Why or why not?

 On this day in 1938, Dr. William Henry Cosby, Jr., was born in Philadelphia, Pennsylvania. When Bill Cosby was in fifth grade, he performed his first comedy routine for his classmates. In sixth grade, his teacher said that he would "rather be a clown than study." In high school, teachers placed Cosby in classes for gifted students because he had a high IQ. When he had to repeat the tenth grade, he dropped out of school. Later, he noticed that other young men who weren't as bright were completing their education. He decided to go back to school. Do you think it's important to get an education? Give three reasons.

 While back in school, Cosby began his acting career. At first, he worked as a comedian. He told stories about his childhood and about the funny things he learned at school and in church.

Think of something funny from your childhood. *Example*: the first time you washed your dog. Create your own comedy routine using your funny situation.

 Librarian Anna Carroll Moore was born on this day in 1871 in Limerick, Maine. Moore thought that children and young adults should have their own section of the library. In 1895, she entered the Library School of Pratt Institute in Brooklyn, New York, and became the head of its new children's department. Eight years later, she wrote *A List of Books Recommended for a Children's Library*. She encouraged librarians around the world to set up areas in their libraries specifically for children and young adults.

Write your own list of books that you'd recommend for a children's library. Why would you recommend these books?

 Write about something you did that was adventurous.

 If you'd like to send Harrison Ford a birthday card, write to:

Harrison Ford
P.O. Box 5617
Beverly Hills, CA 90210

 Watch the video *Raiders of the Lost Ark* or read more about the adventures of Indiana Jones in *Raiders of the Lost Ark: The Story Book Based on the Movie* by Les Martin.

 Every summer, the Japanese Buddhists believe, the spirits of the recently dead return to visit their families. To prepare for these visits, families clean and decorate their homes. They set a place at the table for any family member who has recently died. They light special lamps, lanterns, or bonfires to guide the spirits back home. For three days, families of the deceased celebrate as though they were having a reunion with their relatives. On the third evening, they set the lanterns out again to guide the spirits back to the spirit world. What do you think of this tradition? Is it a good way to honor someone who has died? Write about why or why not.

....

RESOURCES

Raiders of the Lost Ark video (Paramount/Lucasfilm, 1981).

Raiders of the Lost Ark: The Story Book Based on the Movie by Les Martin (New York: Random House, 1981).

....

JULY 13

On this day in 1942, actor Harrison Ford was born in Chicago, Illinois. Ford is famous for his role as Han Solo in the space adventure *Star Wars*. In the *Indiana Jones* movies, he played an archaeologist who found adventures as he searched for lost treasures.

JULY 14

Florence Bascom was the first woman to earn a Ph.D. degree from an American university. She was born on this day in 1862 in Williamstown, Massachusetts. In 1893, Bascom earned her degree in geology from Johns Hopkins University in Baltimore, Maryland. Three years later, she was appointed to the United States Geological Survey. Geology is the study of Earth's history. Geologists study rocks and minerals to find out what the Earth is made of and what changes have taken place on its surface.

 Would you want to study rocks and minerals? Why or why not?

 Today is Bastille Day in France. On this day in 1789, an angry mob stormed the Bastille (prison). They wanted to free the people who were unjustly kept inside. Read the book *Revolution! France 1789-1794* by Sarel Eimerl to learn more about the French Revolution.

 In honor of Bastille Day, learn a French word or two. "Bonjour" (bohn-zhoor) means "good morning." "Au revoir" (oh ruh-vwahr) means "good-bye." "Merci beaucoup" (mehr-ssee boh-koo) means "thank you very much."

Here's how to count to five in French: 1 un (uhn); 2 deux (duh); 3 trois (trwah); 4 quatre (kah-truh); 5 cinq (sank)

 On this day in 1912, Woodrow Wilson "Woody" Guthrie was born in Okemah, Oklahoma. He was a U.S. folksinger, guitarist, and songwriter. Woody traveled around the United States, worked odd jobs, and played the harmonica in pool halls. He performed on radio stations in Los Angeles and Tijuana, Mexico. Woody wrote more than a thousand songs, including "This Land Is Your Land," "Hard Traveling," and "So Long, It's Been Good to Know You." In honor of Woody Guthrie, pick one of his songs and sing it.

....

RESOURCE

Revolution! France 1789-1794 by Sarel Eimerl (Boston: Little, Brown, 1967).

....

JULY 15

The first woman to win an Oscar award for songwriting was Dorothy Fields. She was born on this day in 1905. Fields began writing lyrics for Broadway shows in 1928. In 1937, she won her award for the song "The Way You Look Tonight." By 1968, she had written 400 songs. In 1971, Fields became the first woman elected to the Songwriters Hall of Fame.

 Write about something—a person, pet, or place—that you'd like to write a song about.

 The author who wrote one of the most well-known Christmas poems was born on this day in 1779 in New York City. The poem is called, "A Visit from Saint Nicholas." Clement Clarke Moore, the author, wrote it for his children.

Moore's poem begins, " 'Twas the night before Christmas and all through the house, not a creature was stirring, not even a mouse...." Take a break from the summer heat and read the rest of the poem in *A Visit from St. Nicholas* by Clement C. Moore.

 On this day in 1606, Dutch artist Harmenszoon van Rijn Rembrandt was born. During his lifetime, he painted more than 100 portraits of himself. Rembrandt's life's work consisted of more than 600 paintings, 300 etchings, and nearly 2,000 drawings. Take some paper and a pencil, sit in front of a mirror, and draw your own self-portrait.

 St. Swithin's Day is celebrated in England and Canada on this day. Swithin, the Bishop of Winchester, died in A.D. 862. He wanted to be buried outside the city's cathedral so he'd always be close to the townspeople.

After awhile, monks thought that Swithin should be buried in the cathedral where the other holy people were buried. When the monks started to move the Bishop's remains, a storm began. It lasted for 40 days. The monks decided to leave St. Swithin where he was.

Today, some people say that the weather on St. Swithin's Day, rainy or fair, will continue for 40 days. Write down what the weather is like today. In 40 days, it'll be August 24. Keep track of the weather and see if it stays the same.

RESOURCE

A Visit from St. Nicholas by Clement Clarke Moore (New York: Simon & Schuster, 1971).

JULY 16

Today, people who live in Dinkelsbuhl, Germany, commemorate Children's Reckoning Day. According to legend, in 1632 an army of Swedes was approaching the town of Dinkelsbuhl. The townspeople couldn't agree on how to keep the soldiers from invading. A young girl named Lore offered to go directly to the Swedish colonel and ask him to spare the town. The adults didn't think a child could help. When the army entered the town, Lore led a group of singing children to the Swedish soldiers. The children knelt in front of the colonel and asked him to spare the town. The colonel agreed and the town was saved.

 Write about something you can do that adults think you can't do.

 At 5:30 a.m. on July 16, 1945, the first atomic bomb was exploded. It was located on top of a steel tower at the Alamagordo Air Base in New Mexico. The resulting mushroom cloud went 40,000 feet high and could be seen 400 miles away. The explosion vaporized the 100-foot tower where the bomb had been placed. The desert surface around the blast fused to glass. To learn more about the atomic bomb, read *The History of the Atomic Bomb* by Michael Blow.

 On this day in 1969, *Apollo 11* was launched. People around the world watched the take-off and the first moon landing. They watched eagerly as the astronauts returned safely to Earth. In honor of this moon landing, this week is Space Week. To celebrate this week, find out about an astronaut. (Neil Armstrong was the first person to walk on the moon. In 1983, Sally Ride was the first American woman in space.)

 Do you think the space program is important? Should we keep sending rockets, satellites, and people into space? Why or why not?

RESOURCE

The History of the Atomic Bomb by Michael Blow (New York: Harper & Row, 1968).

JULY 17

"Isn't this Los Angeles?" asked pilot Douglas Corrigan to the ground crew. On this day in 1938, Corrigan took off from an airport in Brooklyn, New York. He wanted to fly west to Los Angeles but his plane had no radio and only a simple compass. Corrigan read his compass wrong and headed east across the Atlantic Ocean. Twenty-eight hours later, he landed in Dublin, Ireland. When he returned to the United

States, he was nicknamed "Wrong Way Corrigan."

 Write about a time you became lost or went the wrong way.

 If you'd like to know more about how to use compasses, maps, and nature signs to help you find your way, find these books: *Finding Your Way in the Outdoors* by Robert L. Mooers, Jr., and *Compass* by Paula Hogan.

 On this day in 1861, the U.S. government authorized the first paper money. The five dollar bill had Alexander Hamilton's picture on it. The ten dollar bill had Abraham Lincoln's picture. To learn more about U.S. money, read *From Gold to Money* by Ali Mitgutsch.

 How can you make some extra money? Make a list of some money-making ideas. *Examples*: Walk a neighbor's dog, start a grocery carrying service for older people, do yard work.

R E S O U R C E S

Finding Your Way in the Outdoors by Robert L. Mooers, Jr. (New York: Outdoor Life Books, 1972).

Compass by Paula Hogan (New York: Walker Publishing, 1982).

From Gold to Money by Ali Mitgutsch (Minneapolis: Carolrhoda Books, 1985).

JULY 18

On this day in 1976, Nadia Comaneci from Romania became the first gymnast to receive a perfect score of 10 from Olympic judges. Comaneci was 14 years old when she faced the judges and performed so well in the gymnastics competition that she received seven perfect scores and three gold medals.

 Write about something you've done that deserves a medal.

 To learn more about Nadia Comaneci, read *Remarkable Children: Twenty Who Made History* by Dennis B. Fradin.

 Although gymnasts can make their sport look easy, walking, jumping, and tumbling on a four-inch balance beam takes practice. Create your own practice balance beam using masking tape. You'll need two pieces of masking tape, each 10 feet long. Stick them on a smooth floor or sidewalk, parallel to each other and 4 inches apart. Practice walking between the tape. Is it hard to stay between the two pieces of tape?

 If it's a hot summer day, plan to cool down. Make a list of all the ways you know to stay cool. *Examples*: wear shorts and a light shirt, drink lots of water, run underneath a sprinkler.

R E S O U R C E

Remarkable Children: Twenty Who Made History by Dennis B. Fradin (Boston: Little, Brown, 1987).

JULY 19

Sitting Bull was the chief of the Northern Hunting Sioux. In 1868, he signed a treaty with the U.S. government that stated Native Americans could live in a reservation above the North Platte River. But the United States broke their treaty promises by letting settlers live and hunt on the land. Sioux, Arapaho, and Cheyenne Native Americans gathered around Sitting Bull to fight. In 1876 at Little Big Horn, this force wiped out Colonel George Custer and the 7th Cavalry detachment. Five years later, on this day in 1881, Sitting Bull finally surrendered to the U.S. Army.

 Write about a time when someone broke a promise to you. How did you feel? What did you do?

 To learn more about Sitting Bull, read *Sitting Bull and the Battle of the Little Big Horn* by Sheila Black or *Sitting Bull: Champion of His People* by Doris S. Garst.

 Native Americans respect life; war was not always their first reaction to a problem. Most tribes resorted to war only after the Europeans broke agreements. Discuss how books and movies often portray Native Americans. Do you agree or disagree with the way these people are portrayed?

 On this day in 1885, novelist Mary O'Hara was born in New Jersey. O'Hara began writing when she was eight years old. In addition to books, she wrote movie scripts and composed songs. Some of her songs were about Wyoming. O'Hara wrote the popular books *My Friend Flicka*, *Thunderhead*, and *Green Grass of Wyoming*. Ask someone to read you a chapter from one of Mary O'Hara's books.

RESOURCES

Sitting Bull and the Battle of the Little Big Horn by Sheila Black (Englewood Cliffs, New Jersey: Silver Burdett, 1989).

Sitting Bull: Champion of His People by Doris S. Garst (Englewood Cliffs, New Jersey: Julian Messner, 1946).

Some books by Mary O'Hara

My Friend Flicka, *Thunderhead*, and *Green Grass of Wyoming* (Philadelphia: Lippincott).

JULY 20

The first moon landing occurred on this day in 1969. Commander Neil Armstrong and Air Force Colonel Edwin Eugene "Buzz" Aldrin, Jr., landed the *Eagle* on the moon's surface. Six hours after landing, Armstrong set foot on the moon. Armstrong and Aldrin remained on the lunar surface for 21 hours, 36 minutes, and 16 seconds. They were outside the spacecraft, walking on the moon's surface, for about 2 hours and 15 minutes.

 Although the moon walk time was less than three hours, scientists took years to prepare for the experience. Write about a time you carefully planned for something.

 When Neil Armstrong set foot on the moon, he said, "That's one small step for man, one giant leap for mankind." Later, he said that he had meant to say, "That's one small step for *a* man, one giant leap for mankind." His size 9 1/2 boots left footprints that have never disappeared from the moon's surface. With your friends and family, talk about why Armstrong's words were so important.

 During the first moon walk, the two astronauts had many tasks to complete. They picked up pieces from earlier experiments, set up seismic equipment, and took photographs. To learn about what the astronauts saw on their moon walk, read *What the Moon Is Like* by Franklyn M. Branley.

 In honor of this first moon walk, draw a rocket blasting off for the moon.

RESOURCE

What the Moon Is Like by Franklyn M. Branley (New York: Harper & Row Junior Books, 1987).

JULY 21

On this day in 1856, Louise Blanchard Bethune was born. She was the first woman architect in the United States. Bethune was also the first woman elected to the American Institute of Architects. Throughout her life, Bethune worked for fair laws to govern her profession. She also worked for equal pay for equal service.

 Write about why you think people should be treated equally.

 On this day in 1899, author Ernest Hemingway was born in Oak Park, Illinois. In 1952, he won a Pulitzer Prize for his story *The Old Man and the Sea*. In 1954, he won the Nobel Prize for Literature. He received that award for "his powerful mastery of the art of storytelling."

Hemingway generally used few adjectives in his writing. An adjective is a word that describes another word. *Examples*: nice, quick, helpful, pretty, strong, and young are all adjectives. Writers use these words to describe someone or something. Make a list of some other adjectives.

 Create a round-robin story. Ask a friend or family member to write a sentence. Have another person read that sentence and add another sentence to continue the first person's idea. Keep asking people to read the previous sentences and add their own sentence. When everyone has had a chance to write a sentence, read your story out loud from beginning to end.

 On this day in 1873, Jesse Woodson James committed his first train robbery near Adair, Iowa. James and his gang took $3,000.

Nine years later, in St. Joseph, Missouri, Jesse James was killed when Robert Ford shot him in the back. Learn more about Jesse James in *Wanted: Frank and Jesse James; The Real Story* by Margaret Baldwin.

R E S O U R C E

Wanted: Frank and Jesse James; The Real Story by Margaret Baldwin (Englewood Cliffs, New Jersey: Julian Messner, 1981).

JULY 22

On this day in 1822, Gregor Johann Mendel was born. Mendel, an Austrian monk and botanist, was the first person to study the laws of heredity. (Heredity means the characteristics that are transferred from a parent to a child.) Mendel's experiments began in 1856 in the monastery gardens.

 Describe the characteristics that you inherited from your parents. If you are adopted, write about other ways you are like your parents.

 Read *Why You Look Like You; Whereas I Tend to Look Like Me* by Charlotte Pomerantz to find out more about Mendel's studies.

 In 1376, a strange man arrived in Hamelin, West Germany. He told the leaders of the town that he could get rid of its rats. When he played his pipe (an instrument like a flute), the rats followed him straight into the Weser River. Not a single rat was left, but the town refused to pay the piper his fee. So, the story goes, the piper played his pipe again, and this time all the children followed him out of Hamelin and never came back. At noon every Sunday during the summer, the town reenacts the story. With a few friends, act out the story of the pied piper.

On this day in 1884, the Reverend William Archibald Spooner was born in London, England. Whenever Spooner spoke, he transposed, or changed around, the first letters of his words. When Spooner went to say "crushing blow," he would say "blushing crow." And "half-formed wish" became "half-warmed fish." These transpositions were called "slips of the tongue," because they were said accidentally. The term "spoonerism" has come to describe them.

Turn these phrases into spoonerisms: hot summer day; jump in a pool; drink lemonade; ride a bike.

....

RESOURCE

Why You Look Like You; Whereas I Tend to Look Like Me by Charlotte Pomerantz (Los Angeles: Young Scott, 1969).

....

JULY 23

On this day in 1715, the first lighthouse in North America was completed. The colonists built the Boston Light on Little Brewster Island near the entrance to Boston Harbor. On September 14, 1716, it was lit for the first time. When the British left Boston in March 1776, they blew up the lighthouse. The newly independent Americans rebuilt it in 1783.

Write about why ships need lighthouses.

A meteor shower is the appearance of hundreds of meteors. On this date, as the Perseus Constellation rises, the Perseid Meteor Showers begin. They are among the most spectacular meteor shows—spectators can see between 50 and 100 meteors in one night. The Perseid Meteor Showers continue every night until August 20. Find out more about these showers by looking up "meteor" in an encyclopedia. Plan to see the Perseid showers if you can.

Many people make a wish when they see the first star at night. Some make a wish on a falling star. During the Perseid Meteor Shower, people will be making many wishes. Write about what you'll wish for when you see a "falling star."

The astronomical and astrological zodiac divide the sun's orbit into twelve sections. The days between July 23 and August 22 are for Leo, the Lion. Survey your friends to find the number of people you know who were born a Leo.

JULY 24

On this date in 1783, Simón Bolívar was born in Caracas, Venezuela. He dreamed of independence for the Spanish colonies of South America. In 1819, during the rainy season, he led 2,500 soldiers across ten rivers and over the Andes mountains. Bolívar attacked the Spanish. They were so completely surprised that after a brief battle they surrendered. Bolívar had become "The Great Liberator." Under his leadership, independence for Venezuela, Ecuador, Bolivia, and Peru soon followed.

Write about a time when you had an unpleasant surprise.

To learn more about Venezuela, read *Enchantment of the World, Venezuela* by Marion Morrison. The book contains colorful pictures of the country and its people.

On this day in 1802, author Alexander Dumas was born. He wrote many romantic historical plays but is best remembered for his swashbuckling historical novels. In 1844, he wrote *The Three Musketeers*; the next year he wrote *The Count of Monte Cristo*. Those two books are known as classics. Find out the names of other classics. Ask a librarian for help. Do any of these titles interest you? Pick one to read—or pick another book of your choice.

 Today is Pioneer Day in Utah. On this day in 1847, the first settlers arrived in the area. Brigham Young had led a group of Mormons out of Illinois where they were being harassed because of their beliefs. Young and his followers settled in present-day Salt Lake City, Utah. On a map of the United States, find Salt Lake City, Utah. Now find the state of Illinois. Using the mileage chart on the map, figure out how many miles the Mormons traveled.

RESOURCE

Enchantment of the World, Venezuela by Marion Morrison (Chicago: Childrens Press, 1989).

July is National Picnic Month. Many people enjoy packing picnic baskets, then finding some special place—a park, lake shore, or country field—to eat their food.

 Write about why you would—or wouldn't—want to eat outside.

 Pretend you're in charge of planning the best picnic ever. Make a list of everything you'd pack. What food would you bring? What would you drink? What would you bring for entertainment? Now think about the best picnic places. Maybe you can go on a picnic with your family or friends.

 Thomas Cowperthwait Eakins was an American painter, teacher, and photographer. He was born on this day in 1844 in Philadelphia, Pennsylvania. Many people think Eakins is the most outstanding American painter of the nineteenth century. When he painted people, Eakins preferred to use live models for his work rather than paint from memory. He wanted his paintings to look as real as possible. To see some of Eakins' paintings, look trough the book *Eakins* by Sylvan Schendler.

 One of Thomas Eakins' famous works is titled *The Thinker*. It's a full-length portrait of Louis Kenton, Eakins' brother-in-law. In the painting, Kenton has his hands in the pockets of his baggy pants and is looking down at the floor as if he's thinking of something.

Draw a life-sized portrait of someone you know—or of yourself. You'll need a large sheet of paper and crayons, pens, or markers. Don't forget to draw the top of the person's head and the tips of that person's shoes.

RESOURCE

Eakins by Sylvan Schendler (Boston: Little, Brown, 1967).

JULY 26

Many people have tried to develop an international language, one that everyone could speak. One of the best-known attempts at an artificial language was called Esperanto. Dr. Ludwig L. Zamenhoff of Poland developed this new language. His textbook on Esperanto was first published on this date in 1887. Today, about 2 million people around the world speak Esperanto.

Do you think everyone in the world should speak the same language? Why or why not?

Ludwig Zamenhoff designed Esperanto to be simple, flexible, and logical. Grammar for Esperanto contains only 16 basic rules. It has 28 letters in its alphabet. Each letter only has one sound. Here's an example of Esperanto:

"Bonan matenon! Kion vi dezirus fari?" That means "Good morning! What would you like to do?"

Would you like to learn another language? Why or why not? If you already know another language, write about why you like speaking two languages.

 If you'd like to learn more about Esperanto, write a letter to:

ELNA
P.O. Box 1129
El Cerrito, CA 94530

 Today is National Day in the Republic of Maldives, an independent island nation in the Indian Ocean. Maldives is located southwest of Sri Lanka near the southern tip of India; it's made up of 2,000 coral islands. On a world map, find Maldives.

JULY 27

On this day in 1922, Norman Lear was born in New Haven, Connecticut. He's an American television scriptwriter and producer who has written many long-running comedy shows. Many of his hits, including "Good Times" and "All in the Family," appeared in the 1970s. Norman Lear once said, "I want to entertain, but [I want to write about] subjects that matter and people worth caring about."

 Write about an idea you have for a new comedy show.

What is your television-watching schedule? Create a chart of the TV shows you watch. Across the top of a sheet of paper, write the days of the week. Underneath each day, write the titles of the TV shows you watch.

Once your chart is done, look at it closely. Do you think you spend too much time watching TV? Perhaps you could pick two shows that you really like to watch. Watching those shows could be your TV time. What could you do with your remaining free time?

 Peggy Gale Fleming, an American figure skater, was born on this day in 1948. When she was 15, she competed in the 1964 Olympics and placed sixth. In the 1968 Olympics, however, she won the only U.S. Gold Medal.

The sport of figure skating has three parts: free style, skating with a partner, and ice dancing. To learn more about this sport, look up "skating" or "figure skating" in an encyclopedia.

 On this date in 1921, Sir Frederick Grant Banting and his assistant, Charles Best, separated insulin from other materials for the first time. Banting was a Canadian physician, born in 1891. He shared the 1923 Nobel Prize in physiology and medicine for his work in extracting the hormone insulin from the pancreas. Today, people with diabetes can control their disease by giving themselves insulin injections. Find out more about this medical breakthrough by looking up "Frederick Banting" in an encyclopedia.

On this day in 1866, author and illustrator Helen Beatrix Potter was born in Bolton Gardens, Kensington, England. Potter studied her pet rabbit and spiders, flies, ducks, and mice. She created many animal characters based on real animals. Her characters include Peter Rabbit, Jemima Puddle-Duck, Squirrel Nutkin, Benjamin Bunny, and Mrs. Twiggywinkle.

 Write a description of your favorite animal character from a book, movie, TV show, or your own imagination.

 In the 1890s, Beatrix Potter began to send her animal stories to a friend's sick child. In 1902, she published her first book titled *The Tale of Peter Rabbit*. You'll find many of Beatrix Potter's stories in *Beatrix Potter Giant Treasury* or the *Peter Rabbit Giant Treasury*. Read one today.

 On this day in 1964, the spacecraft *Ranger 7* televised 4,308 close-up photographs of the moon back to Earth. Also on this day in 1973, Alan L. Bean, Owen K. Garriott, and Jack R. Lousma started a 59-day mission in *Skylab 3* to test people's space flight endurance. Discuss the things you'd do if you were in space for almost three months.

 On this day in 1945, a B-25 Army bomber airplane, lost in the fog, crashed into the Empire State Building in New York City. It crashed into the seventy-ninth floor. Thirteen people were killed.

Shreve, Lamb and Harmon Architects designed the Empire State Building and it was completed in 1931. The Empire State Building is featured in a book called *Unbuilding* by David Macaulay. Look for the book in your library to see a fictional account of workers taking apart the building.

....

RESOURCES

Some books by Beatrix Potter:

Beatrix Potter Giant Treasury and *Peter Rabbit Giant Treasury* (Southbridge, Maine: Crowne Publications).

Unbuilding by David Macaulay (New York: Houghton Mifflin, 1980).

....

On this day in 1877, Charles William Beebe was born in Brooklyn, New York. He was an American naturalist, writer, and explorer who made hundreds of detailed descriptions of tropical jungle, undersea, and bird life. Beebe loved everything about nature and led scientific explorations deep into the jungles and forests of Central and South America, the West Indies, and the Orient.

 Write about the types of animals you'd study if you were a naturalist.

 In 1934, Charles Beebe and his partner, Otis Barton, built a hollow steel ball 5 feet in diameter. With this bathysphere the two men descended 3,028 feet into the Bermuda waters. Beebe saw wondrous deep-sea creatures during his trip underwater. Would you—or any of your friends or family—like to go deep, deep down into the waters of the ocean? Talk about what you think you'd find there.

 On this day in 1938, Peter Charles Jennings was born in Toronto, Canada. When he was nine years old, Jennings hosted a weekly radio program called "Peter's People." On September 5, 1983, Peter Jennings became the anchor person for ABC's "World News

Tonight." Since he began working at ABC, he has won many awards for his outstanding reporting. Interview a friend as if you were a TV reporter.

Create a radio show for young people. Think about the types of stories you'd report on. What kind of music could you play to introduce your show? Would you advertise something? With a tape recorder, record a broadcast.

On this day in 1947, Arnold Schwarzenegger, an actor and bodybuilder, was born in Graz, Austria. When he was 12, he was considered a good soccer player. By the time he was 15, he began to lift weights to develop his legs for soccer. Schwarzenegger kept on lifting weights and taking care of his body. People in his native country called him the "Austrian Oak" because of his huge muscles.

Write about why you think it's important to take care of your body.

When he was in top form in his bodybuilding, Arnold Schwarzenegger's arms measured 22 inches around. Using a tape measure, measure your arms and the arms of your friends. How do those measurements compare with Schwarzenegger's? Hold the tape at 22 inches to see how large his muscles were.

During the 1960s and 1970s, Arnold Schwarzenegger won the title of Mr. Universe five times. He was named Mr. Olympia six times. In 1975, he retired from competition because, he said, he wanted to give "others a chance" to win. Do you think

you get enough exercise? Do you eat enough healthy foods? Talk about why people should exercise and eat right.

On this day in 1890, Charles Dillon "Casey" Stengel was born in Kansas City, Missouri. After playing baseball from 1912 to 1925, he managed the Brooklyn Dodgers and the Boston Braves. He had his most successful managing years with the New York Yankees. He coached that team from 1949 to 1960; the Yankees won seven World Series during that time. To learn more about Casey Stengel and his career, read *Casey! The Sports Career of Charles Stengel* by James Hahn.

··

R E S O U R C E

Casey! The Sports Career of Charles Stengel by James Hahn (New York: Crestwood House, 1981).

··

On this day in 1790, the first U.S. Patent Office was opened. The first U.S. patent was issued to Samuel Hopkins of Vermont. Hopkins had invented a machine that would process potash (from wood ashes) and soap. The patent was signed by George Washington and Thomas Jefferson.

Write about an invention you feel will be needed in the future.

If you'd like more information on how to apply for a patent, write to:

United States Patent and Trademark Office
U.S. Department of Commerce
Washington, DC 20231

Adolph Sax invented the saxophone; his instrument was officially introduced to the military band of the French army on this day in 1840. The saxophone is a wind instrument with a curved metal pipe and holes with keys. In the late 1920s, jazz musicians began using the saxophone in their music. Read more about the saxophone in the book *The Clarinet and Saxophone Book* by Melvin Berger.

 In honor of the saxophone, make your own simple instrument. You'll need a cardboard tube, waxed paper, a rubber band, and a pencil. With the pencil, poke two or three holes into the side of the cardboard tube. Wrap the tube in waxed paper. Make sure one end is totally covered with the waxed paper and hold it in place with the rubber band. Hum into the open end for a kazoo sound.

R E S O U R C E

The Clarinet and Saxophone Book by Melvin Berger (New York: Lee Lothrop and Shepard Books, 1975).

In 1847, Maria Mitchell discovered a new comet. At the time, she was looking up at the sky with a small, two-inch telescope. Mitchell became famous because of her discovery and in her honor the comet was named "Miss Mitchell's Comet." The following year, she became the first woman elected to the American Academy of Arts and Sciences. In 1873, Mitchell founded the American Association for the Advancement of Women. Her group's purpose is to promote the work and achievements of women. Maria Mitchell was born on this day in 1818.

 Write about a group you'd like to organize. What would the purpose of your group be?

 On this day in 1936, Yves St. Laurent was born. He's a French fashion designer who encouraged women to wear pants for all occasions and promoted the short skirts of the 1960s. Some of St. Laurent's clothing designs use fur and leather. He has also used metallic and transparent fabrics and large shapes and prints in his designs.

Be a fashion designer for a day and design a fancy outfit. Draw a picture of yourself in your new creation.

 This is National Clown Week. Did you know that there are three types of clowns? *Traditional* clowns wear simple white makeup on their faces. You can spot *grotesque* clowns by their wild, colored costumes, large painted eyebrows, and huge noses. *Character* clowns dress up as someone else such as mothers, babies, or hobos. Dress up as your favorite type of clown.

 On this date in 1819, Herman Melville was born in New York City. He was an author whose greatest work is *Moby Dick*, which he wrote in 1851. During Melville's lifetime, many people did not read his stories. After his death, a number of his unpublished poems were discovered. Today, many people think of Melville as one of America's greatest writers.

Moby Dick is the story of a Great White whale. Create a list of words that you use to describe whales. Did you list the word "endangered"?

On this day in 1876, James Butler "Wild Bill" Hickok was killed. Someone shot him while he was playing poker in a saloon in

Deadwood, South Dakota. Hickok was born in 1837 in Troy Grove, Illinois. He served in the Union Army during the Civil War and was a scout for General George Custer. In the late 1860s, he worked as a U.S. marshal in Kansas. In 1872 and 1873, he toured the country with Buffalo Bill as a sharpshooter and trick rider.

 Write a list of "wild" names for yourself, such as "Wild Tom," "Wacky Wendy," or "Tina the Terrific."

 In his lifetime, Wild Bill Hickok was also a stagecoach driver on the Santa Fe and Oregon trails, a frontier scout, and a spy. Draw a picture to illustrate some part of Wild Bill's life.

 On this day in 1983, the National Center for Atmospheric Research announced that it was launching a $3.5 million program to study the effects of acid rain in the United States. Acid rain forms when sulfur oxides, nitrogen oxides, and other air pollutants dissolve into rainwater. It can severely damage both plant and animal life. To learn more about acid rain, read the book *Acid Rain* by Mary Turck in the Earth Alert Series.

 Acid rain is just one of the many environmental problems people today are facing. To learn about others—and to find out ways you can help the Earth— read *50 Simple Things Kids Can Do to Save the Earth.*

RESOURCES

Acid Rain by Mary Turck (New York: Crestwood House, 1990).

50 Simple Things Kids Can Do to Save the Earth by John Javna (Kansas City, Missouri: Andrews & McMeel, 1990).

AUGUST 3

n this day in 1970, Commander Juliane Gallina was born in Pelham, New York. When she was 21 years old, she became the first woman to be named Brigade Commander by the U.S. Naval Academy. She is the second woman ever to hold this kind of position in a military service academy.

 Would you want to join the military? Why or why not?

 Every year on the first Monday in August, National Smile-Week begins. It lasts through the following Sunday.

On a large sheet of paper, draw as many faces as you can. Draw each face with a different expression and label it. You can create smiling, frowning, worried, frightened, laughing, puzzled, and pouting faces.

 On this day in 1958, the *Nautilus*, an atomic-powered submarine, traveled under the North Pole ice pack. It was the first submerged crossing of the North Pole. The *Nautilus* started out from the southern tip of Great Britain and traveled north to Reykjavik, Iceland. From there the submarine continued north through the Greenland Sea. After its exploration under the North Pole, the *Nautilus* traveled south to Barrow, Alaska, and through the Bering Strait past the Aleutian Islands. Using a map of the Arctic region, trace the route of the *Nautilus* and its crew.

The longest time a submarine and its crew worked and lived under water occurred from November 1982 to March 1983. The crew of the British submarine *Warspite* spent 111 days in the South Atlantic Ocean. Would you like to live in a submarine? Why or why not? Talk about this with your family.

August 4

On this day in 1963, the United States, the former Soviet Union, and Great Britain signed the Nuclear Test Ban Treaty. The treaty prohibited testing of nuclear weapons in space, above ground, and under water. In more recent treaties, officials have agreed to take apart certain weapons and destroy them.

 Do you think that countries should destroy their weapons? Why or why not? Write a paragraph on this topic, giving your point of view.

 On this day in 1985, baseball greats Tom Seaver and Rod Carew reached career milestones. Seaver won his 300th game. Rod Carew got his 3,000th base hit. You can find these and other facts on baseball cards. Over 200,000 people collect baseball cards. To learn more about baseball cards and collecting them, read *Baseball Cards* by David Plaut.

 Create a card about yourself. On a sheet of paper draw a picture of yourself doing something that you love to do (like playing the piano, reading a book, or kicking a soccer ball). On the other side, write down facts about yourself. Include your birth date, color of your eyes and hair, and the name of your parents and brothers and sisters. Write down the name of your town and school. Describe the picture on the other side of the card and include information about it.

 On this day in 1821, the first issue of *The Saturday Evening Post* appeared on newsstands. For 148 years, this monthly magazine reported on the movie stars, cities, and towns in the United States. For over 40 years, artist Norman Rockwell's realistic paintings appeared on the magazine's cover. The final issue of *The Saturday Evening Post* came out in 1969.

Visit the library and look at three different magazines you've never seen before. Did you like them? Why or why not? See if you can find some issues of *The Saturday Evening Post*.

RESOURCE

Baseball Cards by David Plaut (Philadelphia: Running Press Book Publishers, 1989).

August 5

On this day in 1790, Congress established the Coast Guard to enforce maritime (sea) law. The Coast Guard is a branch of the U.S. Armed Forces and its duties include search-and-rescue missions and safety and environmental protection. The Coast Guard also provides navigation assistance such as buoys, lightships, and beacons. The Coast Guard operates over 250 ships, 160 aircraft, and 2,000 small craft with 37,000 military and 6,000 civilian personnel.

 Would you want to be a part of the Coast Guard? Write about why you would (or wouldn't) want to be a member of the Coast Guard.

 To learn more about the Coast Guard, write a letter to:

The U.S. Coast Guard
2100 Second Street SW
Washington, DC 20593

 On this day in 1991, Russian athlete Sergei Bubka vaulted 20 feet 1/4 inch. He was the first pole-vaulter to pass the 20-foot barrier indoors. Until Bubka's vault, people thought it was impossible to jump over 20 feet.

Make a list of things you think are impossible. What could you do—or what machine could you invent—to make these things possible?

 On this day in 1914, the first electric traffic signal lights were installed in Cleveland, Ohio. What do you think people did before there were traffic signals? Why do drivers and pedestrians need traffic signals?

August 6

On this day in 1911, Lucille Desiree Ball was born in Jamestown, New York. Ball began her career as a dancer in New York City. In 1931, she went to Hollywood to star in movies. Her greatest success came when she starred in the TV series "I Love Lucy" with her husband Desi Arnaz. The series was the first sitcom to be filmed in front of a live audience. "I Love Lucy" became one of the longest running series in television. The final episode was broadcast on April 1, 1960.

 In her shows, Lucille Ball's characters were always getting into silly situations. Write about the silliest situation you've been in.

 Although the "I Love Lucy" shows were shown on television in the 1950s, you can watch them today on video. Enjoy an "I Love Lucy" show today.

 In 1984, Lucille Ball became one of the first inductees into the Television Academy Hall of Fame. Think about the TV shows you watch. Which actor or actress do you think should be in the Television Academy Hall of Fame? Why?

 Lucille Ball was a businesswoman and actress. She became the first woman to head a major motion picture and TV studio. Her company set new trends in show business, including filming in Hollywood, California, while other companies were still filming in New York. To learn more about Lucille Ball, read *Lucille Ball: Pioneer of Comedy* by Katherine Krohn.

RESOURCES

I Love Lucy Collection, Vol. 1, video (Fox Video, 1952).

Lucille Ball: Pioneer of Comedy by Katherine Krohn (Minneapolis: Lerner Publications, 1992).

August 7

On this day in 1869, Professor Edward Charles Pickering took the first photograph of a total solar eclipse. Pickering used a portrait lens to photograph the eclipse as it crossed diagonally from Alaska to North Carolina. In 585 B.C., a total solar eclipse blacked out the sky over Mesopotamia during a war between two armies. The soldiers were terrified by the eclipse; they thought it was an omen. They put down their weapons and made peace on the spot.

 Write about why you think an eclipse used to be so frightening to people. Why is it not as frightening today?

 In a solar eclipse, the moon passes between the sun and earth. In a lunar eclipse, the earth passes between the sun and the moon. To learn more about eclipses, read *Eclipse: Darkness in Daytime,* edited by Franklyn M. Branley.

 On this day in 1904, Ralph Johnson Bunche was born in Detroit, Michigan. Bunche was the grandson of a slave but grew up to be a diplomat. As the Secretary of the Palestine Commission, he helped to settle the Arab-Israeli dispute of 1950. Because of his work, he was awarded the 1950 Nobel Peace Prize. Learn more about the many things Bunche did as an internationally known diplomat in *The Value of Responsibility: The Story of Ralph Bunche* by Ann D. Johnson.

 Diplomats handle relations between their country and other countries of the world. Diplomats must know what to do or say in order to maintain good feelings between people. Have you ever had to break up a fight between two people? Or settle an argument with someone? If you have, you've been a diplomat. Write about a time when you had to be a diplomat.

RESOURCES

Eclipse: Darkness in Daytime, edited by Franklyn M. Branley (New York: Harper & Row Junior Books, 1988).

The Value of Responsibility: The Story of Ralph Bunche by Ann D. Johnson (San Diego: Oak Tree Publications, 1978).

 Can you think of something from your life that would make a good story? Write a brief description of that time. Maybe later you'll write the story.

 The Yearling was set in northern Florida. It tells the story of a farmer, his wife, and his son Jody. Jody adopts an orphaned fawn and vows to raise it himself. Ask someone to read *The Yearling* to you and find out what happens when the fawn begins to eat the family corn.

 Do you have wild animals around your home? Perhaps rabbits, squirrels, ducks, raccoons, or deer live near you. If you've ever seen a young or hurt animal, you may have wanted to help it. Write about the problems that might occur when you shelter a wild animal.

 On this day in 1968, the Republicans nominated Richard Nixon for President. Six years later, in 1974, on this day, he announced his resignation from the presidency. Find out why Richard Nixon resigned by looking up his name in an encyclopedia or other reference books.

RESOURCE

The Yearling by Marjorie K. Rawlings (New York: Macmillan, 1985).

Auguſt 8

On this day in 1896, Marjorie Kinnan Rawlings was born in Washington, D.C. After working as a newspaper reporter, she moved to Cross Creek, Florida. In 1933, she published *South Moon Under,* her first book. *The Yearling*, published in 1938, became her best-known book and won the 1939 Pulitzer Prize for fiction.

Auguſt 9

On this day in 1956, women in South Africa demonstrated against their country's policy of apartheid. In an apartheid government, people are separated and treated differently because of their skin color. In 1981, the United Nations General Assembly asked all governments to observe this day annually.

Write about what you think would happen if everyone had the same skin color.

 To learn more about the struggle against apartheid, send a letter to:

The United Nations Centre
Against Apartheid
Department of Public Information
United Nations Headquarters
New York, NY 10017

 Today is National Day in Singapore, an island republic in southeast Asia. On this day in 1965, Singapore became an independent nation. To learn more about this country, read *Singapore* by Marion M. Brown.

 On this day in 1988, hockey player Wayne Gretsky left the Edmonton Oilers to join the Los Angeles Kings. Gretsky had played for the Oilers since the beginning of his career in 1978. When he announced his trade, the Edmonton fans were crushed. They couldn't believe that their star player was leaving.

Think of someone important in your life—such as a friend, teacher, neighbor. Write about how you'd feel if that person left and went somewhere far away.

RESOURCE

Singapore by Marion M. Brown (Chicago: Childrens Press, 1989).

Agnes Gonxha Bojaxhiu, known as Mother Teresa, was born in Skopje, Yugoslavia, on this day in 1910. Mother Teresa is a Roman Catholic missionary who worked as a teacher in Calcutta, India. In 1948, the Vatican in Rome gave her permission to leave her convent and tend to the homeless, starving, and sick people in Calcutta's slums. "We can do no great things," said Mother Teresa, "only small things with great love."

 Write about the small things you do with great love. If you don't feel you do anything like that now, write about what you'd like to do.

 In 1950, Mother Teresa established her Order of the Missionaries. The order's work expanded beyond India to other countries including Australia, Britain, Sri Lanka, Jordan, Tanzania, and Venezuela. To learn more about Mother Teresa, read *Mother Teresa: A Sister to the Poor* by Patricia R. Giff.

 In 1971, Mother Teresa won the first Pope John XXIII Peace Prize. In 1979, she was awarded the Nobel Peace Prize. Both of these awards are given to people who work to help others. Think about people in your neighborhood or in your family who try to help others whenever they can. Which of these people do you think should win a special prize? Why?

 On this day in 1890, Fay Fuller reached the summit of Mount Rainier in west central Washington. She was only 20 years old and became the first woman to scale the mountain. Pretend you're a mountain climber and scale the jungle gym at a playground.

RESOURCE

Mother Teresa: A Sister to the Poor by Patricia R. Giff (New York: Viking Penguin, 1986).

AUGUST 11

Mars is the fourth planet from the sun. Scientists say that it's the only other planet that might support life. On this day in 1877, Asaph Hall discovered the first of Mars' two moons. At the time, Hall was in charge of a 26-inch telescope at the Naval Observatory in Washington, D.C. Scientists named the moon Deimos; it's the smaller of Mars' two moons. Deimos is about 14,600 miles from Mars. It takes 1.26 days for Deimos to circle the planet.

 Write about what you'd see if you looked through a powerful telescope into the night sky.

 To learn more about Mars and its moons, read *Mars: Our Mysterious Neighbor* by Isaac Asimov.

 On this day in 1921, Alex Palmer Haley was born in Ithaca, New York. He began his writing career while he served in the U.S. Coast Guard. In 1976, after 12 years of research and travel, Haley finished *Roots: The Saga of an American Family*. The book told the story of Haley's ancestors who were from Africa but were brought to America as slaves.

The book and its TV series helped to create a new interest in genealogy, the study of one's ancestors. Ask your parents to tell you something about your grandparents or other ancestors.

 Create a family tree. At the top of a sheet of paper, write your name. On the next line, write the name of your parents. Below those names, write the name of your grandparents. Talk to your relatives including your mother, father, aunts, uncles, and grandparents. Ask them the names of your great-grandparents and your great-great-grandparents. If you want, add the names of your brothers or sisters, cousins, aunts, and uncles. Share your family tree with other family members.

RESOURCE

Mars: Our Mysterious Neighbor by Isaac Asimov (Milwaukee, Wisconsin: Gareth Stevens, 1988).

AUGUST 12

On this day in 1881, Cecil Blount deMille was born in Ashfield, Massachusetts. He was a U.S. film producer and director. DeMille made showy, dramatic epics. While filming, he hired hundreds of extra people to fill stadiums and walk across deserts. With his first film, *The Squaw Man*, in 1913, he established Hollywood as the film-production capital of the world. DeMille went on to create over 70 epics.

 Describe a movie you'd like to make someday.

 Cecil B. deMille thought up the idea of "sneak previews." He wanted to get people interested in his movies, so he showed them a short scene. He hoped that people would get so interested in the scene that they'd go to see the whole movie. What movie previews have you seen lately on TV or in the movie theater? Is there any movie you want to see as soon as it comes out? Tell about it and why you want to see it.

 To learn more about Cecil B. deMille, read *Cecil B. deMille: Young Dramatist* by Hortense Myers and Ruth Burnett.

Create a movie poster for your favorite movie. Include a picture of the movie's stars on your poster. Think of one scene in the movie that you really liked and draw it. Put the name of the movie in large letters.

RESOURCE

Cecil B. deMille: Young Dramatist by Hortense Myers and Ruth Burnett (New York: Macmillan, 1963).

Sir Alfred Hitchcock, a renowned maker of mystery films, was born in England on this day in 1899. He began working in the United States in 1940. He created movies that were suspenseful and thrilling. Some of his classic movies were *The Birds*, *Psycho*, and *North by Northwest*. In each of his films, Hitchcock himself appeared, usually very briefly in one scene.

 Write about a thrilling or scary movie you've seen.

 Hitchcock once said about moviegoers, "Give them pleasure—the same pleasure they have when they wake up from a nightmare." Write about why you think people like to watch scary movies.

 Moviemakers have their own lingo—their own words—to describe what they do. "Cut" means to stop filming a scene. "Take Five" means take a rest. Here is some more movie lingo: print, special effects, and agent. Find out what these movie-related terms mean. List a few movie terms of your own.

 On this day in 1818, Lucy Stone was born near West Brookfield, Massachusetts. She spent her life working for women's rights and against slavery. In 1847, she became one of the first women in the United States to graduate from college. In 1850, she helped to organize the first U.S. Women's Rights Convention. Visit the library and find out about some other people who worked for women's rights or against slavery.

Today marks Victory Day or V-J Day, the end of World War II. It's the anniversary of President Harry Truman's announcement that Japan had surrendered to the Allies. The official signing of the surrender occurred aboard the USS *Missouri* on September 2, 1945.

 Write about a time you thought it was time to surrender or give up on something.

 National Recreational Scuba Diving Week takes place every year during the second week of August. It's a week to try out some scuba gear if you've never had the chance or go diving again if you have. To learn more about this underwater sport, read *Scuba Diving* by Norman Barrett.

 This is La Torta dei Fieschi Day in Italy. On this day in 1240, Count Fieschi of Lavagna in Genoa was married. He surprised his guests and the villagers by offering a slice from a cake that was more than ten yards high. On this day, the people of Lavagna dress up in costumes and gather in the town square. They eat cake and celebrate.

Draw a cake and decorate it for a special event.

 Six months ago it was February 14. You were probably wearing warmer clothes, looking forward to summer, and celebrating Valentine's Day. Make a list of things that have changed in your life since that February day.

RESOURCE

Scuba Diving by Norman Barrett (New York: Franklin Watts, 1988).

Chef Julia Child was born in Pasadena, California, on this date in 1912. In the 1940s she lived in Paris, France, and mastered the art of French cooking. In 1961, she published her first cookbook. Two years later in Boston, she began to star in the TV program "The French Chef." For each episode, Child prepared ingredients, talked about food preparation, and cooked a meal while her TV audience watched.

 Write about the type of recipes you'd include in a cookbook. Why would you choose those recipes?

 Today is National Relaxation Day. It's a day to sit back, rest, and take it easy. It's also a day to think about new ways to have fun. For more information about National Relaxation Day, write to:

National Relaxation Day
12079 Belann Court
Clio, MI 48420

 On this day in 1914, the Panama Canal opened. Between 1904 and 1914, the United States built this waterway in the Isthmus of Panama, the narrowest part of Central America. The United States built the canal to connect the Atlantic and Pacific oceans and open a shorter route for trade to the Far East. The canal begins at Limon Bay near Colon,

Panama, and zigzags south across the isthmus to Panama City. For more information about this huge project, read *Panama in Pictures* by the Lerner Publications Department of Geography Staff.

 To build the Panama Canal, workers cleared a path through the jungle and dug deep into the earth. One of the worst obstacles facing the workers was a strange disease called malaria. Colonel William C. Gorgas realized that mosquitoes carried and spread the disease. He told workers to drain swampy areas along the canal route to kill the mosquito larvae. Look up "Panama Canal" in an encyclopedia to find out the other obstacles workers faced as they dug the canal through the jungles of Panama.

RESOURCE

Panama in Pictures by the Lerner Publications Department of Geography Staff (Minneapolis: Lerner Publications, 1987).

August is usually one of the hottest months of the summer. Tall-growing flowers of late summer, such as goldenrod, brighten fields and neighborhoods. Insects are noisier and more numerous in August than in other months. By this time, public swimming pools are full almost every day. Summer fruits, such as watermelon, are juicy and delicious.

 Write about your favorite part of summer.

 During August, people who live in far northern regions and high mountain areas know that summer is coming to an end. In those areas, the temperature drops at night and frost appears in the morning. Some birds

are already preparing to fly south for the coming winter. With your friends or family, talk about how you'll enjoy the rest of this summer month. Are you looking forward to fall and winter? Why or why not?

 Have you noticed that August is a month without a major holiday? In honor of this holiday-less month, create your own. Make today a holiday. Give this holiday a name and think of how people could celebrate it. Would there be parades, fireworks, and special food? Perhaps you could think of a holiday to celebrate the hot days of August or a day of fun in the sun.

 On this day in 1896, George Washington Carmack discovered gold in the Klondike region of the Yukon in Canada. During the following year, over 30,000 people joined the gold rush in that area. Today, Canadians celebrate Klondike Discovery Day. Write about what you'd do if you discovered gold.

August 17

On this day in 1929, Francis Gary Powers was born in Jenkins, Kentucky. In 1960, Powers flew a U-2 airplane over the Soviet Union. The Soviets shot down his plane and captured him. They accused Powers of spying and sentenced him to ten years in prison. The U.S. government claimed that Powers was only taking pictures to study the weather.

 Do you think we need spies to keep an eye on other countries? Why or why not?

 In 1962, the Soviets freed Francis Powers in exchange for an imprisoned Soviet spy. Powers was not very welcome when he returned to the United States. He died in a helicopter crash near Los Angeles, Cali-

fornia, on August 2, 1977. Find out more about this spy story by looking up "U-2 Incident" in an encyclopedia.

 On this day in 1786, legendary pioneer David "Davey" Crockett was born in Limestone, Tennessee. He was a scout, an army officer, and a member of Congress for three terms. In February 1836, Crockett and about 180 Texans defended the Alamo against several thousand Mexicans. Crockett died, with the last of the defenders of the Alamo, on March 6, 1836. Read more about this frontier settler in *Davy Crockett: Young Rifleman* by Aileen W. Parks.

 In 1954, Walt Disney created a TV series about Davy Crockett. By 1955, children all over the United States were buying coonskin caps like the one Crockett wore. They also bought Davy Crockett swimsuits, toy guns, pajamas, bedspreads, lunch boxes, and guitars. The fad didn't last long, however. By the end of 1955, children had stopped wanting Davy Crockett souvenirs.

What's the latest fad? Make a list of clothes, games, or toys that are "in" right now. Save your list and, in a few months, you can look at it and see if these fads are still popular.

RESOURCE

Davy Crockett: Young Rifleman by Aileen W. Parks (New York: Macmillan, 1986).

August 18

On this day in 1939, MGM Studios released *The Wizard of Oz*. The movie was the first sound version of L. Frank Baum's 1900 classic book. It was not expected to do well, but it contained lavish sets, fun characters, and singable tunes, which made audiences fall in love with it.

 Write about your favorite part of *The Wizard of Oz*. If you've never seen the movie, write about what you think it's about.

 Take a summer break and watch the video of *The Wizard of Oz*.

 Dorothy meets the good witch. The Scarecrow sings and dances. The Emerald City lights up the sky. There are many fun and beautiful scenes in *The Wizard of Oz*. Draw a picture of your favorite.

 Roberto Walker Clemente was born on this day in 1934. He was a U.S. baseball player who was born in Carolina, Puerto Rico. Clemente's major league career lasted 18 years. During his career he made 3,000 hits. In 1972, while flying with supplies to earthquake victims in Managua, Nicaragua, he died in a plane crash. The next year, he was elected to the Baseball Hall of Fame. To learn more about Roberto Clemente, read *Pride of Puerto Rico: The Life of Roberto Clemente* by Paul Robert Walker.

·····································

R E S O U R C E S

The Wizard of Oz video (MGM Studios, 1939).

Pride of Puerto Rico: The Life of Roberto Clemente by Paul Robert Walker (New York: Harcourt Brace Jovanovich, 1988).

·····································

On this day in 1991, a group of Communists tried to remove Soviet President Mikhail Gorbachev from power. The group claimed that Gorbachev was too ill to be president. In fact, Gorbachev was on vacation and soldiers held him hostage in his vacation home. When the

Soviet people heard the news, they filled the streets of Moscow. They gathered together to voice their opinions—peacefully. On August 21, the conspirators gave up their idea of taking over the country. Gorbachev returned to Moscow and the presidency.

 Write about the last time you solved a problem peacefully, without fighting.

 In the 1880s, Mary Ellen Pleasant fled from her life of slavery and moved to San Francisco. There, she became an influential and respected businesswoman. Pleasant donated money to the Underground Railroad, a secret network of people in the South who helped slaves escape to freedom in the North. Pleasant was born on this day in 1814. By the time of her death in 1904, people in California called her the Mother of Civil Rights. With your family or friends, talk about the rights you have.

 On this day in 1902, Ogden Nash was born in Rye, New York. Nash wrote humorous and satirical verses filled with clever, outrageous rhymes. Among his many volumes of poetry are *Free Wheeling*, *The Face Is Familiar*, and *You Can't Get There from Here*. Read some of Ogden Nash's work in *Poems by Ogden Nash*, selected and illustrated by Quentin Blake.

 On this day in 1909, the Philadelphia Phillies established a major league record. They were rained out for the tenth day in a row. Write about why weather during a baseball game isn't as big a problem today as it was in the early 1900s.

·····································

R E S O U R C E

Poems by Ogden Nash, selected and illustrated by Quentin Blake (Little, Brown, 1980).

·····································

August 20

On this day in 1946, Connie Chung was born in Washington, D.C. Chung is the youngest of ten children and the only one of her family who was born in the United States (her brothers and sisters were born in China). Chung is a broadcast journalist and correspondent who has worked for both CBS and NBC. In 1993, she became a co-anchor for the "CBS Evening News with Dan Rather and Connie Chung."

 Write about your family.

 A reporter once asked Connie Chung who she admired most. Chung answered, "My mother. She is strong." Write about the person you most admire and why you admire him or her.

 Donald Yetter Gardner, an American composer, was born on this day in 1913. One of his most famous songs is "All I Want for Christmas Is My Two Front Teeth." Draw a picture of yourself without your two front teeth.

 Spend a lazy summer day staring up at the sky. Take a notepad and pencil and find a quiet spot to relax. If there are clouds in the sky, make drawings of them. If there aren't any clouds, write down what you think about as you look around you.

August 21

The first debate between Abraham Lincoln and Stephen A. Douglas took place on this day in 1858. Both men were running for the U.S. Senate. Both Lincoln and Douglas discussed slavery and its political, legal, and moral issues. Although Lincoln lost the election, his view of slavery as a "moral, social, and political wrong" enhanced his standing as a national figure.

 Write about why it's important to hear both sides of an issue.

 One definition of the word "debate" is a talk or argument. A debate takes place between two or more people who disagree on a topic. In a debate, everyone can have an opinion as long as they have reasons and facts to back up their opinions. Hold a debate with your friends. Decide on a topic and have each person take a different side of the issue. You could debate on which ice cream flavor is the best or which music groups sound better.

 On this day in 1959, Hawaii became the fiftieth state. Hawaii is located in the Pacific Ocean about 2,400 miles southwest of California. It's an archipelago or group of islands. Eight large and 124 small islands, many of them uninhabited, make up the state. Because volcanoes formed the islands, they are mountainous, with low valleys and steep cliffs. To learn more about Hawaii, read *Hawaii: In Words and Pictures* by Dennis Fradin or do some activities in the *Hawaii Fun Activity Book* by Dux Missler.

 Learn some Hawaiian words. Each syllable and each word in the Hawaiian language end with a vowel. Two consonants are never together in a word. Here are some Hawaiian words and their pronunciation and meaning. Practice saying them.

yes: ae (EYE); eat: ai (AH ih); welcome, good-bye, love: aloha (ah LOH hah); dance: hula (HOO lah); sea: kai (KAH ee); child: keiki (KAY kee).

RESOURCES

Hawaii: In Words and Pictures by Dennis Fradin (Chicago: Childrens Press, 1980).

Hawaii Fun Activity Book by Dux Missler (Hilo, Hawaii: Petroglyph Press, 1986).

On August 22, 1991, a day after the Soviet Communist coup had been stopped, a crowd gathered in Moscow. The 10,000 Muscovites watched cranes dismantle a 14-ton statue of Felix Dzerzhinsky. He was the founder of the Soviet secret police. Trucks hauled the massive statue away.

 Write about a huge statue that you've seen either in person or in a photograph.

 Samuel Pierpont Langley was an astronomer, physicist, and pioneer in the design and construction of airplanes. He was born on this day in 1834. In 1896, Langley successfully flew the first mechanically propelled heavier-than-air machines. In 1903, he failed to launch an operated plane (shortly afterward, the Wright Brothers made the first successful flight). Langley Air Force Base, Virginia, was named after this talented aviator. Draw your favorite aircraft or design a plane of your own.

 On this day in 1920, science-fiction author Ray Douglas Bradbury was born in Wauke-

gan, Illinois. Some of Bradbury's sci-fi stories make people think about the harm they're doing to the environment. Have someone read Bradbury's short story, "All Summer in a Day," to you. Draw a picture to illustrate this story and talk about what lesson Bradbury was trying to teach with the story.

 Summer is nearly over. It's the perfect time to think back on what you've done to enjoy your vacation. Make a list of the things that you enjoyed doing this summer. Then make a new list of the things you look forward to doing this winter.

RESOURCE

"All Summer in a Day," found in *The Golden Apples of the Sun* by Ray Bradbury (New York: Doubleday, 1959).

On this day in 1869, Edgar Lee Masters, an American poet, was born in Garnett, Kansas. As a child, Masters lived near the Spoon River in Illinois. From his experiences, he wrote *Spoon River Anthology* about the people living in a small town.

 Write about what it would be like to live in a small town. If you live in a small town, write a paragraph on what you like about your town.

 On this day in 1989, Victoria Brucher became the first girl to play in the Little League World Series. Write about how Victoria might have felt being the first and only girl in the Little League World Series.

 Gymnastics, baseball, tennis, soccer, and ice skating are just some of the sports that both girls and boys enjoy. Do you think that some sports should be played only by girls and some only by boys? With your family or friends, talk about girls and boys playing any sport they want.

 On this day in 1970, an American swimmer broke the 100-meter freestyle record with a time of 51.9 seconds. His name was Mark Andrew Spitz. He won seven gold medals at the 1972 Olympics. What's your favorite Olympic sport? Visit the library and find out who has won medals in your event.

British forces invaded Washington, D.C., on August 24 and 25 in 1814. Soldiers burned the Capitol building, President's house, and other public buildings. President James Madison and other officials fled to safety until the British troops left the city. The British did not realize the strength of their position and left the city two days later.

 Write about what you'd take if you suddenly had to leave home—and you weren't sure you'd be coming back.

 Today is Vesuvius Day in Italy. In A.D. 79, Mount Vesuvius, which had been quiet for 1,500 years, erupted. For eight days and nights, the volcano erupted and buried the nearby city of Pompeii under 20 feet of ash and rock. Almost 1,600 years later, in 1748, the buried city was discovered. The paint was still colorful on Pompeii's buildings and walls.

Today, Mount Vesuvius remains an active volcano on the Bay of Naples in southern Italy. On a map, locate Italy and Mount Vesuvius.

 On this day in 1989, baseball manager Pete Rose was banned for life from the game. He had gambled on a game, which is against the rules of professional baseball. What do you think about gambling? Write down your thoughts on this risky business.

 Here's an activity to do on some rainy summer day: Look through an old magazine and cut out a picture. Glue the picture at the top of a sheet of paper and write a story about it. You could cut out a picture of a car and write about the people who will drive it. If you find a picture of sneakers in a shoe ad, you might write about what would happen if the shoes had magical powers.

Today is UFO Day. On this day in 1951, two Texans saw a flash of light outside of Lubbock. They said that as they watched the sky, an enormous spaceship with blue lights silently passed overhead. The Texans phoned the police. Twenty minutes later, four scientists from the Texas Technical Institute also sighted strange blue lights in the sky. The scientists took pictures to show the authorities. No one has ever been able to explain these happenings.

 Write about how you'd react if someone told you they'd seen a UFO.

For years, people have sent photographs of alleged UFOs to investigators and scientists. Each photograph is sent to a special lab and examined. Of the 1,000 photos that were sent to the lab in the late 1980s, 605 proved to be hoaxes. (People had photographed Frisbees and spaceship models claiming they were UFOs.) Most of the other photographs were of regular objects, such as balloons and airplanes, which people had thought were UFOs. With your family or friends, talk about why someone would fake a photograph to look like a UFO.

 On this day in 1981, the U.S. spacecraft *Voyager 2* sent pictures and data about Saturn back to Earth. Scientists had launched *Voyager 2* in 1977 and hoped that it would travel through the galaxy collecting data on the planets. Learn more about this planet in the book *Saturn* by Dennis B. Fradin.

 Allan Pinkerton was born in Scotland on this day in 1819. Pinkerton immigrated to the United States in 1842 and became a detective for the Chicago Police Force in 1850. Shortly afterward, he established Pinkerton's National Detective Agency, which still exists.

Imagine that you're a detective. Make a list of the things you'd need to help you find and keep track of clues. *Examples*: magnifying glass, bloodhound, notepad, pencil.

R E S O U R C E

Saturn by Dennis B. Fradin (Chicago: Childrens Press, 1989).

 Pretend you're an actor. Write about the types of movies you'd like to star in.

 Make a list of some safety measures that you can take if you find yourself home alone. *Examples*: Keep the door locked. Don't open the door to anyone you don't know. What else can you do to keep yourself safe until your parents return?

 Today is the anniversary of the biggest explosion in recorded history. On this day in 1883, Krakatoa exploded—people 3,000 miles away heard the loud eruption. Krakatoa is a small volcanic island in the center of Sunda Strait, Indonesia, between the islands of Java and Sumatra. The explosion caused a 200-foot tidal wave and hurled 5 cubic miles of earth fragments into the air. It killed 36,000 people and produced atmospheric effects that were experienced around the world for months afterward. On a world map, locate the island of Krakatoa.

 During the 1960s, Krakatoa became active again. To learn more about this island, read *Krakatoa* by Don Nardo. The book is part of the World Disasters Series.

R E S O U R C E

Krakatoa by Don Nardo (San Diego: Lucent Books, 1990).

August 26

On this day in 1980, Macaulay Culkin was born in New York City. He's the star of *Home Alone* and *Home Alone 2*. After breaking box office records, the movies are now popular videos. In an interview, Mack said that he really liked acting in those movies. He had fun running around the house, yelling, eating junk food, and sledding down the stairs.

August 27

The East Coast Surfing Championships take place this week in Virginia Beach, Virginia. For over 30 years, Easterners have competed for the first prize surfing awards. Many people think that surfers only practice their sport on the sunny, sandy West Coast. But surfers from Maine to Florida and down to the Virgin Islands enjoy catchin' a wave.

Pretend you're a surfer. Write about the feel of the water and the smell of the ocean as you stand up and ride your surfboard to the shore.

In honor of this week's surfing championships, learn some surfing lingo. Here's a list of words and their surfing definitions to try out on your friends: gnarly (wild, rough, and dangerous); surfin' safari (a trip a surfer takes in search of good waves); ankle-snappers (waves); shore break (small waves that break close to the beach).

One of the greatest surfers of all time is Margo Oberg. She began surfing in California when she was ten years old. A year later she entered her first surfing contest and won first place. She went on to win the Women's World Championship seven times. Write about a sport you're interested in. How could you practice your sport?

Some historians believe that ancient people invented surfing when they rode the waves on driftwood planks from banana trees. Look up "surfing" in an encyclopedia to find out more about this ancient sport.

August 28

Today is Dream Day. On this day in 1963, Dr. Martin Luther King, Jr., gave a famous speech. He said that he hoped one day all races could live, work, and play as equals. He hoped that his children would grow up in such a world.

Write about what would happen if everyone lived, worked, and played as equals.

If you'd like more information about Dream Day and Dr. Martin Luther King, Jr., send a letter to:

Global Committee Commemorating King
Days of Respect
P.O. Box 21050
Chicago, IL 60621

On this day in 1969, British scientists using sonar detected several huge objects speeding through the water of Loch Ness in Scotland. Loch Ness is a freshwater lake in northern Scotland that's 23 miles in length and 754 feet deep. It's also the legendary home of one or more aquatic monsters.

Do you believe in monsters? Why or why not? Talk about this with your family.

The first rumors of a monster living in Loch Ness occurred in the sixth century. Today, many scientists believe that there are no large unknown animals living in the lake. Nevertheless, in every summer since 1963, people have conducted investigations. To learn how others feel about the Loch Ness Monster, read *Loch Ness Monster: Opposing Viewpoints* by Robert San Souci.

R E S O U R C E

Loch Ness Monster: Opposing Viewpoints by Robert San Souci (San Diego: Greenhaven Press, 1989).

August 29

On this day in 1958, Michael Jackson was born in Gary, Indiana. When he was five years old, he became the lead singer of his brothers' group the Jackson Five. Wherever the group performed, young Jackson carefully watched the other performers. He said he wanted to learn everything about show business. Today, Michael Jackson is a superstar; he's famous around the world.

Would you want to be in show business? Write about why you would—or wouldn't—want to be a star.

 In 1990, CBS Records announced that Michael Jackson had sold 100 million recordings worldwide. He was officially named the top-selling musical artist of the 1980s. To learn more about this singer's career, read *Michael Jackson, Superstar* by Patricia McKissack.

 On this day in 1966, the Beatles gave their last public concert at Candlestick Park in San Francisco, California. The English rock and roll group was hugely successful from 1962 to 1971. In honor of their last concert, listen to some Beatles music.

 On this day in 1896 in New York, Chinese Ambassador Li Hung-Chang's chef invented chop suey. The dish was made to appeal to the Ambassador's American and Chinese guests. The chef created the dish from chopped meat and vegetables. In Chinese the word "shap" means "miscellaneous" and the word "sui" means "bits." Write about your favorite Chinese food. Do you like to use chopsticks to eat it?

R E S O U R C E

Michael Jackson, Superstar by Patricia McKissack (Chicago: Childrens Press, 1984).

 Mary Wollstonecraft Shelley was famous for writing novels. Write about something you'd like to be famous for.

 Frankenstein is the story of a medical student named Victor Frankenstein who creates a monster in his laboratory. At first, the monster is gentle. But because it is ugly, people act unfriendly toward it. The monster becomes dangerous and takes revenge on its creator, Dr. Frankenstein.

In Shelley's book, people were afraid of something they didn't understand. Talk with your friends about something you don't understand. Are you afraid? What could you do to try and understand?

 For a scary good time, watch the 1931 movie *Frankenstein*. Its spooky black-and-white images are sure to give you chills.

 It's time to start thinking about the new school year and all its exciting possibilities. Start the school year by making some school resolutions. You might resolve to make a new friend this year or join a new club or sports team. You could resolve to ask more questions in class or volunteer to help your teacher in the classroom. Make a list of your own School Resolutions.

R E S O U R C E

Frankenstein video (MCA, 1931).

August 30

On this day in 1797, Mary Wollstonecraft Shelley was born in London. When she was 19, she married the English poet Percy Shelley. That summer, when she and her husband moved to Italy, she began to write *Frankenstein*, a novel that would make her famous.

August 31

On this day in 1935, Frank Robinson was born in Beaumont, Texas. He was the first African-American to became a major league manager of a baseball team. He managed the Cleveland Indians from 1975 to 1977. Robinson was elected to the Hall of Fame in 1982.

Write about something you'd like to be first in.

 With some friends, brainstorm a list of unusual ways to use a baseball. How about covering it with cloth, drawing a face on it, and creating a puppet? What else can you think of?

 Now that a new school year is almost here, take some time out to think about teachers. Make a list of things you liked about your teacher last year. Write about what you think your new teacher will be like.

 Pretend you're a teacher and you've just walked into a classroom full of kids. Write about what you'd do on the first day of school to get to know your students.

On or near this day, children all over the world begin a new school year. Israeli children begin the school year in early September. Children in Morocco begin about September 15. Australians, however, don't begin a new school year until late January. In Chile, school starts in March. Children in Japan began their school year back in April.

 If you could choose the day school starts, what would it be? Why?

 September is National Honey Month. More than 211,600 beekeepers raise bees and harvest honey in the United States. The 4.2 million honey bee colonies produce over 227 million pounds of honey every year. Read *Bees* by Christine Butterworth to learn more about these useful insects.

 Every bee has its own job. The drones (male bees) fertilize the eggs the queen bee lays. The workers gather the honey and pollen and watch over the young bees. If you'd like more information about bees and beekeeping, send a letter to:

The National Honey Board
421 21st Avenue, #203
Longmont, CO 80501

 Honey is the thick, sweet liquid the bees make in their hives. What's your favorite way to eat honey?

RESOURCE

Bees by Christine Butterworth (Englewood Cliffs, New Jersey: Silver Burdett, 1988).

On this day in 1838, Lydia Kamekeha Liliuokalani (Lee-lee-oo-o-ka-la-nee), the last monarch of Hawaii, was born in Honolulu. In 1891, she became queen of Hawaii after the death of her brother. During her reign, Americans living in Hawaii wanted to elect people into government positions. They didn't want to be ruled by just one person. Because Liliuokalani refused to give up her throne, the Americans put her in prison for nine months and established a new government.

 Would you want to be the leader of a country? Why or why not?

In England, 11 days disappeared from the calendar in 1752. People went to bed on September 2 and woke up on September 14. King George II decided to adopt the Gregorian Calendar that Pope Gregory XIII had created. In order to catch up with the dates on the Gregorian calendar, English citizens had to lose those 11 days.

Write about how you'd feel about losing 11 days. What would you have done if your birthday was September 7, 1752, and you had missed it?

 Create a calendar for this school year. Look at other printed calendars to see how the days of the week and the numbers for each day appear in small boxes. For your calendar, you'll need 12 sheets of ruled paper; markers, pens, or crayons; and a ruler. At the top of the first page write the word "September." Underneath that word, write the days of the week across the first line. Make boxes and fill in the numbers for that month. For each month of the year, use a new sheet of paper. When all the months are done, decorate your calendar with your own drawings or pictures cut out from magazines showing the different seasons and the holidays.

 September is an important month in the Muslim religion. In the ninth month of their calendar year, Muslims observe Ramadan. During the month, adult Muslims do not eat or drink from sunrise to sunset. Families read the Koran, the Muslim's holy book. When Ramadan comes to an end, Muslims rejoice in the Feast of Fastbreaking. Families gather for the first daytime meal in a month. They eat special foods made just for this time of year.

Find out if there are any Muslim students or teachers in your school. Ask them how they celebrate Ramadan. If you are a Muslim, tell your friends about how you are celebrating Ramadan.

eptember 3

On this day in 1920, reporter Maggie (Marguerite) Higgins was born in Hong Kong. Higgins liked to be where news was happening—she thought that she could report the news more accurately if she was there to see it in person. She reported directly from the battlefields during World War II, the Korean War, and the Vietnam War. During her reporting career, she also interviewed many famous people and national leaders. In 1951, she became the first woman to win the Pulitzer Prize for international reporting. She died in 1966 and was buried in Arlington National Cemetery in Washington, D.C.

 Write about someone in your school or neighborhood you would like to interview. Why would you want to interview that person?

 Near this day, Cherokee Native Americans celebrate a national holiday. They meet in Tahlequah, Oklahoma, to celebrate the establishment of the Cherokee Nation. To learn more about the Cherokee National Holiday, send a letter to:

Cherokee National Historical Society
P.O. Box 515
Tahlequah, OK 74465

Native Americans are given descriptive names. These names express their individuality or birth celebration. One Native American named Red Jacket got his name because he often wore a red jacket.

Give yourself a special name. Think of things about you that are special. You could be Morning Star if you get up easily in the morning. Perhaps you could be Happy Spirit because of your personality. Write about the name you would choose for yourself.

On this day in 1856, Louis Henry Sullivan was born in Boston, Massachusetts. He was an architect who was famous for the way he designed office buildings. Sullivan was one of the first architects to design tall sky-scrapers with iron frames and straight lines. He once said that a skyscraper should be "a proud and soaring thing." He is credited with "inventing" the skyscraper.

Today's skyscrapers contain office space, apartments, stores, and restaurants. Pretend you're asked to design a 50-story office building. Decide what offices, shops, or living spaces would go on each floor. *Examples*: Would a restaurant be on the first or fiftieth floor? Would your skyscraper include a pool? How about a card shop or post office? Draw your skyscraper.

September 4

On this date in 1886, Geronimo, an Apache Indian, surrendered to the U.S. Army at Skeleton Canyon in the Arizona Territory. Geronimo and his followers agreed to live on a reservation in Florida. Geronimo died in 1909, but not before he became a national celebrity. In 1904, he appeared at the St. Louis World's Fair. In 1905, he participated in Theodore Roosevelt's inau-guration parade. Despite his fame, however, he was never allowed to return to Arizona.

Write about how you'd feel if you were forced to leave your home and not allowed to return.

George Eastman patented his Kodak camera on this day in 1888. He invented photo-

graphic film and paper and other items that enable people to take photographs. In 1892, Eastman founded the Eastman Kodak Company. To learn about taking pictures, send a letter to:

Eastman Kodak Company
Photo Information, Department 841
Rochester, NY 14650-0811

Put together a class album. Ask your class-mates to bring in a picture of themselves. If your teacher has a Polaroid camera, take photos of your classmates doing things at your school. Create captions for each pic-ture. If you don't want to use snapshots, ask each class member to draw themselves on a piece of paper and include those pictures in your album.

Happy Birthday, Los Angeles! On this day in 1781, 44 people from Mexico founded this city in southwest California. Today, L.A. is the largest city in California and the second largest in the United States (New York is the first largest). By the late 1980s, L.A.'s popu-lation was 3 million.

Find out five more facts about Los Angeles by looking in reference books.

September 5

The first Labor Day parade was held in New York City on this day in 1882. Over 10,000 people marched in it. After the parade, people gave speeches about the need for better working conditions. Since so many people watched the parade and listened to the speeches, officials decided to honor workers every year. On June 28, 1894, President Grover Cleveland made the first Monday in September the official Labor Day. It's now a national holiday that Canadians also observe.

Write about how you'll celebrate Labor Day.

In 1892, a special Columbian Exposition orchestra performed a piece of music titled *Festival Jubilate* to celebrate the opening of the Women's Building at the World Columbian Exposition in Chicago. That same year, the Handel and Haydn Society performed a *Mass in E Flat*. Composer Amy Marcy Cheney Beach wrote these works and many others throughout her long career. She was born on this day in 1867 in Henniker, New Hampshire. Her last piece, Opus 150, was written in 1938, when she was 71 years old.

Have you ever heard a song that you couldn't get out of your head? Write about the song and why you like or dislike it.

September is National Clock Month. If you'd like information about alarm clocks, grandfather clocks, or watches, write to:

Clock Manufacturers
and Marketing Association
710 East Ogden Avenue, Suite 113
Naperville, IL 60540

On this day in 1963, Norman Bridwell first published *Clifford the Big Red Dog*. To celebrate, read a Clifford book today.

···

R E S O U R C E

Clifford the Big Red Dog by Norman Bridwell (New York: Scholastic, 1988).

···

september 6

On this day in 1860, Jane Addams was born in Cedarville, Illinois. She worked for peace, social welfare, and women's rights. In 1889, she cofounded Hull House, a community center for the poor in Chicago. Addams and her staff watched children while their parents worked in the factories. They helped to improve the neighborhood by asking city officials to collect the garbage that piled up on the streets.

Write about something you'd like to do for your community.

In 1931, Addams was awarded the Nobel Peace Prize. Read more about her in *Jane Addams* by Cynthia Klingel and Dan Zadra.

On this day in 1979, President Jimmy Carter issued a proclamation. It stated that in September the first Sunday that follows Labor Day will be National Grandparents' Day. Although people had celebrated Grandparents' Day before, on this day the holiday became official.

Describe your grandparents. Write about what they look like and the things you like to do with them. If you don't have grandparents, write about other older adults in your life.

If you'd like more information about National Grandparents' Day, write a letter to:

National Grandparents' Day
140 Main Street
Oak Hill, WV 25901

···

R E S O U R C E

Jane Addams by Cynthia Klingel and Dan Zadra (Mankato, Minnesota: Creative Education, 1987).

···

 **September 7**

On this date in 1860, Anna Mary Robertson Moses was born in Greenwich, New York. When she was 78 years old, she began painting pictures of farms and small towns in the United States. She signed her paintings "Grandma Moses." Her 100th birthday on September 7, 1960, was officially named Grandma Moses Day. She died on December 13, 1961.

 Think about a painting you've seen. Write about why you liked or didn't like it.

 According to the *Guiness Book of World Records*, Shigechiyo Izumi of Japan was the longest-living person. When he died in 1986, he was 120 years and 237 days old.

Talk with your classmates about why you think some people live longer than others. What would you like to be doing when you're 100 years old?

 On this date in 1909, Indianola Junior High in Columbus, Ohio, opened its doors to seventh, eighth, and ninth graders. This made it the first junior high school in the United States. Write about your school. When did you start going there? Write about the things at your school that you like and dislike.

 Raggedy Ann and Raggedy Andy dolls have been around since 1915. On September 7 of that year, Johnny Gruelle received a patent for the design. Read his *Raggedy Ann & Andy Giant Treasury: Four Adventures Plus 12 Short Stories* in honor of these lovable characters.

RESOURCE

Raggedy Ann & Andy Giant Treasury: Four Adventures Plus 12 Short Stories by Johnny Gruelle, retold by N. Golden (New York: Outlet Book Company, 1985).

 **September 8**

Today is International Literacy Day. Literacy means the ability to read and write. More than 25 percent of the adults in the world do not know how to read and write. The United Nations sponsors this day to celebrate and encourage worldwide reading and writing.

 Write about why you think it's important to read.

 To learn more about International Literacy Day, send a letter to:

United Nations
Department of Public Information
New York, NY 10017

 September is National Courtesy Month. Throughout this month, try extra hard to use good manners and be polite. Have you ever been in a situation where it wasn't easy to be courteous? Talk with your classmates about your hard-to-be polite situations.

 The first episode of the original "Star Trek" TV series aired on this day in 1966. The science-fiction show about Captain Kirk and the starship *Enterprise* wasn't popular when it first aired. But when the networks showed the reruns, viewers tuned in. There are many books based on the series. One you might enjoy is *Star Trek III: Plot-It-Yourself Adventure Stories, the Vulcan Treasure* by William Rotsler.

RESOURCE

Star Trek III: Plot-It-Yourself Adventure Stories, the Vulcan Treasure by William Rotsler (New York: Simon & Schuster, 1984).

september 9

Harland Sanders was born on this day in 1890. His face is one of the most recognized in the world. You might know him as Colonel Sanders, the man who started the Kentucky Fried Chicken restaurants. When Sanders was 69 years old, he began selling the rights to his special fried chicken. Today, you can find 8,000 Kentucky Fried Chicken restaurants in 58 countries.

 Write about your favorite way to eat chicken. If you don't like to eat chicken, write about another food.

 Have a crowing or clucking contest. Can you crow like an early-morning rooster? How about clucking like a hen trying to find some food? What sound do small chicks make?

 In 1985, there were 8,295,760,000 chickens in the world. In 1989, the United States produced 11.9 million tons of chicken meat. September is National Chicken Month. For more information about chicken and how it can be a healthy meal, send a letter to:

National Broiler Council
1155 15th Street NW, Suite 614
Washington, DC 20005

 Starting a new school year usually means meeting new people and learning new names. To help you learn names, try this activity. Have someone in your class say her name and do a simple action (like clapping, jumping, or stomping feet). The next person says the first person's name and does the first person's action. Then the second person says his own name and does an action. The third person has to say the names and do the actions of the two previous people before saying her name and doing an action. Keep adding names and actions until everyone has had a turn. Can anyone in your class say all the names and do all the actions?

september 10

On or near this date National Hispanic Heritage Week begins. It's the time to recognize the people and cultures from Spain, Portugal, and Latin America. Many English words come from the Spanish language (poncho and rodeo are two of them). Many foods we eat are borrowed from the Hispanic countries. Tacos, chili, guacamole, and burritos are just a few foods.

 Write about your favorite Hispanic food.

 To celebrate Hispanic Heritage Week, learn to count to five in Spanish:

1 uno (oo-noh); 2 dos (dohs); 3 tres (trehs); 4 cuatro (kwah-troh); 5 cinco (seen-ko).

 The Lincoln Highway, the first coast-to-coast paved road, opened today in 1913. Drivers could now travel from New York to San Francisco on a smooth surface. Today, most of this road exists and is known as U.S. Highway 30. It's 3,385 miles long and runs through 13 states. Using a map of the United States, see if you can locate U.S. Highway 30.

Today is Swap Ideas Day. Write down an idea for an after-school activity or a game to play at recess. Have everyone in your class do the same. Put all the ideas in one pile and have someone read the activities out loud. Maybe you'll get a new idea for something to do.

september 11

Today is National Neighborhood Day. On this day, many people go out on their front lawns or walk down apartment hallways to talk to the people who live nearby.

 Write about one thing in your neighborhood that you really like.

 Some people build fences or plant bushes to set boundaries for their yards. Some people set boundaries because they want their dog to stay in the yard. Others build fences because they don't want people getting hurt in their pool. Talk about the kinds of boundaries people use in your neighborhood.

 On September 11, 1862, William Sydney Porter was born in Greensboro, North Carolina. When he was in his 30s, he was sent to prison for embezzlement (a kind of stealing). While in prison, he wrote several short stories. He signed many of his stories O. Henry, instead of using his real name. As O. Henry, Porter wrote stories with creative plots and surprise endings. Have you ever been surprised by the ending of a story, book, or movie? Write brief description of what happened and why you were surprised.

 Rosh Hashanah, the first day of the Jewish New Year, occurs on or near this date. Rosh Hashanah is a happy celebration. People worship in the synagogue and eat special foods. They tell each other "Hatimah Tovah!" (pronounced Ha-tea-ma To-vah), which is Hebrew for "May you be inscribed for a good and sweet year." The wish is for a positive entry in the Jewish Book of Life. To learn more about Jewish holidays, ask a Jewish classmate to tell you how he or she celebrates holidays or read *Celebrate: A Book of Jewish Holidays* by Judith Gross. If you are Jewish, tell your friends about how you are celebrating Rosh Hashanah.

....
RESOURCE
Celebrate: A Book of Jewish Holidays by Judith Gross (New York: Putnam, 1992).
....

september 12

On this day in 1984, Rhoshaandiaatellyneshiaunneveshenk Koyaanfsquatsiuty Williams was born in Beaumont, Texas. According to the *Guinness Book of World Records*, Williams has the longest name that appears on a birth certificate. In October 1984, Mr. Williams expanded his daughter's first name. Williams' first name is now 1,019 letters long and her middle name is 36 letters long.

 If you could choose any first name, what would you chose? Write about why you'd choose that name.

 On this day in 1940, five boys playing in a cave in southwestern France discovered prehistoric paintings on the cave walls. As archaeologists studied the paintings, they gave names to different parts of the cave. In the Great Hall, animal paintings, including four huge bulls, cover the ceiling. The most interesting room in the cave is the Chamber of Felines; it's decorated with cats.

With your class, create your own wall painting. Tape a large sheet of paper onto a wall. Ask everyone in your class to draw on the paper using crayons, markers, paints, or chalk.

 "The Smurfs" cartoon show began today in 1981. These blue-skinned creatures live in their own little village. To learn more about the Smurf family, read *Smurf ABC Book* by Peyo.

 On this day in 1913, Jesse Owens was born in Oakville, Alabama. During the 1935 Olympics, the 21-year-old Owens broke five world records and tied a sixth. Berlin, Germany, hosted the Olympic games. Adolf Hitler, the country's leader, believed that white people were superior to African-American people. Owens proved that Hitler was wrong. Read more about Jesse Owens and his running career in *Jesse Owens: Champion Athlete* by Rick Rennert.

··

RESOURCES

Smurf ABC Book by Peyo (New York: Random House, 1983).

Jesse Owens: Champion Athlete by Rick Rennert (New York: Chelsea Juniors, 1992).

··

Milton Snavely Hershey was born on this day in 1857 in Derry township, Pennsylvania. Hershey manufactured caramels in New York City and Chicago. In 1903, he moved back to Pennsylvania and began to make chocolate bars. Today, Hershey, Pennsylvania, near Harrisburg, is home to the Hershey Foods Corporation.

 Write about your favorite way to eat chocolate. Do you like it plain, on ice cream, or surrounding something like peanut butter, caramel, or mint? If you don't like chocolate, write about another dessert.

 On this day in 1916, Roald Dahl was born in Llandaff, Wales, England. He became famous for writing short stories and novels for adults. When he began writing for children, many of his books gained special recognition. He wrote *Charlie and the Chocolate Factory*, *James and the Giant Peach*, and many others. Read some of his *Revolting Rhymes* to celebrate his birthday.

 Roald Dahl wrote many of his stories from a tiny brick hut 200 yards from his house in Buckinghamshire, England. Dahl wrote in this hut because he could get away from all distractions. Describe your favorite place to go and be quiet and alone without distractions.

 The U.S. Army's general hospital in Washington, D.C., is named to honor a man who was born on this date in 1851. Walter Reed was born in Gloucester County, Virginia. He was a doctor and bacteriologist. In the early 1900s, Reed discovered that a mosquito carried the yellow fever disease. Look up the name "Walter Reed" in an encyclopedia and find out more about his life.

··

RESOURCE

Revolting Rhymes by Roald Dahl (New York: Bantam Books, 1986).

··

september 14

Today is National Anthem Day. "The Star-Spangled Banner," the U.S. National Anthem, was written by Francis Scott Key during the war of 1812. Key wrote his poem when he was a prisoner on a British ship that bombarded Fort McHenry. The British hurled bombs at the fort all night. Early the next morning, Key saw that the U.S. flag still waved above the fort. Key's poem was put to music and titled "The Star-Spangled Banner."

 Write about how you feel when you see your country's flag.

 Here are the first few lines of "The Star-Spangled Banner":

"Oh, say can you see by the dawn's early light
What so proudly we hailed at the twilight's last gleaming?
Whose broad stripes and bright stars through the perilous fight
O'er the ramparts we watched were so gallantly streaming?"

With your classmates, talk about the meaning of this verse. Look up any words you don't know.

 The flag that Francis Scott Key looked at was gigantic. Americans had made the flag so that the British would have no trouble seeing it from a distance. The Fort McHenry flag measured 42 feet by 30 feet. It was constructed of 400 yards of material that weighed 200 pounds. Mary Pickersgell, her mother, and her daughter sewed this huge flag.

Find out how big 42 feet by 30 feet really is. On the gym floor or outside, measure these dimensions. Walk around outside. Walk around inside. Find out the measurements of your school flag. Compare that flag to the one Francis Scott Key saw.

 In 1931, President Herbert Hoover said that the "Star-Spangled Banner" would be the U.S. national anthem. You may have heard the song played at the beginning of sporting events. For more information on this song, read *The Story of the Star-Spangled Banner* by Natalie Miller.

RESOURCE

The Story of the Star-Spangled Banner by Natalie Miller (Chicago: Childrens Press, 1965).

september 15

Today is a national holiday in Japan. It's known as Old People's Day or Respect for the Aged and Elderly Day.

 In honor of this Japanese holiday, write about an elderly person you like and respect.

 On this day in 1857, William Howard Taft was born in Cincinnati, Ohio. He was active in Republican politics from an early age. He became one of Roosevelt's closest advisers. Taft wanted to serve on the Supreme Court, but President Theodore Roosevelt, Taft's wife, and his brothers encouraged him to run for president instead. In 1909, Taft became the twenty-seventh president of the United States. Write about a time a family member or friend encouraged you to do something. Did you do it? Were you glad? Why or why not?

In 1912, Woodrow Wilson was elected president and Taft's term ended. When he left the White House, Taft said, "I am glad to be going. This is the lonesomest place in the world."

Presidents must make many decisions, which can affect millions of people. Sometimes, only a few people agree with a president's decision. Why do you think Taft said that the White House was a lonesome place?

 Tomie de Paola is an author and illustrator who has provided the words and pictures for almost 200 books. He was born on this day in 1934 in Meriden, Connecticut. De Paola writes his own stories and retells folk tales and legends. In honor of his birthday, read his book *The Comic Adventures of Old Mother Hubbard & Her Dog* or another book by de Paola.

RESOURCE

The Comic Adventures of Old Mother Hubbard & Her Dog by Tomie de Paola (New York: Harcourt Brace Jovanovich, 1981).

T he *Mayflower* left Plymouth, England, on this day in 1620. The ship carried 95 adults, 32 children, and two dogs. Because the Pilgrims couldn't worship as they wanted in Europe, they had decided to travel to the New World. Bad storms and rough water made many of the travelers sick; some wondered if they had made the right decision. The *Mayflower* finally reached Provincetown, Massachusetts, two and a half months after leaving England.

 Pretend you're one of the Pilgrims. Write a journal entry about the first day of your voyage. Date it September 16, 1620.

 Tisquantum (known to the Pilgrims as Squanto) and Samoset helped the Pilgrims endure the harsh winter of 1620. Without them, most of the new settlers would have died. Read *Squanto, Friend of the Pilgrims* by Clyde R. Bulla to find out more about these brave men.

 On this day in 1898, Hans Augusto Rey was born in Hamburg, Germany. When he was young, Rey lived near the Hagenbeck Zoo and visited it often. As he grew up, he always found time to visit the zoo. In 1941, Rey published a story about a little monkey. Since then, books about his mischievous monkey, Curious George, have been published in many different languages.

Draw a picture of Curious George being curious about something. If you don't know what Curious George looks like, read *Curious George* by H. A. Rey.

 September is National Breakfast Month. During this month, think about the best foods to eat to start your day. If you need some help deciding what to eat for breakfast, write to:

Great Starts Breakfast
Campbell Soup Company
Communications Center
Campbell Place
Camden, NJ 08103-1701

RESOURCES

Squanto, Friend of the Pilgrims by Clyde R. Bulla (New York: Scholastic, 1985).

Curious George by H. A. Rey (New York: Houghton Mifflin, 1941).

september 17

On September 17, 1787, delegates from 12 states at the Constitutional Convention in Philadelphia, Pennsylvania, voted to approve the Constitution of the United States. Thirty-nine out of the 42 delegates present signed the document. The Constitution outlines the country's basic laws. In honor of the signing, this is Constitution Week.

 Write about why a country needs laws.

 Create your own class constitution. Include in your constitution the kind of government you wish to have and the leaders you'll need (*examples:* room monitor, hall monitor). Decide how your class will choose the leaders. How will your class enforce the rules? If necessary, how will the rules be changed?

 On this day, many people who have not been born in the United States attend special swearing-in ceremonies to become U.S. citizens. For months, these people have studied the history and laws of the United States. They have taken a special test. When they pass the test, they are able to become U.S. citizens. Today is Citizenship Day in their honor. Ask your teacher if he or she knows someone who moved to the United States from another country and became a U.S. citizen. Invite that person to speak to your class. If you moved to the United States from another country, share some of your memories and experiences.

 On this day in 1988, a ceremony was held in Washington, D.C. The ceremony honored the Iroquois Indian Confederacy. Some people believe the Constitution of the Iroquois Confederacy was the model for the way the U.S. government was set up. To learn more about the Iroquois Native Americans, read *Iroquois Stories: Heroes and Heroines, Monsters and Magic* by Joseph Bruchac.

RESOURCE

Iroquois Stories: Heroes and Heroines, Monsters and Magic by Joseph Bruchac (Freedom, California: The Crossing Press, 1985).

september 18

On this day in 1891, Native Americans made Harriet Maxwell Converse chief of the Six Nations Tribe. (The Seneca, Mohawk, Oneida, Onondaga, Cayuga, and Tuscarora tribes form the Six Nations Tribe.) Nine years before, the Senecas had adopted Converse because of all the work she had done to help the tribespeople. The ceremony took place in the Tonawanda Reservation in New York. The Indians named her Ga-is-wa-noh, which means "The Watcher."

 Write about something you have done to help others.

 September is National Library Card Sign-Up Month. It's celebrated during the month of September to remind everyone to get a library card. For more information about libraries, send a letter to:

American Library Association
Public Information Office
50 East Huron Street
Chicago, IL 60611

 Get a library card today (or this week) if you don't already have one. Just visit your library and ask the librarian at the front desk how you can sign up to get one.

On this day in 1709, Samuel Johnson was born in Lichfield, Staffordshire, England. He was a lexicographer, a poet, and a critic. Many people consider him to be one of the greatest English writers of all time. His book *The Dictionary of the English Language* was the first dictionary of English. It was published in 1755.

Hold a dictionary contest. Have someone in your class call out a word. (You might want to start with the word "lexicographer.") See how quickly you can look up the word. See who can find the most interesting dictionary entry.

ſeptember 19

alter Elias Disney's first success with an animated character appeared in a cartoon called *Steamboat Willie*. On September 19, 1928, Mickey Mouse made his debut when Disney first showed that black-and-white cartoon. The film was the first cartoon to use sound. Mickey Mouse became the world's most famous cartoon character.

 Describe your favorite cartoon show. Is it funny or serious? Tell why you like it.

 How many cartoon character names can you list? Do you know which characters the Disney Company created?

 The Walt Disney Company has created a book of fun activities for you to do. Their book is titled the *Mickey Mouse Make-It Book*. Check it out at your library.

 Create a flip book starring your own cartoon characters. You'll need 15 pieces of white paper about the same size (2" x 2"), scissors; pens, markers, or crayons; and a stapler.

On the first sheet of paper, draw a simple background scene. Include flowers, a house, or whatever you can think of. Put the second sheet of paper over the first one and trace your background scene onto the second sheet of paper. Keep tracing the background until all 15 sheets of paper look the same.

Now add your characters. Go back to the first page and draw a person standing on the right. On the second page, draw your figure with one foot up in the air. On the third page, draw your figure with the other foot up. Keep adding actions to your figure on the other pages.

Staple the sheets in order along the left side of the page. Hold that side firmly with your left hand. Flip the other side with your right hand. The faster you flip, the faster your figure will move. Once you get the hang of this flip book, add colors and more characters.

· ·

RESOURCE

Mickey Mouse Make-It Book by the Walt Disney Production Staff (New York: Random House, 1975).

· ·

September 20

If you could attach an adjective to your name, what would you choose? Would you be the Nicest, Smartest, or Friendliest? Make up a list of words that describe yourself.

On this day in 1519, Ferdinand Magellan, a Portuguese explorer, set sail from Sanlucar de Barrameda, Spain. Under the Spanish flag, he led the first expedition to travel completely around the globe. In November 1520, he sailed through the strait that was later named for him. He reached the Philippines in March 1521 but, unfortunately, he was killed there. One of his ships and 18 of his crew members finally returned to Spain after a three-year voyage.

If you were an early explorer, where would you have gone? Would you have climbed mountains? Crossed deserts? Sailed the seas?

Using a world globe, map out Magellan's adventure. Start in Spain and head west to Brazil. Continue south down the coast of South America around the southern tip through the Straits of Magellan. Head northwest to the Philippines then north and west through the Indian Ocean to the east coast of Africa. Travel south around Africa and the Cape of Good Hope then north along the west coast of Africa back to Spain.

Alexander III of Macedonia was called Alexander the Great. He was born on this day in 356 B.C. Many people thought Alexander was the greatest general in ancient history. When he was 20 years old, Alexander became king. Within three years, he had conquered West Asia Minor, Egypt, Babylon, Media, and central Asia. He also invaded India. He was buried in a golden coffin in Alexandria in 323 B.C.

Do you think you'd make a good king, queen, or president? What qualities make someone a good leader?

September 21

Herbert George Wells, an author and historian, was born on this day in 1866. He was born in Bromley in Kent, England. Wells loved to write science-fiction stories—tales about creatures from outer space and life on other planets. He became known as one of the fathers of science fiction. He wrote the science-fiction classics *The Time Machine* and *War of the Worlds*. He died in London on August 13, 1946.

Write the opening paragraph of a science-fiction story. If you want, use one of H. G. Wells' titles to begin your story.

Finish your story and illustrate it. If you like, work with a partner.

The Pennsylvania Packet and Daily Advertiser appeared on September 21, 1784. It was the first daily newspaper. David C. Claypoole and Jon Dunlap published the paper in Philadelphia, Pennsylvania.

Create a classroom newspaper. Have small groups write different articles. One group could ask your teacher questions and write a biography about him or her. Another group might write a story about a new person or someone's hobby. Are there students in your class who like to draw? They could draw pictures to go along with the articles. Think of a name for your newspaper. You could send photocopies home to your parents so they know more about your class.

September 21 is World Gratitude Day. The purpose of this day is to encourage people throughout the world to think about the good things. It's also a day to remember the things you're grateful for and to express your gratitude. If you'd like more information about World Gratitude Day, send a letter to:

Gratitude Day
132 West 31st Street
New York, NY 10001

september 22

In 1885, Florence Merriam Bailey became the first woman to be named an associate member of the American Ornithologists' Union. In 1908, the chickadee was given a scientific name in her honor: *farus gambeli baileyae*. Bailey and her husband, Vernon Bailey, explored the western and southwestern United States documenting the birds they found there. Florence Bailey was born in 1863 and died on this day in 1948.

 Do you enjoy bird watching? Why or why not?

 The Autumnal Equinox begins on or about this day. It marks the beginning of fall in the Northern Hemisphere. Today, there will be 12 hours of daylight and 12 hours of darkness. The Equinox occurs when the sun crosses the equator as it moves toward the Southern Hemisphere.

Write about your favorite part of fall. Is it the weather, smells, or colors?

 Create a leaf print. You'll need a leaf from outside, a piece of notebook paper, and crayons. Turn the leaf so that its veins are facing up. Place the sheet of paper over the leaf. Rub firmly with a crayon over the leaf while you hold the paper. Use fall colors. Once you've made your tracing, cut it out and hang it on your class bulletin board.

 On this day in 1891, the U.S. government opened up 900,000 acres of land in Oklahoma for anyone who wanted to settle out west.

If you were a settler traveling to Oklahoma, what kind of site would you choose? Would you build your home near a creek? Or in the middle of the forest? Would you look for an acre that was up on a hill? Write about the spot you'd choose.

september 23

On this date in 1800, William Holmes McGuffey was born near Claysville, Pennsylvania. In the early 1800s, McGuffey developed reading textbooks called *McGuffey's Eclectic Readers*. He also wrote spellers and primers that taught grade school students good English skills. Teachers loved the books and by the mid-1800s, every student learned to read from McGuffey's books.

 Write about how you learned to read. Can you think of an easier or different way to learn reading?

 Take a good look at one of your textbooks. Look on the first few pages of the book to find the name of the author and the date it was published. Look through the table of contents. Find the index at the back. Read ahead a few chapters to see what you'll be learning in the next months.

Create a reading textbook to help younger students learn how to read. You'll need some construction paper, lined notebook paper, crayons, a pencil, and a stapler.

On a piece of notebook paper, draw a picture of a cat. Underneath the drawing write the word CAT. On another sheet, draw a ball. Write the word BALL under the drawing. Think of other drawings and easy words to add to your reader. *Examples:* DOG, PEN, FOOT, BED. Draw a cover for your book and staple all the pages together. Give your reader to someone who's learning to read. Maybe you could read your book to that person.

J. C. Galle and H. d'Arrest, two German astronomers, first saw Neptune on this date in 1846. Neptune is the eighth planet from the sun (Earth is closer; it's third from the sun). Neptune's diameter is 31,200 miles (Earth's diameter is only 7,927 miles). It takes 164.8 years for Neptune to revolve about the sun (Earth takes only one year). Neptune has two moons, Triton and Nereidi. Read more about Neptune in *A Book about Planets and Stars* by Betty P. Reigot.

....

R E S O U R C E

A Book about Planets and Stars by Betty P. Reigot (New York: Scholastic, 1988).

....

september 24

On September 24, 1957, President Dwight Eisenhower sent federal troops to Central High School in Little Rock, Arkansas. For the first time, African-American and white students attended the same school. Some people were upset with this change. The federal troops protected the African-American students from the angry crowds.

What's the best thing about going to school with people of different colors or ethnic or cultural backgrounds? Write down your opinion.

Fifteen days before President Eisenhower called troops to Arkansas, officials had signed the civil rights legislation for integration. Integration means making something open to people of all races. In Arkansas, that meant opening public schools to all students, regardless of their race. Look up "Civil Rights Movement" in an encyclopedia and read more about the fight for equality.

On this day in 1960, "The Howdy Doody Show" aired on TV for the last time. Howdy was a puppet with red hair and freckles. Buffalo Bob and Clarabelle the Clown were Howdy's friends. For 13 years the show entertained kids with cartoons and funny skits. "Howdy Doody" was one of the longest-running and most popular children's programs.

Write about the children's programs that are on TV today. Do any of them have a cute puppet or special characters? Which puppets or characters do you like? Which ones do you dislike?

September is National Cable Television Month. It seems you can find almost any type of show on cable television: shopping, music, comedy, and drama.

Although it can be fun to watch TV, make a list of things to do besides changing channels and watching shows. The next time you're sitting in front of the TV and there's nothing interesting on, take out your list and do something different.

september 25

On this day in 1931, news reporter Barbara Walters was born in Boston, Massachusetts. She started her career as a writer for NBC's "The Today Show" in the early 1960s. In 1976, she was offered a job as co-anchor of "The ABC Evening News." She became the first woman to co-anchor a nightly news show. After four years she moved on to "20/20," another news program. Walters is probably best known for her specials, in which she interviews famous people.

 Write about something you'd like to be first in.

 On this day in 1890, Yosemite National Park was established. Yosemite is a 761,320 acre park in central California. It's a mountainous, glacial area of outstanding beauty. At Yosemite, visitors can gaze at the highest waterfall in the United States, hike through Yosemite Valley, and admire breathtaking gorges. Visitors can also discover the three groves of giant redwood trees.

Write why you think it's important to have national parks. If you don't feel parks are important, support your answer.

 Over 3 million people a year visit Yosemite National Park. If you're planning a visit or just want information about this park, write to:

National Park Service
Western Region
600 Harrison Street, Suite 600
San Francisco, CA 94107

 On this day in 1988, the Day Butterfly Center opened in Pine Mountain, Georgia. For its butterflies, the center's observatory has 8,000 square feet of glass. Employees have brought in special plants to make it look like a rain forest.

In late September, many butterflies migrate. The monarch butterflies of Canada and the northern United States fly hundreds of miles south for the winter. They fly at speeds of 10 to 30 miles per hour. When they reach the Southern California/Mexico area, the monarchs stop their journey on the same trees in the same places as they stopped the year before. No one can explain why. To learn more about these migrators, read *Butterflies* by Hidetomo Oda.

R E S O U R C E

Butterflies by Hidetomo Oda (Milwaukee, Wisconsin: Raintree Publishers, 1986).

september 26

On this day in 1774, folk hero John Chapman was born in Leominster, Massachusetts. Chapman was nicknamed "Johnny Appleseed" because he planted apple trees throughout the midwestern United States. He traveled hundreds of miles to scatter his apple seeds. Legends say he wore a tin cooking pot for a hat and went barefoot even in winter. As he traveled, he also cared for animals and cured illnesses with herbs. He handed out saplings to settlers and asked them to plant his apple trees as they traveled west.

 Sometimes apples are pictured with little green worms smiling as they crawl out from a hole. Pretend you're a little green worm in an apple. Write about how your apple feels, looks, tastes, and smells.

Think of five words that describe an apple. Choose words that begin with the letters in the word APPLE.

Plant your own apple seeds and watch them grow. You'll need apple seeds that have been allowed to dry out for a few days, small pebbles, dirt, a knife, paper cups, and a small aluminum tray. With the knife, poke some small holes in the bottom of the paper cups. Now cover the bottom of the paper cup with some pebbles. Fill the paper cup three-quarters with dirt. Put two or three apple seeds in each paper cup and cover with a little more dirt. Put the paper cups and seeds on the tray and place in front of a window that gets lots of sun. Keep the soil moist, but be careful not to soak the seeds.

To learn more about apples, read *Apple Tree through the Year* by Claudia Schnieper. Read more about Johnny Appleseed in *Johnny Appleseed: A Tale Retold*, a wonderfully illustrated book by Steven Kellogg.

RESOURCES

Apple Tree through the Year by Claudia Schnieper (Minneapolis: Carolrhoda Books, 1987).

Johnny Appleseed: A Tale Retold by Steven Kellogg (New York: Morrow, 1988).

september 27

Native American Day is celebrated on the last Friday of September. The day honors the contributions of Native Americans of North America.

Write about why it's important to honor many cultures.

Many Native Americans grew up hearing myths and stories that had been told from one generation to another. In some of the stories, animals act like humans. Many stories try to explain some natural occurrence, like the seasons, the snow, or the sun.

Think of an animal, such as an eagle, beaver, or coyote, to star in a myth you make up. Imagine that your animal can talk. How would it explain thunder, shooting stars, or tornadoes?

A pictograph is a drawing that stands for a word. The Sioux Indians kept track of their tribal history by drawing pictures of important events on buffalo skins. People used the pictographs to communicate and carry on traditions.

Create a code in pictographs. You'll need a sheet of paper and a pencil, crayons, or markers. First, think of a message. *Example:* I like spaghetti. Now, instead of spelling out your message, draw it. *Example:* Draw a plate of spaghetti piled high with meatballs and sauce. Now draw a picture of yourself with a big grin on your face. Draw one of your hands pointing to the spaghetti. Share your message with your classmates. Can they guess your message?

Research the life of a Native American who has made a contribution to history. *Examples*: Squanto, Chief Joseph, Tecumseh, Sacagawea, Sequoya, Pocahontas, or Jim Thorpe. Tell your classmates about the information you've discovered.

september 28

Today is a national holiday in Taiwan. It's Teachers' Day in honor of Confucius. Confucius was born on this day in 551 B.C. in Taiwan's Shantun Province. He was a teacher for more than 40 years. He died in 479 B.C. at the age of 72. People all over the world still respect and follow his sayings and teachings.

 Write about what you'd teach your students if you were teacher for a day.

 Confucius wrote about many subjects. He wrote about being nice to others: "What you do not want done to yourself, do not do to others." He wrote about wanting to learn: "Ignorance is the night of the mind, a night without moon or star."

Think up your own sayings about friendship and learning. *Example*: "You need a friend so be a friend."

 In 1970, Confucianism had an estimated 370 million followers. Read more about this teacher in *Confucius and Ancient China* by Theodore Rowland-Entwistle.

 A fable is a story that teaches a lesson or a useful truth. Fables usually include animals that speak and act like humans. Create a fable that teaches a lesson or shows a truth. Use one of the quotations from Confucius. For some more ideas, read one of Aesop's fables in the book edited by Kathryn T. Hegeman.

···

RESOURCES

Confucius and Ancient China by Theodore Rowland-Entwistle (New York: Franklin Watts, 1987).

Aesop's Fables, edited by Kathryn T. Hegeman (Monroe, New York: Trillium Press, 1984).

···

O n this date in 1895, Joseph Banks Rhine was born in Juniata, Pennsylvania. Rhine was interested in the mind and how it worked. He wondered if people could use their minds to perform out-of-the-ordinary tasks. Through his research, Rhine thought up the term ESP, which stands for extrasensory perception. Someone with ESP, Rhine said, could sense objects before seeing them or know events that had not yet happened.

 What is something you'd like to know about before it happened?

 For fun, try this experiment to see if you have ESP. You'll need a few objects from your classroom (*examples:* an eraser, chalk, book, notebook, ruler) and a partner. Sit back-to-back with your partner. Have your partner pick up an object and hold it. Tell your partner to think about the object. Without looking, try to read your partner's mind. See how many objects you can guess correctly. Now let your partner try the experiment.

 Joseph Rhine also worked with psychokinesis or PK. He thought that people with PK could influence outside events, such as making a pencil rise in the air or making dice show certain numbers.

Here's a PK experiment you can do with some dice. Hold the dice in your hand and think about the numbers you want to appear. Roll the dice on your desk and see how many times the numbers you want appear on the rolled dice.

 On this day in 1829, Scotland Yard's police officers first appeared in the streets of

London. An act of Parliament established Scotland Yard, which is officially known as the Metropolitan Police Department. Sir Robert "Bobby" Peel passed the act, so the officers called themselves bobbies in his honor. The first headquarters for the Criminal Investigation Department was in Scotland Yard, near Charing Cross. The force kept the name Scotland Yard even though it has since moved. Imagine you're a Scotland Yard detective. Is there something you'd like to investigate?

september 30

On this day in 1962, riots broke out when James Meredith, an African-American, enrolled in the University of Mississippi. Meredith wanted a good education and decided to attend the all-white university. He knew that the U.S. government had passed a law stating that all schools must be integrated and opened to anyone, regardless of race. President John F. Kennedy had to send U.S. troops to the campus to enforce the new integration law. Three people died as a result of the riots.

 James Meredith believed he had the right to attend the school of his choice. Write about something you believe in.

 On September 24, you learned about President Dwight Eisenhower calling in troops when African-American teenagers wanted to attend high school. That incident happened in 1957. Five years later, when James Meredith wanted to attend a school, people were still not used to the integration laws. Imagine that you came to school one day and found out that people with your hair color were not allowed in. With your class, talk about how you'd feel if you couldn't go somewhere just because your hair color was not accepted.

 On this day in 1841, the U.S. Patent Office granted Samuel Slocum patent number 2,275. The patent was for a machine "for sticking pins into paper." Today, we call that machine a stapler. If Samuel Slocum hadn't invented the stapler, how would you put things together? Make a list of some other ways to attach two things.

 Plan a Fall Festival to celebrate the reds, yellows, and browns of autumn. Ask your classmates to bring in anything that reminds them of fall. Set up a display of your fall findings; drink some apple cider or play Pin the Leaf on the Tree (similar to Pin the Tail on the Donkey) to celebrate this season.

october 1

Today is World Vegetarian Day—it's a day meant to make people aware of the benefits of a meatless lifestyle. Vegetarians eat only vegetables and plant products. Some vegetarians choose not to eat meat because they're concerned about animal rights. Others believe that a meatless diet is healthier than one that contains hamburgers, hot dogs, and red meat.

 Write about how you feel about eating meat. Are you a vegetarian? Why or why not?

 October is National Vegetarian Awareness month. To learn more about vegetarians and their diet, send a letter to:

Vegetarian Awareness Network/VEGANET
P.O. Box 321
Knoxville, TN 37901

 A major fast-food chain has introduced meatless burgers in their restaurants in the

Netherlands. The veggie burger is made up of potatoes, peas, carrots, corn, and onions. Restaurant patrons in the Netherlands had asked the food chain for the meatless meals. If the sandwich is a hit, U.S. restaurants might get them, also. Would you want to eat this meatless dinner? Talk with your classmates about your opinions of this kind of burger.

 Julia Wells was born in Walton-on-Thames, England, on this day in 1927. She's better known as actress Julie Andrews, who starred in the film *Mary Poppins*. Watch the video of this Walt Disney movie today—have a supercalifragilisticexpialidocious day.

··

R E S O U R C E

Mary Poppins video (Walt Disney, 1964).

··

On this day in 1869, Mohandas Karamchand Gandhi was born in Porbandar, India. He's known as Mahatma Gandhi ("Mahatma" means "Great Souled"). Gandhi wanted India to become independent from Great Britain. He gathered support for his cause by living simply and believing in nonviolent principles. Instead of throwing rocks and shooting guns, Gandhi talked with people and held peaceful demonstrations. He felt that nonviolence was the best weapon against unfairness.

 Is nonviolence the best way to handle a situation? Write your opinion.

 On January 30, 1948, Gandhi was assassinated. The man who killed him felt Gandhi was too tolerant of other religions. On the anniversary of Gandhi's birth, thousands of people gather at a park on the Jumna River in Delhi. They sing hymns and read from the holy books of the Gita, Koran, and Bible. In honor of Gandhi's birthday, list three nonviolent ways to solve a problem.

 Good grief, Charlie Brown! It's your birthday. The *Peanuts* comic strip first appeared on this date in 1950. Charles M. Schulz created the famous comic strip, which today appears in 2,300 newspapers and 31 languages. Charlie Brown and his friends even have their own animated TV specials. If you'd like more information about the Peanuts gang, send a letter to:

United Features Syndicate
Public Relations Director
200 Park Avenue
New York, NY 10166

 Decorate your bulletin board using the Peanuts gang. Cut out *Peanuts* cartoon strips from the newspaper or draw your own versions of the characters. Let Charlie Brown and his friends help you learn some new vocabulary words or just give you a smile.

On this day in 1873, author Emily Post was born in Baltimore, Maryland. In the late 1800s, Post's publisher asked her to write a book about etiquette and good manners. By 1922, her book *Etiquette: The Blue Book of Social Usage* was one of the best-selling books in the United States. It told the correct ways to act in many situations.

 Are manners important? Why or why not?

 Did you know that there's more to good manners than saying "please" and "thank you"? Good manners also mean talking nicely on the phone and putting a napkin in your lap when you eat a meal. It means sending a thank-you note after you receive a gift. Make a list of some other good manners.

Sometimes, an act that one person thinks is good manners might be considered bad manners by someone else. *Examples:* In some parts of the Middle East, people use their hands to eat. In other societies, diners use forks and spoons. In Japan, people think it's bad manners to put food on top of rice. In China, people heap their food onto beds of rice. Ask your classmates the things they think are good manners. Do you think those things are good manners, too?

In Japan, people bow to one another when they meet. In Paris, people kiss each other on the cheek. In the United States, people shake hands. Emily Post suggests that you add a smile when you greet someone. What's your favorite way to greet someone? Show your class how you like to greet someone. Ask your classmates to show you their way. With a classmate, practice some good manners.

october 4

On this date in 1957, Russian scientists launched *Sputnik I*, the first satellite. *Sputnik I* was about the size of a basketball, and had a radio transmitter inside it. Because of *Sputnik's* successful launch, this day marks the beginning of the Space Age. At the time, Americans were shocked that the United States had not made the first space launch. American parents demanded that schools put more emphasis on math and science so that their children would be able to continue the study of space.

Write about why you like studying science and math. Or write about why you dislike these subjects.

"10-4" is what radio operators say when they mean "okay" or "yes." Each year, the 4th day of the 10th month is a day of recognition for radio operators. On this day, people honor radio operators—whether they're trained dispatchers talking to firefighters or people with CB radios in their homes. Make up your own radio lingo using numbers. Maybe "12-5" could mean "Hello" or "Let's go to the library." What could "1-0" or "2-8" stand for?

On this day in 1862, Edward L. Stratemeyer was born in Elizabeth, New Jersey. Stratemeyer wrote 150 books for kids—and started hundreds of others. He and a group of people called the Stratemeyer Syndicate wrote hundreds of books under 60 different names. Stratemeyer used the name Franklin Dixon to write the Hardy Boy stories. He used the name Carolyn Keene to write the Nancy Drew stories. He wrote the Tom Swift stories under the name Victor Appleton.

Many authors use pseudonyms, or pen names, to write their books. Dr. Seuss' real name is Theodore S. Geisel. Mark Twain's real name is Samuel Clemens. Steven King, author of many horror stories, also wrote under the name Richard Bachman. Think about a pseudonym you'd like to use for your writings. Why would you choose that one?

Edward Stratemeyer died in 1930, but at least four million copies of his books are still in print. Today's Stratemeyer Syndicate authors still write for the same series. They change the characters and situations to keep up with the times. Choose a book from the Hardy Boys, Nancy Drew, or Tom Swift series and ask someone to read part of the book to you.

RESOURCES

Mystery of Smuggler's Cave (A Hardy Boys Mystery) by Franklin Dixon (New York: Wanderer Books, 1980).

The Secret in the Old Lace (A Nancy Drew Mystery) by Carolyn Keene (New York: Wanderer Books, 1980).

The Space Fortress (A Tom Swift Mystery) by Victor Appleton (New York: Simon & Schuster, 1981).

october 5

The first Monday in October is Universal Children's Day. In 1953, the United Nations General Assembly set up this holiday. Over 120 countries celebrate this day with special ceremonies and festivals. Today is also a day to let governments know what children and young people need.

 Write a few sentences on what governments need to know about you and your life.

 One way to learn about the cultures and customs of children from other countries is to become a pen pal. You can write to young people your age in any part of the world. For information about becoming a pen pal, write to:

World Pen Pals
1694 Como Avenue
St. Paul, MN 55108

 October is National Roller Skating Month. It's a month to honor those shoes with wheels or roller blades attached to the soles. Two women hold the record for the most world roller skating speed titles. From 1953 to 1965, Alberta Vianello from Italy skated to eight track and ten road records. From 1964 to 1981, Annie Lambrechts from Belgium earned 1 track and 17 road speed records. Write a few sentences on what you like about roller or in-line skating. If you've never roller or in-line skated, write about why you would—or wouldn't—want to try.

 Tecumseh died on this day in 1813. He was a Shawnee Indian chief born in Old Piqua near Springfield, Ohio, in March 1768. Tecumseh worked to unite the western Indian tribes against the settlers who were moving onto Indian land. After his brother was killed in 1811, Tecumseh joined the British in the War of 1812. He was killed in action at the Battle of Thames in Upper Canada in 1813. To learn more about Tecumseh, read *Tecumseh: Warrior-Statesman* by James McCague.

RESOURCE

Tecumseh: Warrior-Statesman by James McCague (Dallas, Texas: Garrard Publishing Company, 1970).

october 6

On this day in 1927, *The Jazz Singer*, the first full-length "talking" movie, was released. Although the actors didn't say too many words, they performed several musical numbers. Al Jolson was the star of the movie, which was based on his life. The movie was the beginning of today's modern sound movies.

 Write about a movie you saw that had lots of music. What was your opinion of the movie and the music?

 Al Jolson was a comedian and singer who performed on vaudeville and Broadway stages. His most popular songs were "Swanee" and "Mammy." In *The Jazz Singer*, Jolson said, "Wait, you ain't heard nothin' yet!" Write about a time you amazed someone.

Egyptian President Anwar el-Sadat felt strongly about peace. In 1977, he and Menachem Begin worked out peace terms between the Arabs and Israelis. The two men shared the 1978 Nobel Peace Prize for their efforts to end the 30-year Arab-Israeli conflict. On this day in 1981, Sadat was assassinated. He was shot by a man who didn't like the way Sadat helped Israel. Read more about the Egyptian president in *Anwar el-Sadat: A Man of Peace* by Deborah N. Rosen.

 Today is German-American Day. It celebrates German heritage and the things German-Americans have done to help build America. To learn more about German-American Day, send a letter to:

The Society for German-American Studies
Central Library, M.L.33
University of Cincinnati
Cincinnati, OH 45211

··

R E S O U R C E

Anwar el-Sadat: A Man of Peace by Deborah N. Rosen (Chicago: Childrens Press, 1986).

··

october 7

Today is the birthday of Yo Yo Ma, who was born in Paris, France, in 1955. Many people think that he is one of the greatest musical talents alive. When he was still a toddler, Yo Yo's family encouraged him to play the violin. When he was four, he played so well that people called him a musical phenomenon. When he was seven, Yo Yo decided to play a larger instrument, so his father made a cello for him. When his family moved to New York City, more people heard of Yo Yo's talent. In 1978, he won the Avery Fisher Prize, the most important award in classical music.

 Write about a musical instrument you'd like to play. If you don't want to play an instrument, write about one you like to listen to.

 Send a birthday card or a note to Yo Yo Ma and address it to:

Yo Yo Ma
ICM Artists, Ltd.
40 West 57th Street
New York, NY 10019

 In honor of Yo Yo Ma's birthday, play musical chairs. Have everyone in your class put their chairs in a circle with the seats facing out. Take one of the chairs away. Ask one person to play a record or tape of Yo Yo Ma's cello music or some other music. When the music begins, walk around the chairs. When the music stops, try to find somewhere to sit. The person left standing leaves the game. Remove a chair and start the music again. Keep going until only one chair remains.

 If this is the first Monday in October, it's Child Health Day. Have you ever thought about what it's like to live in another country? Pick a country. Find out what children your age do for fun there. Would you like living there?

october 8

On this day in 1872, chemist Mary Engle Pennington was born. She specialized in analyzing bacteria and developed methods to make sure milk was pure. In 1905, Pennington began to work with refrigeration, the idea of keeping foods cold in order to keep bacteria away. She became a pioneer in the safe techniques of freezing foods. When she died in 1952, she was the president of the American Institute of Refrigeration.

Write about how your life would be different if there were no refrigerators or freezers.

 Today is Jesse L. Jackson's birthday. He's a civil rights leader, minister, and politician who was born in Greenville, South Carolina, in 1941. In 1968, Jackson was ordained a Baptist minister. He worked with Dr. Martin Luther King, Jr., and later formed Operation PUSH, an African-American economic group in Chicago. Today, he continues to work for civil rights worldwide.

To learn more about Jesse Jackson, read *Jesse Jackson: A Black Leader* by Patricia S. Martin.

 This is Fire Prevention Week—it's a week for everyone to learn more about the dangers of fire. During this week, people also learn to become safe from fire. If you'd like more information about Fire Prevention Week, send a letter to:

National Fire Protection Association
Public Affairs and Education Department
1 Batterymarch Park
P.O. Box 9101
Quincy, MA 02269-9101

Draw a picture of your home, including all the windows and doors. Share the drawing with your family and talk about how you'd leave your home if it was on fire. With your family, decide on a spot outside your house where you and your family would meet to make sure everyone was safe.

ROPE LADDER

BACK DOOR EXIT

EXIT

EXIT

MEET BY MAPLE TREE

RESOURCE

Jesse Jackson: A Black Leader by Patricia S. Martin (Vero Beach, Florida: Rourke Corporation, 1987).

oday is Alphabet Day in Korea. On this day in 1446, King Sejong proclaimed hangul as the official written language of Korea. Hangul is made up of 24 letters. Traditionally, Koreans write from top to bottom in columns arranged from right to left. The style of writing in the United States and other western countries have influenced Koreans. Today, many write the hangul alphabet on lines from left to right.

 Write a sentence that contains as many letters of the alphabet as possible. Can you use all 26 letters?

 On Alphabet Day, Koreans hold calligraphy contests. Calligraphy is the art of fine handwriting. The letters in a calligraphy alphabet have fancy curves and lines. Write the alphabet and make the letters as fancy as you can. Add an extra squiggle to the capital A, E, or L. Put an extra curl on the end of the small g, j, or y. Try writing your name using the letters on your fancy alphabet.

 Mount Hosmer in Missouri is named for sculptor Harriet Goodhue Hosmer. She was born on this day in Watertown, Massachusetts, in 1830. When Hosmer was a teenager, she decided to become a sculptor and took lessons from a physician who helped her study the human body. As a hobby, she enjoyed climbing mountains. Today, you can find her sculptures in St. Louis, Missouri, and in the Metropolitan Museum of Art in New York City. She is the first successful female sculptor in the United States.

Create your own sculpture with some clay. Poke, press, and mold the clay into anything you can imagine.

On this day in 1915, the Fingerprint Society, also called the International Association for Criminal Identification, was founded. Fingerprinting is used to identify people because no two fingerprints are alike.

Many police officers use fingerprints to help locate missing children. Ask your police department about a fingerprinting project for your school. If one isn't available, hold a fingerprinting day in your class. You'll need a stamp pad, 3" x 5" cards, and plenty of paper towels and water. Write your name on the top of a card. Place one finger on the stamp pad. Press on the pad and then gently place your finger on the card. Do this with all ten of your fingers.

october 10

On this day in 1956, tennis star Martina Navratilova was born in Prague, Czechoslovakia. When she was five years old, her parents and grandparents taught her to play tennis. When she was 20, during the U.S. Open tennis tournaments, she defected to the United States. For three years, from early 1981 through 1984, Navratilova won 235 tennis matches and lost only five.

 Write about something your parents or grandparents have taught you.

 To defect means to leave one place or situation and become a part of another. When Martina Navratilova defected to the United States in 1976, she left her family and home in Czechoslovakia and went to live in a new country. Would you want to leave your country and live somewhere else? Talk with your classmates about why you would—or wouldn't—want to live in another country.

 On this day in 1973, Spiro Theodore Agnew resigned from his job as U.S. vice president. That year, he was charged with bribery, conspiracy, and tax charges. He had committed these crimes while he was governor of Maryland.

Who was the first vice president? Who is the current vice president? Look up "vice president" in the encyclopedia and see if there's a listing of all the vice presidents. Find out which vice presidents went on to become presidents.

 Children's author James Marshall was born on this date in 1942. In 1991, *The New York Times* named his book *Old Mother Hubbard and Her Wonderful Dog* one of the ten best illustrated books. Find this book, or another one by Marshall, and look at the illustrations. Do you think they're good?

··

R E S O U R C E S

Some books by James Marshall:

Old Mother Hubbard and Her Wonderful Dog (New York: Farrar, Straus & Giroux, 1991) and *Mary Alice, Operator Number 9* and *Mary Alice Returns* (Boston: Little, Brown).

··

october 11

On this day in 1884, Anna Eleanor Roosevelt was born in New York City. In 1905, she married her distant cousin Franklin Delano Roosevelt, who became president in 1933. Roosevelt raised a large family and helped her husband who was crippled with polio. She also worked for social causes and became active in the National Association for the Advancement of Colored People. She wrote a newspaper column, lectured on human rights, and was an assistant director of the Office of

Civilian Defense. Because of her many humanitarian pursuits, Eleanor was called the "first lady of the world."

 Write about what the first lady's job should be today.

 Eleanor Roosevelt was the U.S. first lady from 1933 to 1945. Research her life and create a timeline to show the events that occurred during the time she and her husband were in the White House.

 In 1945, Eleanor Roosevelt became a United Nations delegate. She also helped to write the United Nations Declaration of Human Rights. She died in 1962. To learn more about Roosevelt and her life, read *Eleanor Roosevelt, First Lady of the World* by Doris Faber.

 On this day in 1759, Mason Locke Weems was born in Anne Arundel County, Maryland. Weems was a clergyman who traveled around the country selling books. Wherever he visited, he told stories about famous people and made them sound as if they were true facts. Some people say Weems created the story about George Washington cutting down the cherry tree. Weems' stories became popular and were considered best-sellers for many years.

In small groups, create a fictitious story about a historical person. Tell your stories to other groups.

··

RESOURCE

Eleanor Roosevelt, First Lady of the World by Doris Faber (New York: Viking Kestral, 1985).

··

Since 1971, Americans have celebrated Columbus Day on the Monday nearest October 12. On this date, Columbus and his crew sighted San Salvador Island in Central America. Columbus was Italian, but he claimed the new land (now called the Bahamas) for Spain's rulers. The Spanish King Ferdinand V and Queen Isabella I had provided the funds he needed to find a short route to the Indies in Asia.

 Write about how you'll celebrate Columbus Day. Or write about why you *won't* celebrate it.

 When Columbus landed in Central America, he thought he had landed in India. He called the native people Indians by mistake. Read more about Columbus in *Discovering Christopher Columbus: How History Is Invented* by Kathy Pelta.

 Columbus and his crew set sail from Spain in three ships: the *Niña*, *Pinta*, and *Santa Maria*. Draw a picture of three sailing ships traveling on the ocean. Add your own make-believe monsters like those that Columbus was expecting to find. You might also try to draw a flat Earth with ships sailing to the edge of it, which was another fear of Columbus and his crew.

 Some people believe that Viking sailors from the Netherlands were the first people to discover America. Others believe that no one could discover this land because people already lived here. Write about how you'd feel if someone claimed to have "discovered" you.

....

RESOURCE

Discovering Christopher Columbus: How History Is Invented by Kathy Pelta (Minneapolis: Lerner Publications, 1992).

....

october 13

On this day in 1925, Margaret Hilda Roberts Thatcher was born in Grantham, Lincolnshire, England. In 1975, she became the first woman in British history to lead a major political party. After the March 1979 elections, Thatcher became Britain's first woman prime minister. She served for 11 1/2 years, until she was defeated in November 1990.

 Write about the rules and laws you'd create if you ruled a country.

 In college, Margaret Thatcher studied chemistry and hoped to become a researcher. She became interested in politics, however, and went to law school. Two areas she helped to improve were school construction and teacher-development programs.

Make a list of the things you'd like to add to or change in your school building. Ask your classmates about the things they'd like to add or change. Pick the five best ideas and write a proposal to your principal requesting the additions or changes.

 Research the contributions of other women politicians. *Examples*: Geraldine Ferraro, Imelda Marcos, Indira Gandhi, Golda Meir, Eva Peron. Share your information with your class.

 On this day in 1926, Jesse Leroy Brown was born in Hattiesburg, Mississippi. He was the first African-American naval pilot and the first African-American naval officer to lose his life in combat during the Korean War. On December 4, 1950, his plane was shot down. Twenty-two years later, the USS *Jesse L. Brown* was launched on March 18, 1972. It was the first ship to be named in honor of an African-American naval officer. Would you want a ship named after you? Tell your class why you would—or wouldn't—want a ship named after you.

october 14

On this day in 1894, poet e. e. cummings was born. As he wrote his poems, cummings developed his own descriptive words. ("Mud-luscious" was the way he described a time after a rain. He used "greenly" to describe the way leaves look in the summer.) He also used unusual punctuation and capitalization. Whenever he wrote his name, he never capitalized any of the words.

 Write your own description of what it looks like outside after it rains. If you want, turn your description into a poem.

 whaT wouLd HappeN if, there weRE; no punCtuaTion or capitalization Rules? IT would pRobably; be a Lot harder to REad Books and mAgazines" WhY do yOu thinK these ruleS: are ImportanT/ ask Your claSSmates what They THINK.

 "Use a capital letter to start a word at the beginning of a sentence." "Use a question mark with sentences that end in a question." Make a list of other punctuation and capitalization rules. To help others remember these rules, write them on a piece of tagboard and hang it in your classroom.

Today is a national holiday in Malagasy Republic, which is also known as the Republic of Madagascar. It's a nation located in the Indian Ocean about 250 miles east of Africa. Madagascar is the fourth-largest island in the world. It stretches about 980 miles. Its major cities are Antananarivo, which is its capital, and Tamatave. On a map or globe, locate the Republic of Madagascar.

october 15

Mata Hari, one of the most notorious spies in World War I, was executed on this day in 1917. She was executed by a French firing squad. Mata Hari was born Margaret Gertrude Zelle in Leeuwarden, Netherlands. In 1901, she married a Dutch colonial officer and lived on the island of Java in Indonesia. A few years later, she left her husband and traveled to Europe. During World War I, she was a double agent— she spied on French soldiers for the Germans and on German soldiers for the French.

 Pretend you're a spy and write about your most exciting spying adventure.

 Spies often use secret words or actions that only other spies know about. Create a secret handshake with one of your classmates. Make it complicated. Use a certain number of handshakes. Clap hands. Tap elbows. Do a high and low shake. Once you've practiced your handshake, share it with your class. . .or keep it a secret.

 Today is National Poetry Day in honor of the Roman poet Virgil, who was born on this day in 70 B.C. One of Virgil's most famous poems was called the *Aeneid*. It tells the story of a hero who lived through the Trojan War and had many adventures. National Poetry Day is a day to pay tribute to all poets.

Write your own piece of poetry. You could write a poem about poets or poetry.

 Poet Shel Silverstein has written many poems for children. Some of his poems are about acrobats, flying shoes, a stack of pancakes, and old Christmas trees. Ask someone to read one of his poems to you. You can find his poems in *Where the Sidewalk Ends* and *Who Wants a Cheap Rhinoceros?*

....

R ESOURCES

Some books by Shel Silverstein:

Where the Sidewalk Ends (New York: Harper & Row Junior Books, 1974) and *Who Wants a Cheap Rhinoceros?* (New York: Macmillan, 1983).

....

october 16

On this day in 1893, two sisters copyrighted the words to the "Happy Birthday" song. Mildred and Patty Smith Hill, schoolteachers from Louisville, Kentucky, wrote the familiar lyrics and used the tune from a song titled "Good Morning to You."

 Write about some of the fun things you've done at a birthday party.

 Sing "Happy Birthday" to Angela Lansbury. She was born on this date in 1925 in London, England. She is an American stage, screen, and television actress. Her most famous role is that of a mystery writer, Jessica Fletcher, in the TV series "Murder She Wrote." Make a list of the skills that you think a mystery writer needs.

Share your favorite mystery story with your classmates. Either read the story or tell it to others. Don't give away the ending. See if someone can guess it or figure it out from the story.

 Today is World Food Day. It celebrates the day in 1945 when the United Nations started the Food and Agricultural organization. Today, people all over the world think about the world's food problem and work to find solutions to the problems of hunger, malnutrition, and poverty.

With your class, plan to donate cans of food to a local food shelf. Talk about how you will collect the cans and who will take the food to the people who need it.

On this day in 1989, baseball fans were getting ready to watch a World Series game at Candlestick Park in San Francisco. As TV viewers tuned into the pre-game show, an earthquake hit and the broadcast was knocked off the air. The quake injured thousands and killed 67 people. It caused $10 billion in damage.

 Write about what it would be like to feel an earthquake. If you've felt an earthquake, write about where you were and what happened.

 An earthquake is the movement of rocks within the Earth. The weight of the rocks rubbing against each other causes great pressures. When the pressure becomes too great, the rocks move into new positions— causing an earthquake. To learn more about this natural occurrence, read *Earthquakes: Nature in Motion* by Hershell H. Nixon and Joan Lowery Nixon.

 Jupiter Hammon, America's first African-American poet, was born on this day in 1711. Hammon was born into slavery, but unlike most slaves he was taught to read and write. On Christmas Day in 1760, his first poem, "An Evening Thought," was published.

Write about your evening thoughts. If you want, make a poem out of your ideas.

 In Jupiter Hammon's honor, Black Poetry Week falls during the week of his birthday. Find out about the poetry of other African-American poets who we honor this week. These poets include Langston Hughes, Gwendolyn Brooks, James Weldon Johnson, Paul Lawrence Dunbar, Nikki Giovanni, Countee Cullen, Maya Angelou, Le Roi Jones, and Calvin Scott.

....
R E S O U R C E
Earthquakes: Nature in Motion by Hershell H. Nixon and Joan Lowery Nixon (New York: Dodd, Mead, 1981).
....

What's a flat, open-faced pie made of bread dough that's covered with tomato sauce and cheese and baked in a hot oven? Pizza! October is National Pizza Month. According to the National Association of Pizza Operators, pizza is America's number one fun food. You can find pizza that's thick or thin crust, stuffed, round, square, or rectangular.

 Write about your favorite type of pizza. If you don't like pizza, write about a food you do like.

 Make a list of all the pizza toppings that you can think of. What toppings would you put on a vegetarian pizza? Which toppings do you like to put on your pizza?

 Your favorite pizza probably comes topped with cheese and tomato sauce and is delivered to your door in a cardboard box. But there's much more to pizza than that. There are potato pizzas, corn pizzas, and even a dessert version that's made up of cream cheese and fruit. Use your imagination and draw the wildest pizza you can think of.

 The first pizzas were called *picea*. In A.D. 1000, Italians and Greeks ate *picea*, which was a round dough covered with herbs and spices. In 1830 in Naples, Italy, pizza lovers flocked to the first pizzeria. If you'd like to know more about this round pie, read the book *Pizza!* by Teresa Martino.

....

RESOURCE

Pizza! by Teresa Martino (Milwaukee, Wisconsin: Raintree Publishers, 1989).

....

october 19

Today marks the birthday of Annie Smith Peck, who was born in 1850. Peck was one of the first female college professors in the United States. After she visited Switzerland, however, she decided to quit her job and begin mountain climbing. After she climbed the Matterhorn in Southern Switzerland, people called her the "Queen of the Climbers." When she was 60, she scaled Mount Huascarán in Peru.

 Write about what you'd like to be doing when you're 60 years old.

 Today is Evaluate Your Life Day. It's a day to take a few minutes and study your life. When you think about your life today,

remember all the good things. Remember all the things you're thankful for.

 On this day in 1957, Queen Elizabeth II of Great Britain did something she had always wanted to do. She saw an American football game. The queen left Washington, D.C., where she was meeting with the president, and traveled to Maryland. She watched a football game between the University of Maryland and the University of South Carolina.

In one sentence, write down something you've always wanted to do.

 In Japan, the Pickle Market (or Bettara-Ichi) begins today. The market opens to sell large, white pickled radishes called bettara. Worshippers use the radishes in their ceremonies to honor Ebisu, one of the Seven Gods of Luck. Sellers dangle the radishes from ropes and swing them around calling, "Bettara, bettara." To learn more about Japan, read *Japan: Land of Samurai and Robots* by Laurence Ottenheimer or *Japan* by Karen Jacobsen.

....

RESOURCES

Japan: Land of Samurai and Robots by Laurence Ottenheimer (Ossining, New York: Young Discovery Library, 1988).

Japan by Karen Jacobsen (Chicago: Childrens Press, 1982).

....

october 20

On this day in 1818, the 49th parallel was established as the United States-Canadian border. The new border stretched from the Rocky Mountains east to Lake of the Woods in Northern Minnesota. (East of Minnesota, the Canadian border follows the natural border created by the Great Lakes.)

Write what might have happened if there was no border between the two countries.

 On a map of North America, look for the provinces and states that are along the border between the United States and Canada.

 Sir Christopher Wren was born on this day in 1632. He was an English architect, mathematician, and professor of astronomy. After the great London fire of 1666, Wren became a self-taught architect and designed over 53 churches. St. Paul's Cathedral in London, with its magnificent dome, is one of his most well-known creations.

Write about the most magnificent building you've ever seen in person or in a book or magazine. What did you like about it?

 October is Computer Learning Month. For more information on computers and ways to celebrate computer month, write to:

Computer Learning Foundation
P.O. Box 60007
Palo Alto, CA 94306-0007

october 21

Today marks the birthday of Alfred Bernhard Nobel, who was born in 1833. Nobel was a Swedish engineer and chemist who invented dynamite. He received a patent for his idea in 1867. Nine years later, he patented a more powerful form of blasting gelatin. Nobel became very rich from his discovery. Because he wanted to be known as more than just the inventor of explosives, he used his fortune to establish the international Nobel Prizes.

 Write about a time something negative in your life became something positive.

 The Nobel Prizes are awarded each year to the leaders in physics, chemistry, physiology, medicine, literature, peace, and economics. Nobel created these prizes because he wanted to encourage people to find peaceful uses for science and technology. With your class, talk about some of the peaceful uses for science. What have been some of the violent uses?

 October is Popcorn Poppin' Month. In 1988, students at Jones High School in Orlando, Florida, built the largest container of popcorn. Their box measured 25 feet by 25 feet.

Find three facts about this fun food by looking up "popcorn" in an encyclopedia. Share the facts with your classmates.

 In honor of Popcorn Poppin' Month, make a popcorn necklace. You'll need a bowl of popped popcorn (with no butter or salt), a long piece of string, and a needle. Make a large knot on one end of the string and put the other end through the needle. Take one popped kernel and thread the needle through it. Push that kernel all the way down the string to the knot. Keep adding popped kernels until you've made a festive garland.

october 22

On this day in 1844, actress Sarah Bernhardt was born in Paris. She was known as "The Divine Sarah" and became famous throughout the world for playing tragic and heroic roles. She also played some male roles. Bernhardt continued her stage career even after her leg was amputated in 1915.

 Would you want to act on stage in front of an audience? Why or why not?

Divide a piece of paper into two columns. In one column, list things men have traditionally done. In the other column, list things women have traditionally done. Do you think men and women should be allowed to work in only certain types of jobs?

 On this date in 1837, Henry David Thoreau began his personal journal. A journal is a record of events or feelings. By 1862, 25 years after he had begun, Thoreau had filled up 14 thick volumes. On some days, Thoreau wrote only a few sentences; on other days he wrote pages and pages.

Think about some reasons to keep a journal. With your class, talk about some of the everyday activities you do that you could write about in your journal.

 October is National Indoor Games Month. Because October weather can be cloudy and wet, it's the perfect time to try a new board game or replay an old favorite. Ask your classmates to bring their favorite board game to school. Set up the games around your classroom and let everyone take turns playing the different games.

october 23

On this day in 1906, Gertrude Ederle was born in New York City. Ederle loved to swim and practiced her swimming strokes whenever she had the chance. When she was 16 years old, she broke seven world swimming records in one afternoon at Brighton Beach, New York. On August 6, 1926, she became the first woman to swim the English Channel. Ederle swam the 35 miles in only 14 hours, 31 minutes.

 Write about the first time you learned to swim. If you don't know how to swim, write about why you would or wouldn't want to learn.

 Gertrude Ederle had tried to swim the English Channel in 1925, but had failed. In 1926, she was determined to swim the distance. She entered the cold, choppy waters in Cape Gris-Nez, France. Reporters and friends in a small boat followed her. Ederle swam through large waves and cold winds until she reached Kingsdown on the coast of England.

On a map of England, locate the English Channel. Look for Cape Gris-Nez, France, and Kingsdown, Great Britain.

On this day in 1940, Edson Arantes do Nascimento—better known as Pelé—was born. He's a Brazilian soccer player and the best player of his time. He led Brazil to three World Cup victories in 1958, 1962, and 1970. During his career, he was the highest paid athlete in the world. In 1971, Pelé retired from international competition but later joined the New York Cosmos in the North American Soccer League. He helped to popularize the sport of soccer in the United States.

With your class, talk about why you think soccer is becoming a popular sport in the United States.

 A soccer ball contains a geometric shape of six sides called a hexagon. Draw some hexagon shapes like the one found on a soccer ball. Cut out the shapes and use them to create a set of new designs. Change the position of the designs and use other colors. How creative can you be?

october 24

On this day in 1901, Anna Edson Taylor became the first person to travel over Niagara Falls in a barrel and survive. Taylor did the stunt to raise money to repay a loan due on her Texas ranch. Before she crawled into the barrel, she told people that she was 43 years old. She was really 63 when she did this crazy stunt.

 Write about a crazy stunt you have seen, heard about, or imagined.

 Sarah Josepha Hale was born in Newport, New Hampshire, on this day in 1788. In 1830, she wrote *Poems for Our Children*, which included a poem titled "Mary's Lamb." She also wrote a book about the achievements of women. *Woman's Record: Or Sketches of all Distinguished Women from the Creation to A.D. 1654* was published in 1863. It included biographies of more than 2,500 women. In honor of this writer, sing "Mary Had a Little Lamb," a song based on her poem.

 Today is United Nations Day. It celebrates the beginning of this international peace-keeping organization. Before World War II ended, people all over the world believed that there should be an organization that works to prevent future wars. On June 26, 1945, 50 nations signed a charter to create the United Nations. The charter took effect on this day. To learn more about the United Nations, write to:

United Nations
Department of Public Information
United Nations Headquarters
New York, NY 10017

 Today, 159 countries belong to the U.N. Select a United Nations' member country and make a globe to highlight your selected country.

For your globe, you'll need a balloon; about 20 pieces of string, each about 20 inches long; laundry starch; a bowl; newspaper; and a pin.

Spread the newspaper on a table and pour the laundry starch into the bowl. Blow up your balloon. Dip a piece of string in the laundry starch and wrap it around the balloon. Continue dipping string in the laundry starch and wrapping the strands around the balloon until you've used all 20 strands.

As the string on the balloon is drying (it'll take about 24 to 48 hours), look at a map and draw your country on a piece of construction paper and cut it out. When the string has dried, break the balloon with a pin and carefully remove the balloon pieces from inside your globe. Glue your country on the globe in its place. Hang the globes in your classroom to celebrate United Nations Day.

october 25

Each year on this day, Hindus in India celebrate Dewali, the festival of light. It celebrates the return of the Lord Shri Rama to Ayodhya after a 14-year exile. Dewali is the prettiest of all Indian festivals. Thousands of flickering lights light up cities and towns. People set off fireworks to add color and noise to their celebration. Also during the holiday, Hindus worship Lakshmi, the goddess of wealth. People clean their homes and draw fancy designs on the front steps. Hindus exchange presents, go to fairs, and play games on this colorful holiday.

 Lights are often an important addition to a festive time. Write about the most beautiful light display you've ever seen.

On Dewali, friends and families get together to celebrate and exchange gifts of sweets, dried fruits, and nuts. It's the most important Hindu festival and is similar to the celebration of Christmas in Western religions. To learn more about this holiday, ask an Indian classmate to tell you how he or she celebrates Dewali. If you are Indian, share what you know about this holiday with your class.

 On this day in 1881, the artist Pablo Ruiz y Picasso was born in Malaga, Spain. Picasso was known as a Cubist because many of his paintings contain boxlike structures. The years 1900 to 1905 are known as his Blue Period because he used the color blue in so many of his paintings.

To learn more about this artist, read *Pablo Picasso* by Ernest Raboff.

 Picasso also created collages, a technique of pasting cut materials onto canvas. Create your own collage. All you need are scissors, old newspapers or magazines, glue, and paper. Think of a theme for your collage, such as friendship, families, seasons, or pets. Cut out pictures of your theme and fill your paper with the images.

....

R E S O U R C E

Pablo Picasso by Ernest Raboff (New York: Lippincott, 1987).

....

On this day in 1895, the New York Public Library was founded. It officially opened on May 24, 1911. New York was the first state to build libraries for its citizens. It became the model for other libraries around the world.

 Write about the library you go to. Would you change anything in it? Why or why not?

 To learn more about libraries, read the book *I Like the Library* by Anne Rockwell.

 Authors often go to the library to research information for their books. They use the many different resource and reference materials to help them. Visit your library and find the reference section. What kinds of reference books are available in your library? What are you able to find in the books?

 On this day in 1941, illustrator Steven Kellogg was born. Pinkerton, a Great Dane, inspired Kellogg to write and draw some of his funniest stories. Share a dog book with a friend. Have you read a dog story that would make a good movie?

....

R E S O U R C E

I Like the Library by Anne Rockwell (New York: Dutton, 1977).

....

Today is Good Bear Day. It honors Theodore "Teddy" Roosevelt, who was born on this day in 1858. In 1901, he became the twenty-sixth president of the United States. Roosevelt loved to hunt. In 1903, during a trip to Mississippi, he refused to kill a young bear cub. A toy maker heard of his decision and made some small stuffed bears that he called Teddy's bears. Customers loved the toy and the teddy bear was born.

 Pick three people in your life. Write about the animal you'd associate with each of them and why.

During Theodore Roosevelt's time in office, workers began building the Panama Canal. In 1906, he won the Nobel Peace Prize for helping to end the Russo-Japanese War. He died on January 6, 1919. To learn more about this president, read *Bully for You, Teddy Roosevelt* by Jean Fritz.

 Theodore Roosevelt kept a zoological notebook where he described wood spiders, crickets, and other insects. Start your own zoological notebook by writing a description of an insect, bird, or mammal you've seen.

 Today is National Day in the Grenadine Islands, located in the southern Windward Islands at the east end of the Caribbean Sea. The Grenadine Islands extend over 60 miles between Grenada and Saint Vincent. They include about 600 small islands. Locate the Grenadine Islands on a world map. What do you think the climate is like there?

....

R E S O U R C E

Bully for You, Teddy Roosevelt by Jean Fritz (New York: Putnam, 1991).

....

On this day in 1886, the Statue of Liberty was dedicated. The statue is located in New York Harbor on Liberty Island. From the top of the heel to the top of the head, the statue measures 111 feet 1 inch. The statue's index finger is 8 feet long (which is about the height from your classroom floor to ceiling). Her nose is 4 feet 6 inches long. Her mouth is 3 feet wide. The Statue of Liberty wears a crown of seven spokes and carries a law book inscribed "July 4, 1776."

 Would you want to visit the Statue of Liberty? Why or why not? If you've visited this monument, write about what you thought when you first saw the statue.

 The people of France gave the statue to Americans to commemorate 100 years of U.S. independence. Workers built the entire statue in Paris. They took it apart, packed it into 214 crates, and shipped it to the United States. The book *Statue of Liberty* by Leonard E. Fisher contains some interesting pictures and more facts about the statue.

 Today is OHI Day in Greece. In 1944, the Italian dictator Benito Mussolini attacked the country. OHI Day celebrates the Greeks refusal to open their borders to the army. ("Ohi" means "no" in Greek.) People celebrate this national holiday with military parades in the cities of Athens and Thessaloniki.

There are many different ways to say "no" without using the word "no." Make a list of ways to say "no."

 On this day in 1834, the U.S. government ordered the Seminole Indians to move from Florida to Indian Territory, which is now Oklahoma. When the Seminoles refused to leave their homes in Florida, the government sent troops to force them out. A 17-year war between the Seminoles and the U.S. government began. When President Andrew Jackson ordered the Seminoles removed to the West, Osceola, a Seminole chieftain, took his people into the Everglades to continue the fight.

Find out more about this Native American tribe by looking up "Seminole" in an encyclopedia or other reference book.

RESOURCE

Statue of Liberty by Leonard E. Fisher (New York: Holiday House, 1985).

October 29

On this day in 1964, The Star of India, the world's largest sapphire, was stolen from the Museum of Natural History in New York City. It was a 565-carat stone (which is about 4 ounces). A sapphire is a hard, transparent precious stone. It usually is deep blue in color.

 Write about your favorite blue things.

 What is your favorite precious stone? Do you like sapphires, diamonds, emeralds? Use an encyclopedia to find three facts about your favorite stone. Share the facts with your class.

 Today is the birthday of James Boswell, who was born in Edinburgh, Scotland in 1740. Boswell was a lawyer and a biographer. He gathered facts about people's lives and wrote books, called biographies, using those facts. His 1791 biography of Dr. Samuel Johnson is considered a masterpiece. Write a biography about a family member. Ask the person questions about his or her life and use those facts to write a story.

 October is National Dessert Month—a month devoted to sweets and fancy desserts. What's your favorite type of dessert? Talk with your classmates about the most delicious dessert you've ever eaten.

October 30

On this day in 1938, a radio broadcast caused national panic. Actor Orson Welles produced a dramatization of the story *The War of the Worlds*. The story is about Martians who invade Earth. At the beginning of his radio show, Welles announced that the events were not really happening. But the production included so many good sound effects that people thought Martians were actually invading their town. Thousands of terrified people fled to the countryside while many more called police stations and hospitals asking for help.

 Write about what you'd do if you thought Martians were invading your town.

 Think about a real-life news story. Write a script for your own radio broadcast based on that news story.

 In October 1992, NASA and the Search for Extraterrestrial Intelligence (SETI) Institute began listening for radio signals coming from outer space. During the next ten years, scientists will be aiming their radio telescopes at more than 1,000 stars—stars that they think could support intelligent life—and listening for any signs of life.

Think about how old you'll be ten years from now. What year will it be? Do you think that scientists will have heard something from outer space by then?

 Halloween is tomorrow. Orange and black are the colors of this spooky holiday. Divide your class into small groups. Have some of the groups list all the things that are orange. Ask the other groups to list all the things that are black. After five minutes, compare the lists. Can your class think of more orange things or more black things?

october 31

Happy Halloween! In medieval England, this day was known as All Hallow's Eve. People celebrated the eve of All Saints' Day, which is on November 1.

 Write about how you'll celebrate Halloween this year.

 Dressing up in costumes, carving pumpkins, and going to school fairs are some of the ways people celebrate Halloween. To learn more about this fun holiday, read *Halloween* by Gail Gibbons. To learn about the origins of Halloween symbols, look in *Witches, Pumpkins and Grinning Ghosts: The Story of Halloween Symbols* by Edna Barth.

 If you go trick-or-treating, bring along a separate container and collect money for the United Nations Children's Fund (UNICEF). Collecting money on Halloween for this worthy cause began in 1950. It remains a tradition in North America. For more information about UNICEF, write to:

Group Programs
United States Committee for UNICEF
331 East 38th Street
New York, NY 10016

 On this day in 1950, broadcast journalist Jane Pauley was born in Indianapolis, Indiana. After graduating from college, Pauley worked for several small TV stations before becoming a co-anchor on NBC's "The Today Show." For 14 years, she interviewed celebrities on this early morning talk show. In 1990, she decided to leave the show and work on other news shows. If you were a journalist, which celebrity would you interview? Make a list of questions you'd like to ask that person.

RESOURCES

Halloween by Gail Gibbons (New York: Holiday House, 1984).

Witches, Pumpkins and Grinning Ghosts: The Story of Halloween Symbols by Edna Barth (Boston: Clarion Books, 1981).

November 1

Ice hockey is a fast-action game and one of the most popular sports in the United States and Canada. On this day in 1959, Jacques Plante, goalie for the Montreal Canadiens, changed the game of hockey. After getting badly cut early in a game against the New York Rangers, he came back into the game wearing a mask. He became the first hockey goalie to wear a mask.

 In hockey, players often fight with one another. Write about your opinion of violence in hockey. What are your suggestions for playing the game differently?

 In the fall of 1992, Manon Rheaume became the first woman to try out for a spot on a National Hockey League (NHL) team. Along with other would-be players, she tried out for the Tampa Bay Lightnings. Although she didn't make the NHL team, the Atlanta Knights, a minor-league team, signed her up for three years. Rheaume encourages young athletes to try out for a team or play a position even if someone has told them that they can't. Write about a sport you've always wanted to play. Tell why you did—or didn't—try out for the team.

 Ice hockey began in Canada in the 1870s; later, people in the United States began to play the sport. Amateur hockey has been an event in the winter Olympic Games since 1920. To learn more about hockey, read *Hockey Is for Me* by Lowell A. Dickmeyer.

Today is All Saints' Day. In Christian religions, this day honors people who have died, especially those who do not have a saint's day of their own. In Mexico people celebrate the Day of the Dead on the first two days of November. They visit cemeteries and eat "Dead Men's Bread," which is a round loaf decorated with sugar skulls. On this day, Mexicans do not mourn people who have died, they celebrate with friendliness and good humor. Write about a positive way to remember someone who has died.

RESOURCE

Hockey Is for Me by Lowell A. Dickmeyer (Minneapolis: Lerner Publications, 1978).

 On this date in 1947, the H-2 Airplane, better known as the *Spruce Goose*, flew for the first—and only—time. The 200-ton plywood aircraft cost $25 million dollars to build and was the world's largest plane. It flew for only one mile and stayed only 70 feet from the ground. Look through the book *Draw 50 Airplanes, Aircraft and Spacecraft* by Lee J. Ames to give you ideas and suggestions on how to draw the *Spruce Goose* and other aircraft.

RESOURCE

Draw 50 Airplanes, Aircraft and Spacecraft by Lee J. Ames (New York: Doubleday, 1971).

The game of checkers originated in Europe in the sixteenth century. The game ends when all of a player's pieces are removed from the board. On this day in 1977, Alan M. Beckerson of Great Britain figured out that the shortest possible game of checkers requires only 20 moves.

 What's your favorite board game? Write about why you like it.

 Play a game of checkers. It you don't know how, pair up with someone who can teach you. Have a third person keep track of how many times each player moves a piece. Record the results. Did anyone take less than 20 moves to finish a game?

 Organize a checker tournament with the members of your class. As you win a game, you continue to play other people. How many games will have to be played before one person is the champ?

Today is Sandwich Day in honor of John Montague, the Fourth Earl of Sandwich. Montague was born on this day in 1718. He was a gambler who liked to play cards, but he didn't like to stop for meals. In 1744, he found that putting meat between two slices of bread allowed him to eat with one hand and continue to play cards with the other.

 Describe your favorite sandwich.

 Make a list of as many different sandwiches as you can think of. Here are a few to start your list: peanut butter on toast, bologna on wheat bread, and ham and cheese with tomato on white bread.

 Ask your classmates to write their favorite type of sandwich on a slip of paper. Gather all the pieces of paper and sort them by sandwich type. What is the favorite sandwich of the members of your class?

On this day in 1966, President Lyndon B. Johnson signed a truth-in-packaging law. This law says that manufacturers of prepared foods have to identify the ingredients in the food. These ingredients must appear on the food's label. That way, the person who buys the product will know what's in it.

Collect some empty product containers. Compare ingredients according to the packages. Use a dictionary to look up any ingredients you aren't familiar with.

November 4

O n or near this date, National Chemistry Week begins. During this week, people are encouraged to learn more about chemists and their contributions to modern life. National Chemistry Week is meant to help the public understand more about chemistry.

 Write about a school subject you'd like to know more about.

 For more information about National Chemistry Week, send a letter to:

American Chemical Society
1155 16th Street, NW
Washington, DC 20006

 Chemistry is the science of studying all kinds of substances. Chemists study substances to learn what they're made of and their characteristics. Chemists also look for changes that occur when they mix substances together. Glass, aluminum (used to make soft drink cans and aircraft bodies), batteries, and silverware are some of the many products that chemists have developed.

Imagine what your life would be like without one of the above items. Write about the other materials you'd have to use instead.

 On this day in 1968, a U.S. postage stamp honoring Chief Joseph, a Nez Percé warrior, went on sale. In 1877, Chief Joseph decided to lead 800 of his people (men, women, and children) from their Idaho reservation through Montana to Canada. He thought they could live on their own land there. The U.S. Army tried to stop him. Chief Joseph was finally forced to surrender to Colonel Nelson Miles 40 miles from the Canadian border. To learn more Chief Joseph and other Native American leaders, read *The Great Chiefs* by Benjamin Capps.

RESOURCE

The Great Chiefs by Benjamin Capps (New York: Time-Life Books, 1975).

November 5

O n this day in 1857, Ida Minerva Tarbell was born in Erie County, Pennsylvania. She was an American writer, editor, and historian who liked to investigate companies. She asked questions to find out all she could about people and large corporations. In 1904, she wrote a history of the Standard Oil Company and told her readers about the wrongdoings of the oil industry. As a result, people demanded that officials pass laws to regulate the oil businesses.

 Write about a company or business you'd like to learn more about.

 To learn more about Ida M. Tarbell and her investigations, read *Ida M. Tarbell, Pioneer Woman Journalist and Biographer* by Adrian A. Paradis.

On this day in 1924, the first book of crossword puzzles appeared on bookstore shelves. Try creating your own crossword puzzle. Decide on a topic (such as cold weather) and think of some words that describe that topic (such as snowflakes, hats, November, gloves, white). Now think of some clues for those words (such as "What's white and falls from the sky?" "What do you wear on your head to keep warm?" and "What is the eleventh month of the year?").

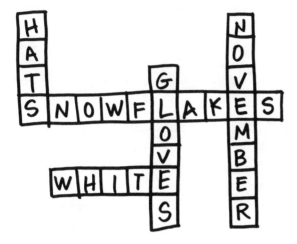

Now you're ready to make your puzzle. In pencil, print the longest word in the center of your paper. Build your crossword puzzle from that word. After you've used all the words, draw boxes around the letters. Copy the boxes—but not the letters—on a sheet of paper. Write your clues on the paper. Give your puzzle to a friend and see if your friend can use the clues to fill in the words.

On this day in 1987, Tania Aebi completed a solo 27,000-mile journey around the world. The 21-year-old sailor became the first woman and the youngest person to make this journey alone. In the spring of 1985, she left New York and sailed south to Central America. She traveled through the Panama Canal and sailed westward across the Pacific and Indian oceans. At the African coast she sailed north through the Red Sea and the Suez Canal to the Mediterranean Sea. She sailed west through the Strait of Gibraltar between Spain and the northern tip of Africa. From there, she continued west to New York across the Atlantic Ocean. She completed the trip in 2 1/2 years. On a world map, follow Aebi's course around the world.

RESOURCE

Ida M. Tarbell, Pioneer Woman Journalist and Biographer by Adrian A. Paradis (Chicago: Childrens Press, 1985).

November 6

On this date in 1854, John Philip Sousa was born in Washington, D.C. He was a composer and bandmaster known as the "March King." Sousa wrote more than 140 military marches—one of his most famous is called "Stars and Stripes Forever."

Describe a marching band. If you've never seen a marching band, write about another music band you've seen or heard.

List as many musical instruments as you can. Label the ones that are used in a marching band. Which ones are used in an orchestra?

Listen to some of Sousa's music (you can find a selection on the recording *The Original All-American Sousa!*) or any marching music. March around the room. Pretend you're in a parade and you're playing your favorite band instrument.

Today at 11:43 a.m., Eastern Standard Time, autumn will be half over. About 44 days have gone by since September 21, when the Autumnal Equinox began the season. The same amount of time remains before December 21, which is the winter solstice, the beginning of winter. Write about what you'll do to enjoy the last weeks of autumn.

RESOURCE
The Original All-American Sousa! recording (Delos, 1990).

November 7

On this day in 1867, Marie Sklodowska Curie was born in Warsaw, Poland. When she was 24, she went to Paris to study math, physics, and chemistry. In their lab, Curie and her husband, Pierre, studied the radiation given off by radioactive substances. In 1903, they were awarded the Nobel Prize in physics for their work.

 Write about something you'd like to study in a lab.

 Marie Curie became the first woman to receive the Nobel Prize. After her husband died, she was appointed to his position at the University of Sorbonne in Paris. In 1911, she won a second Nobel Prize, this one for her work in chemistry. With this second award, she became the first person to win two Nobel Prizes. Learn more about Marie Curie by reading the book *Marie Curie* by Edwina Conner.

 Find out about the work of other women who were chemists. Look up "Dorothy Crowfoot Hodgkin," "Irene Joliot-Curie," or "Ellen Swallow Richards" in an encyclopedia.

 Key Club International Week takes place each year during the first week of November. During this week, the group recognizes the service projects that its members have completed. If there is something in your neighborhood or town that needs changing, start your own service project. Adding a recycling program to your school, planning a food drive, or changing a city ordinance or law are all examples of service projects. Discuss with your classmates something you'd like to change in your school or community. Make that your first step to turning your ideas into actions that can make a difference.

RESOURCE
Marie Curie by Edwina Conner (New York: Franklin Watts, 1987).

November 8

Today marks the birthday of Dorothy Day. She was born in 1897 in Brooklyn, New York. Day was a pacifist, which means she did not support the use of violence in any manner. She opposed nuclear weapons and the war in Vietnam in the 1960s and 1970s. Day also helped the homeless in New York City. She opened a house of hospitality where people without homes could stay and find something to eat.

 Write a few sentences on your feelings about the homeless. What are your ideas for helping these people?

 Today, many people in large cities and small towns are homeless. Discuss with your class one way to help the homeless in your area. Perhaps your class could donate money or clothing to a homeless shelter. Many of these shelters could also use blankets and pillows for the people who stay there. Ask your teacher to contact a homeless shelter in your community and find out how your class can help.

On this day in 1656, Edmund Halley, an astronomer, was born in London, England. Halley studied comets and discovered that they follow certain paths around the sun. He predicted that a certain comet, which had appeared in 1682, would return 76 years later in 1758. Halley died in 1742—16 years before his comet was to appear again—but his prediction was correct. His comet has been appearing every 76 years since then, just as he said it would.

Figure out when Halley's Comet will appear again. It has already appeared in 1758, 1834, 1910, and 1986.

 Singer Bonnie Raitt was born on this day in 1943. She grew up in a musical family; her father still performs with touring musical shows. Her maternal grandfather wrote nearly 600 hymns. When she was younger, she went to a summer camp and became interested in the folk music she heard there. After she got home, she learned to play the guitar. In 1990, Raitt won four Grammy Awards for her music.

Have you ever been to summer camp? If you have, write about the things you did and the people you met. If you've never been to a summer camp, write about why you would—or wouldn't—want to go to one.

November 9

On this day in 1731, Benjamin Banneker was born near Ellicott's Mills, Maryland. He was the son of freed slaves and studied science, math, astronomy, and clock making. Banneker borrowed astronomical instruments and books from a neighbor and taught himself how to use them. Throughout his life, he never stopped trying to teach himself new things. In 1791, he became the first African-American presidential appointee when George Washington asked him to survey the site of the new U.S. capital.

 Write about something you'd like to teach yourself.

 Create a self-help list to explain to someone how to do something. First, think of something you know how to do. *Examples*: mow the lawn, bake some cookies, play soccer, or baby-sit. Next, write the numbers 1 through 10 down the sides of a sheet of paper. For number 1, write down the first thing you need to do with your activity (*example*: Take out the lawn mower). For number 2, write down the next thing you need to do (*example*: Check to see if there's enough gas in the tank). Keep describing your activity. If you need more than ten steps, add more to your list.

 Benjamin Banneker also wrote an almanac. An almanac contains calendar information, weather forecasts, and information about astronomy. It contains useful tidbits of information. It's often reprinted each year. Look through *The World Almanac* or another almanac. Can you find out the capital of Hawaii? How about the number of people who live in Los Angeles?

 On this day in 1805, Dr. Harriet Kezia Hunt was born in Boston, Massachusetts. In 1835, Hunt and her sister began a medical practice to help sick women and children. She became the first woman to practice medicine in the United States. (Elizabeth Blackwell was the first woman to earn a medical degree.) In 1850, she was one of the first women to attend Harvard Medical School.

Throughout her career, Hunt promoted the good health habits of diet, regular bathing, exercise, and rest. With your class, talk about other good health habits.

RESOURCE

The World Almanac (New York: Pharos Books, updated annually).

November 10

On this date in 1988, Los Angeles Dodger Orel Hershiser won the National League Cy Young Award. Each year, sportswriters vote for the pitcher who has been an outstanding performer during the previous baseball season. In 1988, all 24 sportswriters voted for Hershiser. He was the ninth player in National League history to win the award unanimously.

 Write about a time when you were an outstanding performer.

 Look through the sports section in back issues of your newspaper and collect some baseball team logos. The Milwaukee Brewers were named by a fan who won a contest. Other teams named by fans include the Seattle Mariners, Toronto Blue Jays, Texas Rangers, and Kansas City Royals.

 Are there some baseball terms that you'd like more information about? For a dictionary of baseball terms, read *Baseball Talk for Beginners* by Joe Archibald.

 On this day in 1871, Henry Morton Stanley met the missionary-explorer David Livingstone. David Livingstone was a Scottish clergyman and explorer. In 1851, he discovered the Zambezi River and traveled from Africa's east coast to its west coast exploring the river. In 1855, while looking for the source of the Nile River, Livingstone discov-

ered Victoria Falls. Meanwhile, many people were worried that Livingston might be lost, so they sent Henry Stanley to find him. Stanley was a reporter with the *New York Herald* and an explorer himself. Stanley found Livingstone at Ujiji, which is located in central Africa near Lake Tanganyika. When he located him, he said, "Doctor Livingstone, I presume?" The phrase is still heard today when someone is obviously found.

Find the Nile River on a world globe or map. Look in an encyclopedia and learn five interesting facts about this river.

RESOURCE

Baseball Talk for Beginners by Joe Archibald (Englewood Cliffs, New Jersey: Julian Messner, 1974).

November 11

Today is National Young Reader's Day. It's celebrated to encourage young people to read books. This day also begins National Children's Book Week.

 Write about why reading is—or isn't—something you like to do.

 To celebrate National Young Reader's Day, tell your class about your favorite book. Tell your classmates part of the story but not too much—just enough to make them want to read it, too. Tell why the story is your favorite. Hold up a copy of the book. You could even show some of the illustrations.

 To learn more about National Young Reader's Day, send a letter to:

The Carson Group, Inc.
Frick Building
437 Grant Street, Suite 912
Pittsburgh, PA 15219

 Author Anna K. Green was born in Brooklyn, New York, on this day in 1846. She wrote a story titled *The Leavenworth Case*, a detective story with a suspenseful plot. The main characters in the story were Ebenezer Gryce, a detective, and Amelia Butterworth, his assistant. Green was the first woman to write a successful detective story.

Make a list of characteristics you could include in a detective story. Later, you can write a story using these characters.

November 12

On this day in 1815, Elizabeth Cady Stanton was born in Johnstown, New York. She was an American suffragist, women's rights leader, and social reformer. She became a lecturer, writer, and journalist. In 1840, Stanton joined with Lucretia Mott to fight for equality. In 1848, they organized the first women's rights convention at Seneca Falls, New York. In 1851, Stanton joined Susan B. Anthony. The two worked closely in the struggle for women's rights for 50 years.

 Write about a friend you'd like to work with on a project.

 Find out more about these women's struggle for equal rights by looking up "Elizabeth Stanton," "Lucretia Mott," and "Susan B. Anthony" in an encyclopedia or other reference book.

 On this day in 1840, Francois Auguste Rodin, a French sculptor and painter, was born. In 1876, he completed his first major work, "The Age of Bronze." His statue was so realistic that some experts accused him of having cast it from a living figure. One of Rodin's most famous sculptures is "The Thinker," which he created in 1880. "The Thinker" is the statue of a seated man hunched over. His chin rests in his hand; his elbow rests on his knee.

Look for a picture of "The Thinker" in a library book or encyclopedia.

 On this day in 1859, Jules Leotard became the first "man on a flying trapeze." His act was introduced at a Paris circus. His special costume fit him closely so that no part of his clothing would catch on his trapeze. The costume became known as leotards. Learn more about the circus in *Circus* by Mabel Harmer or *Circus!* by Jack Prelutsky.

RESOURCES

Circus by Mabel Harmer (Chicago: Childrens Press, 1981).

Circus! by Jack Prelutsky (New York: Macmillan, 1989).

November 13

On November 13, 1850, Robert Louis Stevenson was born in Edinburgh, Scotland. Because he suffered from tuberculosis, he had poor lungs and spent most of his childhood in bed. When he was older, he traveled around the world searching for places that had mild climates. On one of his trips, he drew a treasure map with his stepson and wrote a story about it. In 1883, *Treasure Island* was published. Three years later, Stevenson wrote *Kidnapped*. *The Strange Case of Dr. Jekyll and Mr. Hyde* is also one of his books.

Would you like to travel around the world? Why or why not?

 You can find pirates, treasure maps, adventure, and voyages on the high seas in Robert Louis Stevenson's books. Ask someone to read part of *Treasure Island* or *Kidnapped* to you.

 Create a treasure map of your school. On a large sheet of paper, draw a map of your school. Include the classrooms, lunchroom, principal's office, and playground. Pretend that a treasure is hidden in your classroom and put a large "X" there. After creating the map, glue it to a stiff piece of paper. Cut the map into some puzzle shapes. Ask your teacher or a classmate to hide the pieces in the room and give you clues on where to find each piece. See how quickly you can put the map together.

 Make a pirate's three-cornered paper hat. You'll need a single sheet of newspaper, some tape, and a stapler.

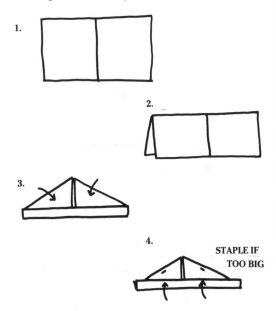

Place the newspaper horizontally on your table. Fold it in half lengthwise. Take the top right corner and fold it down to the middle to form a triangle. Fold down the top left corner to form a second triangle. You should have about a 1 1/2 to 2 inches edge left along the unfolded edge. Separate the bottom edges. Fold up the edge on each side of the hat. Use some tape to help keep the folds in place. If the hat is too big, staple the sides together about halfway up the hat. Open up the hat and place it on your head so that the pointed edges are over your shoulders.

RESOURCES

Some books by Robert Louis Stevenson:

Treasure Island (Scribner, 1981) and *Kidnapped* (Grosset & Dunlap, 1948).

On this day in 1907, William Steig was born. He is an artist and author who didn't start writing for children until he was 60 years old. When he was 62, his book *Sylvester and the Magic Pebble* won the Caldecott Medal (awarded each year to the best American picture book). When he accepted his award, he was nervous about giving his acceptance speech.

 Write about something that makes you nervous.

 Read Steig's book *The Amazing Bone*. It's about a pig named Pearl who finds a magic bone.

 On this day in 1840, the French painter Claude Monet was born. His paintings include many seascapes and city scenes. He was famous for painting the same scene at different times of the day or at different times of the year. He painted several views of the Seine River in Paris.

Take a large sheet of paper and use a marker to divide it into four squares. In the first square, draw an outdoor scene in the fall. *Examples*: you could draw your home, playground, or favorite tree. In the next square, draw the same scene as it will look in the winter. In the other two squares, draw the scene as it will look in the spring and summer.

 In the 1870s, Claude Monet began to use a loose, broken-color brush stroke to create his work. This was called Impressionism because one of his paintings was titled *An Impression: Sunrise*. Look up the word "impression" in your dictionary. How many different meanings does that word have?

. . . .

RESOURCE

The Amazing Bone by William Steig (New York: Penguin Books, 1977).

. . . .

NoVeMBer 15

On this day in 1887, artist Georgia O'Keeffe was born in Sun Prairie, Wisconsin. In her paintings, O'Keeffe looked at natural objects, such as rocks, bones, clouds, and flowers, and painted them in their simplest form. Sometimes she painted close-up views of her subjects. Sometimes she used thin paint and clear colors to emphasize the simple objects.

 Write about things you'd paint if you were an artist. If you are an artist, describe what you like to paint.

 Zebulon Montgomery Pike first sighted Pike's Peak on this day in 1806. Pike was an explorer who traveled throughout the newly purchased Louisiana Territory. He also searched for the source of the Mississippi River. He was leading an army expedition to Colorado and New Mexico when he discovered Pike's Peak.

Pike's Peak is located in central Colorado about 10 miles west of Colorado Springs. Although it isn't the tallest peak in the Rocky Mountains, it is the best-known. It rises 14,110 feet and dominates western Colorado's landscape. On a map of Colorado, locate Pike's Peak.

 On this day in Japan, children visit Shinto shrines to give thanks for good health and fortune. This day is called Schichi-Go-San, which means "seven, five, three." Seven-year-old girls, five-year-old boys, and all three-year-old children are honored. Children dress in traditional Japanese clothing such as a kimono with an obi and geta. An obi is a stiff, belt-like sash. Geta are wooden clog shoes worn with socks.

Find out more information about traditional costumes in the book *Costumes and Customs of Many Lands* by Margaret Oldfield.

 Thanksgiving is about a week and a half away. Make a list of the things you're thankful for.

. . . .

RESOURCE

Costumes and Customs of Many Lands by Margaret Oldfield (Minneapolis: Creative Storytime Press, 1982).

. . . .

NoVeMBer 16

Astrogeology is the study of rocks, craters, and other surface features of the moon and the planets. An astrogeologist is a person who studies these items. Many people became astrogeologists on this day in 1968 when the first moon rock went on display in New York City.

 Write down what you think about rocks. Have you ever looked at one closely? Do you think they're interesting or useful? Why or why not?

 Make your own pet rock. Look outside for a stone about the size of your hand. Wash it clean and let it dry. With markers or paints, draw a face on any part of the stone you choose.

 On this day in 1915, author Jean Fritz was born. She has written many books for young people and received awards and honors for many of them. To celebrate her birthday, choose one of her books to read for yourself. Or have someone read *The Cabin Faced West* to you. It's a good story to hear out loud.

✉ According to the Hindu solar calendar, this is the birth anniversary of Guru Nanak, the founder of Sikhism. Sikhism combines Hindu and Muslim teachings. Today, there are 6 million Sikhs in the world; most live in India. Find out more information about Nanak and Sikhism by writing to:

Government of India Tourist Office
North Mezzanine
30 Rockefeller Plaza
New York, NY 10112

RESOURCE

The Cabin Faced West by Jean Fritz (New York: Penguin Books, 1987).

November 17

On this day in 1805, explorers Meriwether Lewis and William Clark reached the Pacific Ocean. The Lewis and Clark Expedition had explored the Louisiana Purchase and the country beyond it. President Thomas Jefferson had asked the two explorers to keep notes of all they had seen on their journey. Their journals documented 122 animals and almost 200 plants that had never been seen by white people before.

 Study an animal or plant that interests you and write a description of it.

 Sacagawea, a woman of the Shoshone tribe, led the Lewis and Clarke expedition through the territory between the Mississippi River and the Rocky Mountains. Sacagawea and her husband were living in the Dakotas when the expedition reached there. Lewis and Clark knew they would need a guide to help them find the Pacific Ocean, so they asked Sacagawea for her help. To learn more about this remarkable guide, look up "Sacagawea" in an encyclopedia.

 On May 14, 1804, Lewis and Clarke left St. Louis. They traveled up the Mississippi River through the present-day state of Missouri to Sioux City, Iowa. There, they continued on the Missouri River through South Dakota to present-day Bismarck, North Dakota. There they spent the winter and met Sacagawea. In the spring, the explorers continued on the Missouri to Great Falls, Montana. They traveled south to Lemhi Pass in Idaho and crossed the Bitterroot Range near Missoula, Montana. Then they traveled west down the Clearwater, Snake, and Columbia rivers to the Pacific Ocean.

On a map of the United States, trace Lewis and Clark's expedition.

 On this day in 1790, August Möbius was born in Schulpforte, Germany. He was an astronomer and mathematician who pioneered the field of topology. Topology is a branch of mathematics that identifies figures when they are twisted or stretched. Möbius became the first to describe a "one-sided" piece of paper, which he called the Möbius strip.

Create your own Möbius strip. Cut a long strip of paper about 1 inch wide and at least 10 inches long. Color one side of the strip. Hold the strip with the colored side facing you. Twist *one* end so the uncolored side also faces you. Tape or staple the two ends together; make sure the strip stays twisted. Now run your finger along the whole length of one side of your Möbius strip. What happens? Does the paper strip still have a colored side and an uncolored side—or does it only have one side?

November 18

Charles Ferdinand Dowd was a Connecticut teacher who proposed a time zone plan for the United States. He and others convinced the railroads to adopt the time zones on this day in 1883. Dowd and his group divided the United States into four time zones—Eastern, Central, Mountain, and Pacific. Within each zone, local time is standardized, which means that it's the same time everywhere in that zone.

 Write about your favorite time. Maybe it's Saturday morning or Friday afternoon.

 Some people refer to themselves as morning people because they feel the best when they first get up. Others say they're night owls because they feel most energetic in the evenings. Take a survey of your classmates and ask them if they work best in the morning or at night.

 We need time zones because the sun does not rise and set at the same time in every part of the world. Write about what would happen if every state or country decided to have its own time.

 On this day in 1966, *Lunar Orbiter 2*, a U.S. spacecraft, began sending photos of the moon's surface back to Earth. At the time, U.S. scientists were preparing for the first trip into outer space (which would take place in 1969). Scientists studied the photos and looked for a good landing site. To see pictures of the moon and learn more about its surface, read *What the Moon Is Like* by Franklyn M. Branley.

RESOURCE

What the Moon Is Like by Franklyn M. Branley (New York: Thomas Y. Crowell, 1986).

November 19

On this day in 1863, officials set aside 17 acres of the battlefield at Gettysburg, Pennsylvania, for a national cemetery. During the dedication ceremony, a man named Edward Everett spoke for two hours. President Abraham Lincoln spoke next. His speech—called the Gettysburg Address—lasted only three minutes. Many people say that speech is one of the finest ever given in the English language.

Write about the best—or worst—speech you've ever heard. If you've never heard a speech, write about one you'd like to hear. *Examples*: your favorite athlete telling about his or her sport. A rock star telling about what it's like to perform on stage.

Many people feel nervous when they speak in front of an audience. If you get nervous before giving a speech, write down some things you could do to feel better. *Examples*: Take some deep breaths, prepare your speech ahead of time, and write out notes to use while you're speaking.

On this day in 1917, Indira Nehru Gandhi was born in Allahabad, India. In 1975, after nine years as India's prime minister, she was found guilty of using illegal practices in the election of 1971. She refused to resign and arrested many of her opponents. In the 1977 election, she was defeated and faced corruption charges. She came back to politics in 1980, however, and was again elected prime minister. In 1984, she was assassinated.

Find out more information about this political leader by looking up "Indira Gandhi" in an encyclopedia. Visit your library and ask a librarian if there are any books about Indira Gandhi.

James Abram Garfield was the first left-handed president of the United Sates. He was born on this day in 1831 in Orange, Ohio. Other famous "lefties" include Caesar, Napoleon, Michelangelo, Albert Einstein, Ben Franklin, and Leonardo da Vinci. Ten percent of the population is left-handed. Find out how many people in your class are left-handed.

November 20

American astronomer Edwin Powell Hubble was born in Marshfield, Missouri, on this day in 1889. In the early 1900s, Hubble worked at Mount Wilson Observatory near Pasadena, California. In 1923, he studied the brightness of certain stars that had appeared in a photograph. He discovered that these stars were not part of the Milky Way; they were part of a different galaxy.

If you could travel to a different galaxy, would you? Why or why not?

To learn more about Edwin Hubble's work, read *Telescopes and Observatories* by Heather Couper and Nigel Henbest.

As a tribute to Edwin Hubble, the Hubble Space Telescope was named for him. In 1990, astronauts on the Space Shuttle *Discovery* sent the Hubble Telescope into space. With this telescope, astronomers hoped to study other galaxies. Unfortunately, since it was put into space, this telescope has had many problems. To learn more about how astronomers use telescopes to study faraway planets and distant galaxies, look up "telescope" in an encyclopedia or other reference book.

November is International Creative Child and Adult Month. This is a month to help people realize that they can improve and develop their creativity. It's also a month to let people know that being creative can reduce stress and increase well-being.

With your class, think of a creative project you can do together. *Examples*: Create a piece of artwork to hang in the school hallway, or write a play and put on a production for the school.

RESOURCE

Telescopes and Observatories by Heather Couper and Nigel Henbest (New York: Franklin Watts, 1987).

November 21

One of the richest women in America's history was born on this day in 1835 in New Bedford, Maine. Hetty Green managed all of her own financial transactions. She was worth over $100 million dollars. She died in New York City on July 3, 1916.

 Write what you'd do with $100 million dollars.

 Today is World Hello Day. It's a day set aside to promote peace through communication. Today, everyone is encouraged to greet ten people. People in more than 125 countries participate in this annual activity. If you'd like more information about this day, send a letter to:

World Hello Day
Box 993
Omaha, NE 68101

 To celebrate World Hello Day, say "hello" to someone you don't know very well. Greet a person in another class, a school secretary, or a new student.

 Greetings between people differ throughout the world. In some parts of the world people greet each other by saying, "Have you been at peace during the night?" In many countries, people bow to one another as a greeting. Hindus use the namaste (na-MAS-tay) gesture when they bow. To do this gesture, place your palms together. Nod your head slightly and say, "namaste" as you bow. Practice this Hindu greeting.

November 22

Billie Jean Moffit King was born on this day in 1943 in Long Beach, California. She is an American tennis player who won her first tournament at the age of 13. She won her first Wimbledon title at the age of 17. She campaigned to make women's prize money in tennis equal with the prize money that men won. She became the fist sportswoman to earn $100,000 in a single year.

 Write about a sport you enjoy playing.

 On this day in 1906, the International Radio Telegraphic Convention meeting was held in Berlin, Germany. At the meeting, the letters "SOS" were chosen as the signal for help. Contrary to popular opinion, the letters don't stand for anything. They are simply easy to send in the dots and dashes of Morse Code.

Write about a time you needed to send for help.

 Morse Code is a way to send messages over telegraph wires. The code uses a series of dots and dashes. Three short dots stand for the letter "S" and three long dashes stand for the letter "O." In Morse Code, "SOS" looks like this:

To find out how to use other letters in Morse Code, look up "Morse Code" in an encyclopedia or other reference book.

 On this date in 1819, English author George Eliot (whose real name was Mary Ann Evans) was born. In the early 1800s, people had a hard time accepting the fact that women could write books. Mary Ann wrote her novels using the name George Eliot so that companies would publish her work.

Have you ever had trouble getting something done because people thought you couldn't do it? Tell the class about your experience.

November 23

On this day in 1939, the Montgomery Ward Company decided to create something that their store Santa Claus could give to children. Robert May, an advertising copywriter, wrote a poem about a reindeer with a shiny nose. The reindeer uses his glowing nose to guide Santa's sleigh on a foggy Christmas Eve. May originally called his reindeer Rollo, but it was later changed to Rudolph. Montgomery Ward's Santa Claus gave copies of the poem to children who came to talk to him.

 Pretend that you've been asked to create a new character for the upcoming holiday season. Write about what you'd choose.

 Draw a picture of Rudolph the Red Nosed Reindeer getting ready for the holiday season.

 After World War II, Johnny Marks wrote a song about Rudolph. Gene Autry originally recorded it. Today, the total record sales have passed the $1 billion mark. Read *Rudolph the Red Nosed Reindeer* by Robert May. Then listen to the song. How does May's story differ from Marks' song?

 The four Sundays leading up to Christmas are called Advent. In Christian religions, people begin preparing for Christmas during Advent. During this time, everyone can prepare for the December holidays. Make a list of the things you'd like to do before the end of December.

RESOURCES

"Rudolph the Red Nosed Reindeer" recorded by Gene Autry, found in *Billboard's Greatest Christmas Hits: 1935-1954* recording (Rhino Records, 1989).

Rudolph the Red Nosed Reindeer by Robert May (Cambridge, Massachusetts: Applewood Books, 1990).

November 24

Frances Hodgson Burnett, a children's author, was born on this day in 1849. Burnett was born in England but moved to Knoxville, Tennessee, with her family when she was 16 years old. Burnett wrote many novels, but her most popular books were the ones she wrote for children, including *The Secret Garden* and *A Little Princess*.

 Pretend you're a children's author. Write about how you'd make your stories interesting to young children.

 In 1911, Frances Hodgson Burnett published *The Secret Garden*. It's the story of Mary Lennox, a spoiled girl who is sent to live with her uncle after her parents die. Slowly, Mary learns to make friends and accept her new home. One day, she discovers a door in an old wall; the door opens into a long-forgotten garden. Ask someone to read *The Secret Garden* to you and find out what happens when Mary walks through the door.

 On this day in 1888, Dale Carnegie was born in Maryville, Missouri. In 1936, he published a book called *How to Win Friends and Influence People*. Since that first edition, the book has sold almost 5 million copies. Write about how you make friends.

 Thayendanegea, a Mohawk Indian chief, was born in 1742 and died on this date in 1807. In 1777, he was a captain in the British Army and fought on the British side in the American Revolution. After the war, Thayendanegea moved to Ontario and established the Six Nation Reserve along the Grand River. He later translated the Anglican Book of Common Prayer and the Gospel of Mark into the Mohawk language. To learn more about this chief, look up "Thayendanegea" in an encyclopedia or other reference book.

....

RESOURCE

The Secret Garden by Frances Hodgson Burnett (New York: Dell Publishing Company, 1911).

....

NoVeMBer 25

Today is Independence Day in the Republic of Suriname, an independent nation in northeast South America on the Atlantic Ocean. The people who live in Suriname are mostly Indonesian, Creoles, Asian, and Indians. In 1975, Suriname gained full independence from the Netherlands and became a member of the United Nations.

 Write about a time when you were independent and on your own.

 Every day, loggers and land developers destroy plants and animals in the world's rain forests. Many species are in danger of becoming extinct. In South America, people are working to save the rain forest. They are trying to use the rain forest's resources instead of destroying them. Find out more about the destruction of this natural resource in *Tropical Rain Forests* by Cornelia F. Mutel and Mary M. Rodgers.

 Marc Brown is a children's author who was born on this day in 1946. Read his book, *Arthur's Thanksgiving*; it's especially appropriate for this time of year. Brown has two sons, Tolon and Tucker. He hides their names in every Arthur book he writes.

 Join the Arthur Fan Club and Reading Association. You'll receive a membership card and newsletter. Send a letter and a self-addressed, stamped envelope to:

Arthur Fan Club
c/o Little, Brown and Company
34 Beacon Street
Boston, MA 02106

....

RESOURCES

Tropical Rain Forests by Cornelia F. Mutel and Mary M. Rodgers (Minneapolis: Lerner Publications, 1991).

Arthur's Thanksgiving by Marc Brown (Boston: Little, Brown, 1983).

....

NoVeMBer 26

In 1789, President George Washington proclaimed this day to be Thanksgiving Day. Congress had recommended a day of public thanksgiving and prayer. In 1863, President Abraham Lincoln proposed that Thanksgiving be celebrated on the last Thursday in November. In 1939, President Franklin D. Roosevelt moved Thanksgiving Day to the fourth—but not the last—Thursday of November. Since people usually didn't start their holiday shopping until after Thanksgiving, he moved the date up a week to help businesses. Roosevelt's change made the holiday shopping season one week longer.

Do you think the holiday shopping season needs to be one week longer? Why or why not?

 Keep a record of this Thanksgiving. Write down what your family did on this day. Write down any special traditions your family has for this day. Keep your list in a special place and include a picture that was taken on that day. Next year, you can remember what your family did and add any new traditions you may have started.

 To celebrate Thanksgiving Day, many people gather together for a turkey dinner. Some families save the turkey's wishbone and let it dry out. Then two people (each holding one section of the wishbone) make a wish and pull the wishbone apart. The person who ends up with the largest portion of the wishbone will have a wish granted. Write about what you'd wish for on the wishbone. Why would you wish for that?

 Do you think people should eat turkey on Thanksgiving Day? Do you think people should eat some other meat—or no meat at all? Talk about your views with your class.

November 27

In 1983, Cabbage Patch dolls were a huge fad. On this day all over the United States, thousands of people lined up in front of stores waiting to purchase the dolls. The Zayre Corporation had 275 stores throughout the country and stocked their stores with 60,000 Cabbage Patch dolls. All the dolls were sold in less than 30 minutes.

 Write about your favorite doll or toy.

 Cabbage Patch dolls are soft, cuddly, chubby toys with hair made out of yarn and soft fabric skin. They come in all sizes, from newborns to toddlers. Why do you think Cabbage Patch dolls were so popular? Ask your classmates if they ever had a Cabbage Patch doll.

 On this day in 1942, rock and roll star Jimi Hendrix was born in Seattle, Washington. In the 1960s, he changed rock music with his wild guitar playing style. In the 1960s, people began saying things like "groovy" (which meant terrific), "heavy" (which meant something was really meaningful), and "flower power" (which was the idea of changing the world through peace and love). Make a list of any special words and phrases you use and their definitions.

 At this time of year, many cities and towns in the United States organize holiday light parades. Some cities ask all the office buildings to keep their lights on for one night in late November or early December. Other places have parades at night—all the floats are decorated with colorful lights. Write about how you'd like to see your city or town celebrate the holiday season.

November 28

The Japanese poet Matsuo Basho died on this day in 1694 in Osaka, Japan. He developed the three-line Haiku poem. Basho wrote both cheerful and sad Haiku. Here's a translation of one of his poems: "I am one/Who eats his breakfast/Gazing at the Morning-glories."

 Write about what you do while you eat your breakfast.

In English, the Japanese poetry form Haiku has 17 syllables. The first line of the poem has five syllables, the second line has seven syllables, and the third line has five syllables. Write your own simple Haiku poem. You could write about the weather or your favorite book.

 Marie Manning was born in Washington, D.C., in 1873. Using the name Beatrice Fairfax, she wrote an advice column for the *New York Evening Journal* from 1898 to 1905. In the 1930s, she began the column again and continued writing it through the 1940s. She was the first journalist to write an advice column.

Look through the newspaper and find an advice column. After reading the column, decide whether you agree with the advice given.

 Create a thank-you note to give to the person who prepared your Thanksgiving meal. Fold a piece of construction or notebook paper in half and decorate the front with fall colors. Inside, write a short message thanking that person for the good meal.

November 29

Author Madeleine L'Engle was born on this day in 1918. One of her most popular books is *A Wrinkle in Time*. It's about three kids who travel to a strange world to rescue one of their parents. The book, however, wasn't an instant success. "It took two years of rejection slips from 20 or 30 publishers before I found a grown-up editor who could understand *A Wrinkle in Time*," remembered L'Engle. Once published, it became immediately popular with children.

 Write about a time you were rejected or told you couldn't do something, yet you kept going.

 Another children's author was born on this day. Clive Staples Lewis, better known as C. S. Lewis, was born in Belfast, Ireland, in 1898. He wrote the "Chronicles of Narnia" series. These books begin when Peter, Edmund, Susan, and Lucy climb inside a large wardrobe. As they stumble past the coats stored there, they find a door to Narnia, a special world filled with strange creatures.

Find out what a wardrobe cabinet looks like. Draw your version of the one that begins the Narnia stories.

 On this day in 1983, scientists on the Massachusetts coast saw a 45-ton female right whale with a calf. This sighting gave scientists new hope for the future of this rare breed. Right whales were the mainstay of the whaling industry and, because of this, are near extinction today.

Create a whale poster. Find out the different types of whales and their sizes.

 America's first official record keeper was Charles Thomson. He was born on this day in 1729 in Ireland. Thomson was chosen secretary of the First Continental Congress on September 5, 1774. He wrote down everything Congress did—he had tens of thousand of records.

The record keeper, or secretary, of a club or group keeps track of what happens at each meeting. Be a record keeper for your class. Write down everything that happens today. At the end of the day, compare your records to your classmates'. Do they remember events the same way you did?

November 30

On this day in 1924, Shirley Chisholm was born in Brooklyn, New York. After she graduated from college, Chisholm worked as a teacher in New York's nursery schools and day care centers. In the early 1960s, she decided to become a politician. In November 1968, she became the first African-American woman to be elected to the U.S. Congress.

 Write down five things you like about your teacher. Do you think he or she would make a good politician?

 Sir Winston Leonard Spencer Churchill was born on this date in 1874 at Blenheim Palace, Oxfordshire, England. He was born in a palace because his father was a duke. Churchill was a British statesman, political figure, and author. He was England's prime minister from 1940 to 1945 and 1951 to 1953.

Churchill once wrote, "Everyone has his day and some days last longer than others." Write about the longest day you can remember. Why did it seem so long?

 Winston Churchill knew many words—he knew more words than the average person. Increase your vocabulary. Find five words in the dictionary that are new to you. Learn to pronounce and spell them. Use them in sentences.

 Say good-bye to November and hello to December. Create your own ceremony to finish out the month and begin a new one.

December 1

On this day in 1955 in Montgomery, Alabama, Rosa Parks made history. She refused to give up her bus seat to a white man. In 1955, African-Americans were only supposed to sit at the back of buses, but on this day there were no seats left at the back. Parks sat down at the front and refused to give up her seat. The police arrested Parks. Her action began the Civil Rights movement of the 1950s.

 Write about a time you stood up for a person or an idea that was different or unpopular. How did you feel about taking this risk? Were you afraid you would lose friends?

 After Rosa Parks' arrest, African-Americans refused to ride buses in Montgomery. They wanted to change the law that said only white people could sit at the front. To learn more about Rosa Parks and the beginnings of the Civil Rights movement, read *Rosa Parks* by Eloise Greenfield.

 This day begins a month of celebrations. During December, people celebrate Hanukkah, Christmas, or Kwanza. Jewish people celebrate the eight-day festival of Hanukkah, the Feast of Lights. Christians celebrate Christmas, which commemorates the birth of Jesus. African-Americans celebrate Kwanza, which recognizes the traditional African harvest festivals.

Write about a celebration you enjoy. What does your family do to participate in the celebration?

 Plan a December holidays program with your class. Include the traditions of Hanukkah, Christmas, and Kwanza. Find out more about the holidays you aren't familiar with and include their traditions in your program.

RESOURCE

Rosa Parks by Eloise Greenfield (New York: Harper & Row Junior Books, 1973).

december 2

Have you ever wondered how things work? David Macaulay wrote books for people who want to know what things look like from a different point of view. He was born on this day in England in 1946. In his book, *The Way Things Work*, he explains how hundreds of machines and devices work. He explains such things as compact discs and parking meters.

 Look around your classroom and find a gadget, device, or machine that you'd like to learn more about. Write about what catches your interest and why you want to know more.

 Georges Pierre Seurat was a French artist born on this date in 1859 in Paris, France. Instead of painting with lines and strokes, Seurat painted people and things using thousands of dots. His most famous painting is called *A Sunday Afternoon on the Island of LaGrande Jette.*

Create a painting using Seurat's style. Use a paint brush or cotton swab and bright paint colors. Dip the brush or cotton swab in paint and make your painting by dotting the paper. A group of green dots could make the leaves of a tree. A group of brown dots could make the tree trunk. Use your imagination to create a masterpiece.

 Look at a color photograph printed in a magazine or newspaper. Use a magnifying glass to see how dots form the picture.

 Maria Callas was one of the world's most famous opera singers. She sang soprano, which is the highest female voice. Callas made her operatic debut in Verona, Italy, when she was 24 years old. In 1956, she performed at the Metropolitan Opera in New York City for the first time. Callas was born in New York City on this date in 1923. She died in 1977. To learn more about opera, read *Opera! What's All the Screaming About?* by Roger Englander.

RESOURCES

The Way Things Work by David Macaulay (Boston: Houghton Mifflin, 1988).

Opera! What's All the Screaming About? by Roger Englander (New York: Walker and Company, 1983).

december 3

On this day in 1965, figure skater Katarina Witt was born in Karl-Marx-Stadt in the former East Germany. When she was five years old, Witt began skating on an ice rink near her kindergarten. The people in her town saw that she had talent and made sure that she trained with the best coaches. Witt worked to perfect her skating routines. Her hard work paid off when she won gold medals at the 1984 and 1988 Winter Olympic games.

 Figure skaters often wear costumes decorated with bright colors and sequins. What is the most elaborate costume you've ever seen?

The gas neon was first used to light up a sign on this day in 1910. Scientists figured out that if they filled a tube with neon and sent an electrical current through it, the gas would glow. If you could make a neon sign that the whole world could see, what would it say? Draw your sign and color it in neon colors.

On this day in 1968, the National Women's Hall of Fame was founded in Seneca Falls, New York. The hall of fame's purpose is to honor women who have made contributions to the arts, athletics, business, education, government, the humanities, philanthropy, and science. If you'd like to know more about the hall of fame and the women who are honored there, write to:

National Women's Hall of Fame
76 Fall Street
Seneca Falls, NY 13148

On the night of December 3, 1984, toxic fumes leaked from the Union Carbide chemical plant in Bhopal, India. The deadly gas that escaped killed more than 2,000 people and injured 200,000 more.

Talk about how people can prevent accidents. Choose an accidental event like a fall in the bathtub. With your class, think of ways that you could avoid this accident. Think about other accidents and ways to prevent them.

december 4

President Woodrow Wilson boarded an ocean liner headed for France on this date in 1918. He traveled to France to attend the peace conference at Versailles, located near Paris. He became the first U.S. president to visit a foreign country while in office.

Write about why world leaders visit foreign countries.

Look through past issues of newspapers and news magazines for articles about the current president. Find out where the president has traveled.

Lillian Russell was an American singer and actress who appeared in many musicals, operas, and plays in the 1880s and 1890s. She was born on this day in 1861 in Clinton, Iowa. In 1913, Russell toured the country, giving a lecture titled "How to Live a Hundred Years." What's your advice on how to live a hundred years? Write a one-minute speech to give to your class.

What's your favorite holiday song? Draw a picture that illustrates a part of the song.

december 5

On this day in 1986, a new federal government regulation went into effect. The new rule said that office areas should be divided into smoking and nonsmoking areas. Large areas used by many employees, such as auditoriums, conference rooms, classrooms, and libraries, would be nonsmoking areas.

Write about how you feel when people around you smoke.

Many scientific reports link lung cancer in nonsmokers to smokers' smoke, which is called *secondhand smoke*. Create some "Please Don't Smoke" signs so that smokers will know not to smoke around you.

Martin Van Buren, the eighth president of the United States, was born on this day in the village of Kinderhook, New York. One of his nicknames was "Old Kinderhook" or "O.K.," because of where he was born. His supporters in the 1836 presidential campaign used those initials, and soon anything that was "all right" was described as "O.K." After Van Buren was elected, he used the initials to sign bills.

Today, the expression "O.K." is used around the world. People who don't know another word of English understand "O.K." Make a list of things you think are okay.

 In the Netherlands, Sinterklass Avond (SIN-ter-clahs AH-font) means Saint Nicholas Eve. Dutch children look forward to December 5, when Saint Nicholas travels from house to house delivering gifts. Before they go to bed, the children fill wooden shoes with straw and carrots for the white horse that Sinterklass rides. They hope that Saint Nicholas will fill their wooden shoes with goodies.

Pretend that Sinterklass will visit your house tonight. Draw a picture of your shoes before and after Sinterklass has visited.

december 6

Today is St. Nicholas' Day. Saint Nicholas, who lived in the Middle Ages, loved children. In one legend, he brought three boys back to life. In another, he secretly gave gold to three poor girls. From this kind act came the custom of giving presents on the Eve of St. Nicholas. This custom was later transferred to Christmas Eve.

 Write about some of the things you do to prepare for the holiday season.

 In Holland, Dutch children wake up to find toys and treats in their shoes. According to

the story, the Dutch Sinterklass travels on horseback from Spain and enters houses by climbing down the chimney. Because he's a Roman Catholic bishop, Sinterklass is not married. Black Pete, Sinterklass' servant, always rides with his master on the eve of December 6.

How does the legend of Sinterklass compare to the United States' Santa Claus? Talk with your classmates and teacher about the similarities and differences. *Example*: Sinterklass lives in Spain; Santa Clause lives at the North Pole.

 Some children believe that eight tiny reindeer pull Santa's sleigh. Create one of the most famous reindeers—Rudolph the Red Nosed Reindeer. You'll need white, light brown, dark brown, and red construction paper; ruler; scissors; glue; and a marker.

With the light brown paper, cut out a rectangle. With the red paper, cut out a small triangle. On the dark brown paper, spread your right hand out and trace it. Now trace your left hand. Cut out your tracings; these will be the reindeer antlers. Glue the triangle in the middle of the rectangle and glue the antlers on the top of the rectangle, one on each corner. Use the marker to draw a reindeer face.

 Florida's Everglades National Park was dedicated on this day in 1947. It's the third largest national park in the United States. The park stretches from Lake Okeechobee to Florida Bay in southeast Florida. Visitors to the park can see vast swamps, saw grass, hammocks, and coastal mangrove forests. Many protected species such as the alligator, crocodile, egret, and bald eagle live in the park.

For more information on what you can see at this national park, write to:

Everglades National Park
P.O. Box 279
Homestead, FL 33030

december 7

O n this day in 1973, novelist and short story writer Willa Cather was born in Winchester, Virginia. When she was young, her family settled in Red Cloud, Nebraska. She grew up around immigrant farmers, who later became the subject of her books. Many of her characters loved the land, were loyal to their families, and struggled with nature.

 Write about a character in a book you've read. Did you like this character? Why or why not?

 Answer these questions to create a character that you could use in your own short story.

■ What is your character? (*Examples*: girl, boy, hippopotamus, giraffe, eraser)

■ What does your character look like? (*Examples*: has long red hair, wears a small hat, has two brown eyes)

■ What does your character like to do? (*Examples*: drinks from a straw, visits toy stores, reads books in the attic)

■ What's your character's first and last name?

 Create some stationery to give as a gift during this month of giving. You'll need clean paper about 8" x 6" in any color you choose and markers, crayons, or paint. Decorate the edges of the paper with winter scenes or a colorful pattern. Be sure to leave enough room so that someone can write a letter on the stationery.

 This is the anniversary of the attack on Pearl Harbor. On December 7, 1941, nearly 200 Japanese aircraft attacked Pearl Harbor, Hawaii. The raid lasted a little more than one hour. Almost all of the U.S. Pacific Fleet was anchored there; many lives and ships were lost. After the attack, the United States entered World War II. President Franklin D. Roosevelt requested a Declaration of War. It was approved by Congress on this day in 1941. To find out more about why America entered World War II, look up "Pearl Harbor" in an encyclopedia.

december 8

I n 1843, the first Christmas card was produced. Although there is some disagreement, many people believe that the British artist John C. Horsley created the first Christmas card for Henry Cole, a government official. A company published and marketed one thousand copies of the card.

 Write a verse or a message that you'd like to include in a holiday card.

 Eli Whitney was a farmer, college student, inventor, teacher, and gun maker. He began the development of modern industrial methods. He was born on this day in 1765 in Westboro, Massachusetts. Whitney was fascinated with mechanical things. In 1794, he invented the cotton gin, which rapidly separated cotton fibers from seeds. Separating cotton had been done by hand before the cotton gin's invention. Later, Whitney manufactured guns for the U.S. Army. He began the mass production of rifles with interchangeable parts.

Today, many items are made with interchangeable parts. Make a list of things that could be fixed by replacing a broken piece.

 Eli Whitney, a northerner, invented the cotton gin while he was visiting his friend Catherine Littlefield Greene, a southerner. Some people believe that Greene actually invented the new way to separate cotton. Greene lived in the south and knew that it took a long time to separate the cotton fibers from the seeds. Some people think that she gave Whitney her plans for the new invention. To learn more about Eli Whitney, read *Eli Whitney: Great Inventor* by Jean Latham.

 Mexican painter Diego Rivera was born on this date in 1886. During his career, Rivera painted murals, which are large pictures or decorations. Painters create their murals on walls or ceilings. One of Rivera's murals is three stories high. In his paintings, he tried to show the hardships of the Mexican people.

Where could you paint a mural? Is there a blank wall in your school cafeteria that could use some decoration? Talk with your class about where you could put a mural. Work together to come up with a plan for your mural. Get permission before you start painting. If you can't paint on a wall, create your class mural on large sheets of paper taped together.

RESOURCE

Eli Whitney: Great Inventor by Jean Latham (New York: Chelsea House Publishers, 1991).

december 9

Grace Brewster Murray Hopper was born on this day in 1906. During World War II, she enlisted in a branch of the U.S. Navy called WAVES (Women Accepted for Volunteer Emergency Service). While in the Navy, she helped to standardize the military's computer languages and programs. To help in her work, she developed COBOL, a computer language. In 1983, President Ronald Reagan promoted Hopper to the rank of rear admiral. When she retired from the Navy at age 80, she was the oldest officer on active duty in all of the armed services. Hopper died in 1992.

 Write a few sentences on what you think about computers. Have you ever used one? If so, did you like it? If not, would you want to? Why or why not?

 Emmett Kelly was born on this date in 1898. He performed in circuses as a tramp clown, a hobo, and "Charley Clown." Kelly's costume was old, raggedy clothes and a scruffy beard. He wore a red nose and always had a sad or lonely expression on his face.

Design a clown mask or makeup that you might wear if you performed with a circus. On a large sheet of paper, draw a face. Now decorate the face in any way you'd like. You could paint the whole face white and add a red nose and red cheeks. Or you could paint stripes or polka dots on your face.

Create a clown corner in your classroom. Find pictures of various types of clowns in reference books. Find pictures of other circus performers. Write some clown jokes and riddles.

 On this day in 1848, Joel Chandler Harris was born in Eatonton, Georgia. Harris is famous for his Uncle Remus stories, which were retellings of African-American folk literature. Brer Rabbit is one of his famous characters. Read a modern retelling of Harris' tales in *The Tales of Uncle Remus: The Adventure of Brer Rabbit,* retold by Julius Lester.

RESOURCE

The Tales of Uncle Remus: The Adventure of Brer Rabbit, retold by Julius Lester (New York: Dial Books for Young Readers, 1987).

december 10

Emily Dickinson, one of America's greatest poets, was born in Amherst, Massachusetts, on this day in 1830. She lived by herself in Amherst and stayed away from people. In 1860, Dickinson began writing poems. She wrote simple poems about things that she had never experienced. Here's a line from one of them: "I never saw a moor, I never saw the sea; Yet know I how the heather looks, And what a billow be."

 Write about something you'd like to do—or experience—someday.

 Only seven of Emily Dickinson's poems were published during her lifetime. After her death, her sister Lavinia discovered almost 2,000 more poems written on the backs of envelopes and other scraps of paper. Dickinson had locked them in her drawer.

The poems were published gradually over 50 years, beginning in 1890. To read some of Dickinson's poems, find the book *I'm Nobody! Who Are You? Poems of Emily Dickinson for Children.*

 Try writing a simple four-line poem in the style of Emily Dickinson. You can show your poem to your class, if you like—or you can keep it a secret.

 Author Rumer Godden was born on this date in 1907. Dolls are the main characters in many of her books. One of her stories is a Christmas tale titled *The Story of Holly and Ivy.* The story is about a girl, a doll, and wishing. Ask someone to read the story to you.

RESOURCES

I'm Nobody! Who Are You? Poems of Emily Dickinson for Children by Emily Dickinson, illustrated by Rex Schneider (Owings Mills, Maryland: Stemmer House, 1978).

The Story of Holly and Ivy by Rumer Godden (New York: Viking Penguin, 1985).

december 11

On this day in 1863, astronomer Annie Jump Cannon was born in Dover, Delaware. When she was a young girl, she loved to stargaze through a trapdoor in her attic. She also played with crystals and admired the rainbows they made on the wall. As an astronomer, she classified stars and discovered five novas and 300 new stars.

 Describe a rainbow you've seen either in person or in a picture.

 Use a glass triangular prism to make rainbows on the walls. If you don't have a prism, fill a shallow pan almost full of water. At one end of the pan, place a lamp or flashlight. At the other end of the pan, slant a mirror to create a rainbow on the wall.

 Darken the room and shine a flashlight on a wall to create a light show. Learn to make unusual shadow pictures in the book *The Hand Book: All Kinds of Things to Do With Your Hands* by Lassor Blumenthal.

 Make a yarn wreath to use as a holiday decoration. You'll need a plastic lid, scissors, yarn (any color you want), glue, and some beads.

Cut a medium-sized hole in the center of the plastic lid. Take one end of a long piece of yarn and glue it to one side of the lid. Thread the other end through the hole and around the lid, covering up the spot where you glued the first end. Keep threading the yarn through the center hole and wrapping it around the lid until you've covered the entire lid. If you'd like, add a bead to the yarn before you thread it through the hole as an extra decoration. When the lid is covered, cut the string and tuck it into the back of the wreath. Cut an 8-inch piece of string and thread it through the yarn at the top of your wreath. To hang your wreath, make a loop and tie the ends together.

RESOURCE

The Hand Book: All Kinds of Things to Do With Your Hands by Lassor Blumenthal (New York: Doubleday, 1976).

december 12

Today is Poinsettia Day, a day to look at and enjoy the plants with the bright red leaves. On this date in 1828, Dr. Joel Poinsett brought the first plant from Mexico to the United States. Today, the poinsettia has become a favorite holiday season plant.

 Write about your favorite flower or plant. Why is it your favorite?

 Poinsettias begin to appear during the holiday season. For some people, this is also the time to decorate a tree with ornaments and lights. You can make one type of ornament with small pinecones. You'll also need thin wire; scissors; glue; and glitter, sequins, or small beads.

Twist the wire around the topmost knob of the cone and make a loop for hanging. Place lines or spots of glue all over the cone. Sprinkle the glue with the glitter, sequins, or small beads. Let the glue dry overnight and then hang up your ornament.

 Imagine that you discover a rare and beautiful flower or plant. It will be named after you! Draw your flower or plant and write its name.

 At the center of a flower is the part that makes seeds. To learn how to tell the seed part from the other parts of the plants, read *A First Look at Flowers* by Millicent E. Selsam and Joyce Hunt. This book is full of ideas on how to study and learn about flowers.

RESOURCE

A First Look at Flowers by Millicent E. Selsam and Joyce Hunt (New York: Walker and Company, 1977).

december 13

This is Santa Lucia Day in Sweden. Santa Lucia Day is a time for celebrating and thanking Saint Lucia, the Queen of Light, for returning after the darkness of winter. In some families on Santa Lucia Day, the oldest daughter serves breakfast to the other family members and wears a crown of lighted candles. Many schools, offices, and communities have a Santa Lucia procession. They sing carols that thank the "Queen of Light" for bringing hope at the darkest time of the year.

 Think about someone you'd like to thank. Write a thank-you note to that person.

 Following Santa Lucia Day, many people in Sweden start Christmas preparations. They clean their homes and bake holiday bread and cookies. Ask your classmates what they do to prepare for the holidays. What traditions of theirs do you like?

 Leonard Weisgard was born on this day in 1916 in New Haven, Connecticut. He wrote and illustrated dozens of children's books using watercolors, poster paint, crayons, chalk, and ink. The illustrations he created for Margaret Wise Brown's *Little Island* helped that book win a 1946 Caldecott Medal. Read *Where Does the Butterfly Go When It Rains?* by May Garelick and illustrated by Leonard Weisgard to see some of this artist's work.

 Sir Francis Drake started a voyage around the world on this day in 1577. With 160 men and five ships, Drake spent the next three years sailing around South America to California, across the Pacific and Indian oceans, and finally up the coast of Africa. He became the first person from England to sail around the globe. The story of Drake's adventures is told in the picture book *Sir Francis Drake: His Daring Deeds* by Roy Gerrard.

RESOURCES

Where Does the Butterfly Go When It Rains? by May Garelick, illustrated by Leonard Weisgard (New York: W.R. Scott, 1961).

Sir Francis Drake: His Daring Deeds by Roy Gerrard (New York: Farrar, Straus & Giroux, 1988).

december 14

Roald Amundsen's dog sled expedition reached the South Pole, the farthest south one can go from the equator, on this day in 1911. Amundsen had 4 companions and 52 sled dogs. All 5 explorers and 12 of the dogs returned to the base camp safely. At first, Amundsen had wanted to explore the North Pole, but he found out that an American, Robert E. Peary, had already reached it. He headed for the South Pole instead.

 Take a fantasy voyage to the South Pole. Write a story telling how you'd get there, who you'd meet, and what you'd do to keep warm.

 Much of Antarctica lies under solid ice more than 1,000 meters thick. It is the coldest and most desolate place on Earth. It's also one of the larger continents; Antarctica is larger than the United States and Mexico combined. Scientists recorded the coldest temperature on Earth at the Antarctic. In 1957 and 1958, the temperature dropped to 102 degrees below Fahrenheit.

Experiment to find out the temperature in and around your classroom. You'll need a small thermometer, paper, and a pencil or pen. Hold the thermometer in your hand for a few minutes and then check the temperature. Record that number on your paper. Put the thermometer on a desk and let it sit for about five minutes. What's the temperature now? Put the thermometer near a window or light. Put it by the radiator and then by the classroom door. How does the temperature vary in each of these places?

 Margaret Chase Smith has been a teacher, writer, businessperson, member of Congress, and senator. During her 33 years in Washington, D.C., Smith was present for every roll call and participated in every decision. She has always spoken for a strong, fair government. In 1948, she was responsible for an act that said women would receive equal pay, privileges, and rank in the armed services. She is the only woman to be elected to serve in both the House of Representatives and the Senate. Smith was born on this day in 1897 in Skowhegan, Maine.

Write about your attendance at school. Have you missed any days this year or do you hope to have a perfect attendance record?

 Beginning on this day in 1901, the first Ping-Pong tournament was held. Celebrate this event with this silly game: Line up with friends to push Ping-Pong balls across the carpet or gym floor, using only your nose.

december 15

Each year since 1900, the National Audubon Society has sponsored a winter bird census. From December 15 to January 2, more than 41,000 bird watchers in North and Central America count the birds they see. Scientists assign circular areas 15 miles in diameter to small groups. Those groups identify and count as many birds as they can. Then they try to estimate how many birds there are altogether.

 Write about why it's important to keep track of the bird population.

 If you'd like more information about the Audubon Christmas Bird Count, send a letter to:

The National Audubon Society
950 Third Avenue
New York, NY 10022

 The study of birds is called ornithology. You can be an amateur ornithologist by observing the different types of birds that live around your neighborhood. Keep track of the birds that stay around your community during the winter months. Use a bird book to help you identify the birds' names. Keep a list of the birds you see and add to it as you spot new birds.

 Today is the birthday of American billionaire John Paul Getty. He was one of the richest Americans of his time. Getty was born in Minneapolis, Minnesota, in 1892. During the Depression, he was able to use his cash to buy things that others could not. John Paul Getty lived in a 73-room mansion in London, England. He died on June 6, 1976.

Write about how your life would be different if you were a billionaire.

december 16

Margaret Mead was an American anthropologist and author known for her studies of primitive people who lived in the southwest Pacific Ocean area. She was born in Philadelphia on this day in 1901. Mead collected information about the people she studied. She observed the way different people worked and played. She showed that people are affected by the culture they live in.

 Write a few sentences on something you'd want an anthropologist to know about you.

 An anthropologist is a person who studies the customs, beliefs, and development of a group of people. Be a classroom anthropologist. Observe your classmates and write down your observations. Watch what others do while they are thinking or answering a question. Watch the different ways people act when someone new is around or when they're talking to friends.

 George Santayana, a philosopher and author, was born in Madrid, Spain, on this day in 1863. When he was nine, he and his family emigrated to the United States. In 1912, he returned to Europe and settled in Italy. Santayana once said, "Those who cannot remember the past are condemned to repeat it."

Write about why it is important to learn about historical events.

 The Mexican celebration of Las Posadas (Lahs Poh-SAAH-thahs) begins today and lasts for nine days. Each evening, a group of friends reenact the journey of Mary and Joseph, Jesus' parents. They search for a posada or inn. They knock at their friends'

doors for a place to rest. Their friends invite them in for games and fun. One of the special activities is breaking a piñata that's filled with treats, including paper banners called papel picado.

Create your own paper banner. You'll need a rectangular piece of tissue paper, scissors, string, and glue. Follow the instructions shown in the illustration.

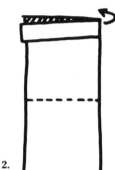

1.

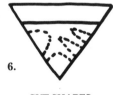

2.

3.

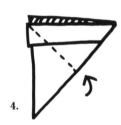

4.

5.

6.

CUT SHAPES

7.

UNFOLD AND HANG

december 17

On this day in 1760, Deborah Sampson Gannett was born in Plympton, Massachusetts. During the Revolutionary War, she used the name Robert Shurtleff Sampson and enlisted in the Fourth Massachusetts Regiment. In 1783, she developed a fever and was hospitalized. There, the doctors found out that she was a woman. Soon after, the army discharged her. After leaving the army, she made public appearances dressed in her fighting uniform and talked to people about her military experiences.

 Write about a time you wished you were someone else.

 On this day in 1790, the Aztec Calendar—one of the wonders of the western hemisphere—was found. Workers repairing Mexico City's Central Plaza unearthed the stone calendar. The centuries-old, intricately carved stone was 11 feet, 8 inches in diameter. It weighed nearly 25 tons. The Aztecs created the calendar as a monument to the sun. They buried it along with other Aztec idols soon after the Spanish conquest in 1521. The calendar's 52-year cycle recorded many Aztec ceremonies.

Write about a special day you'd like to remember.

 The Aztecs carved their calendar in A.D. 1479. This extraordinary time-counting tablet originally stood in the Great Temple of the Aztecs. It remained hidden for 311 years. Today, it is over 500 years old. To learn more about the calendar and the people who created it, read *The Mighty Aztecs* by Gene S. Stuart or *Aztecs* by Jill Hughes.

 Create a birthday calendar to keep track of your friends' birthdays. You'll need pens, markers, or crayons and 12 sheets of lined paper, with the lines numbered from 1 to 31. (Just number one sheet and make several photocopies. For the shorter months, cross out the extra days.) At the top of each sheet of paper, write the name of a month. Now fill in the birthdays of your friends, parents, brothers and sisters, grandparents, and anyone else special in your life. (Don't forget yourself.) As each month begins, you can look at your calendar and see who's celebrating a birthday that month. Add new birthdays as you make new friends. Because this calendar includes dates but not days, you can use it for many years.

RESOURCES

The Mighty Aztecs by Gene S. Stuart (Washington, DC: National Geographic Society, 1981).

Aztecs by Jill Hughes (New York: Gloucester Press, 1979).

december 18

Movie director and producer Steven Spielberg was born on this day in Cincinnati, Ohio, in 1947. He is a moviemaker whose famous films include *Jaws*, *E.T.*, *Close Encounters of the Third Kind*, *Poltergeist*, *Raiders of the Lost Ark*, and *Jurassic Park*. His teachers didn't think he was a good student. When he was young, Spielberg spent most of his time going to the movies. He became interested in moviemaking when he used his father's eight-millimeter camera to create his own films.

Write about a Steven Spielberg movie you saw and liked. If you haven't seen any of his movies, write about another movie you have enjoyed.

Pretend you're going to make a movie about your life. List the names of the characters in your movie. *Examples*: you, your parents, best friend, grandparents, a pet, your teacher. Think about an opening scene for your movie. *Examples*: Your movie might begin by showing you as a newborn baby or on your first day of kindergarten. List the other events in your life that you'd include in a movie about you.

On this day in 1929, musician Toshiko Akiyoshi was born in Ryoyo, Manchuria, China. While living in Japan, Toshiko developed an interest in jazz. In 1956, she came to the United States to study this type of music and to play in clubs. In 1984, she led her own orchestra called Toshiko Akiyoshi's New York Jazz Orchestra. Toshiko is one of very few women who have led jazz orchestras.

Listen to a jazz recording. Do you like it? Why or why not?

Antonio Stradivari, a celebrated violin maker, was born about 1644 and died in Cremona, Italy, on this day in 1737. Musicians consider the violins he made to be perfect musical instruments. In his career, he made more than 1,000 instruments. Half of his handmade violins are still around today.

Invite a violinist to your class. Perhaps your school's music teacher knows a violinist from a local orchestra who will come and demonstrate the art of playing the violin.

deceMBer 19

On this day in 1958, the U.S. Earth satellite *Atlas* broadcast the first radio voice message from space. President Dwight Eisenhower had recorded a 58-word message to Americans that was relayed to the satellite. In his message, he wished for peace on Earth and good will to all people.

If you could send a message that everyone in the United States would hear, what would you say?

A satellite is an object that moves around the Earth, moon, or other bodies in space. Scientists use satellites to forecast the weather and connect radio and television communications around the world. A satellite that scientists have sent out of Earth's orbit can provide information about conditions in space.

Find out more about satellites by looking up "satellite" in an encyclopedia or other reference book.

British Arctic explorer Sir William Peary was born on this date in 1890. He was the first man to reach the North Pole, a feat he accomplished in 1909. The Arctic includes the Arctic Ocean, Greenland, and the northernmost regions of Asia, Europe, and North America. These lands partially surround the ice-covered Arctic Ocean and vary from low coastal plains to high ice plateaus and mountains.

The North Pole is a *very* cold place. List five things you do to keep warm. If you live where the weather is hot, list five ways you try to keep cool.

The official first day of winter is approaching. In some areas, the temperature falls and so does snow. Windows are covered with white frost. When this occurs, children all over the world have different ways of explaining it. In Russia, children say that Mother Frost has been there. In Germany, it's Father Frost. In the United States, children say Jack Frost has painted the windows. In Norse mythology, the son of the god of winds was called Jokul Frosti. Maybe that's where Jack Frost came from. What other winter legends do you know? With your class, talk about other winter legends you've heard.

december 20

The Louisiana Purchase, one of the greatest real estate deals in history, was completed on this day in 1803. The United States bought the large area of land from France for $15 million. In a ceremony in New Orleans, the people took down the flag of France and replaced it with a U.S. flag. The 825,000 square miles of territory spans from the Mississippi River to the Rocky Mountains. All or part of 15 states were formed from this territory.

 Write about something really *big* you would buy if you could.

 Using a blank map of the United States, label each of the 15 states included in the sale. The states were: Montana, North Dakota, South Dakota, Wyoming, Minnesota, Nebraska, Iowa, Colorado, Kansas, Missouri, New Mexico, Arkansas, Texas, Oklahoma, and Louisiana.

 The Louisiana Purchase doubled the area of the United States. To learn more about this real estate deal, read *The Louisiana Purchase* by Robert Tallant.

 During this holiday season, many people exchange gifts—so it's the perfect time to create your own wrapping paper. All you'll need are some large sheets of paper (newsprint, butcher paper) and markers, crayons, or paint. Decorate your paper with a holiday theme. *Examples*: include green trees, white snowflakes, or write the word "Happy Holidays" over and over on your paper in different colors. If you like creating your own wrapping paper, draw some that could be used to wrap a birthday gift (include a birthday cake with candles or balloons).

R E S O U R C E

The Louisiana Purchase by Robert Tallant (New York: Random House, 1952).

december 21

The first day of winter begins on or about December 21. Today, the sun is at its greatest distance from the equator. In the Northern Hemisphere, today is the shortest day of the year. In the Arctic Circle, the sun will not appear at all today.

 Write about the sights, sounds, smells, tastes, and the way things feel during this time of year.

 Many people in the Northern Hemisphere look forward to this day. It means that slowly the days will get longer. Read a winter story to celebrate the beginning of a new season. *Up North in Winter* by Deborah Hartley is a good choice.

 Write a winter poem. Down the left side of your paper, write the word WINTER. Begin the first line of your poem with a word that begins with a "W" and the second line with a word that begins with an "I." Keep going until you have a six-line poem.

 While people living in the Northern Hemisphere get ready to wear warmer coats, people in the Southern Hemisphere head to the beach. In Australia and other countries in the Southern Hemisphere, today is the first day of summer. Pretend you're spending the holiday on the warm, sunny shores of Australia or New Zealand. Draw a picture of your holiday picnic on the beach.

RESOURCE

Up North in Winter by Deborah Hartley (New York: Dutton Children's Books, 1986).

december 22

Hanukkah is a Jewish holiday that's observed during midwinter. Jewish people celebrate the time long ago when their ancestors rebelled against a Syrian king and retook the Temple of Jerusalem. When they rededicated the temple, they found that there was only enough oil to light their lamp for one day. Amazingly, however, it stayed lit for eight days.

 Write about something you thought was amazing.

 Each day during Hanukkah, people light one candle on the eight-branch Menorah, which represents the oil lamp. Draw eight candles on a sheet of paper to represent the candles in a Menorah. Do not show them lit. "Light" one each day by writing a message of peace on the candle. Then "light" the candle by coloring it yellow.

 During Hanukkah, people continue to work during the day but at night they sing, play games, and tell jokes and riddles. Spinning a dreidel is one of the games Jewish children play. (A dreidel is a top with four sides; each side has a different Hebrew letter on it.) To play this game, each player starts out with the same number of items (*examples*: pennies, nuts, beans) and puts one of the items in the center. Each player takes turns spinning the dreidel and, depending on where the dreidel lands, either puts or takes something from the pile. When the center pot is empty, everyone adds one item to the pot.

To create a simple dreidel, you'll need tagboard, a marker, scissors, and a pencil. Cut a two-inch square out of the tagboard. With the marker, divide the square into four sections. In one section, print the Hebrew word "Nun" (which means to do nothing); in another section, print "Gimmel" (which means take the whole pot); in the third section, print "Sheen" (which means place an item into the pot); and in the last section, print "Hay" (which means take half the items). Punch a hole in the middle of the square and insert a pencil through the hole. Now it's ready to twirl.

 Children enjoy spinning tops in all parts of the world. In Malaysia and New Guinea, people use tops as charms to ensure a good harvest. Just like circular wreaths, the spinning tops symbolize the seasonal cycles. In many communities, there are even top spinning competitions. You can make your own tops from a variety of materials. Stick a sharpened pencil through the center of a plastic coffee can lid (or through a hole drilled in a large plastic screw top from a jar). Do you notice how the larger and heavier the top is, the longer it will spin?

december 23

Many pilots have flown around the world trying to break speed and distance records. On this day in 1987, two more pilots added their names to the record books. Dick Rutan and Jeana Yeager became the first pilots to fly around the world without stopping to refuel. On December 14, Rutan and Yeager left Edwards Air Force Base in California in their specially designed plane, the *Voyager*. They spent the next 216 hours flying 24,986 miles around the globe without landing once.

 Pretend you're on the *Voyager* flying for 216 hours without landing. Write about the things you'd do to keep yourself from being bored.

 On this day in 1860, poet Harriet Monroe was born in Chicago, Illinois. When she was 28 years old, she wrote *Valeria and Other Poems*, her first book of verse. In 1892, her poem titled "Columbian Ode" was read at the ceremonies dedicating the World Columbian Exposition in Chicago. In October 1912, she began *Poetry: A Magazine of Verse*. That was the first magazine devoted only to poetry.

Create your own poetry magazine. Collect some poetry that you and your classmates have written. With some construction paper, make a front and back cover for your magazine (include a title for your magazine). Gather the poetry pages together and staple them to the front and back covers. Keep your magazine on a shelf in the classroom so anyone can read the book when they want.

 On this day in 1975, the U.S. Congress passed Public Law 94-168, which is known as the Metric Conversion Act of 1975. This act declared that the International System of Units would be the United States' basic system of measurement. By the early 1990s, however, the public law was still not in full use. Today, the United States, Liberia, and Myanam are the only three countries in the world that do not use the metric system. Do you study the metric system in your math class? Do you think we should study the metric system? Tell your class your opinion.

 Create some holiday place mats to decorate your dinner table. You'll need some large sheets of paper (at least 11" X 17"); pens, markers, or paints; clear plastic laminate; scissors; and a stapler.

First, draw some holiday scenes on the paper. *Examples*: a snowy forest, Santa Claus, a bright Menorah, or a colorful holiday wreath. Cover the front and back of the place mat with a sheet of laminate. (The laminate will make the place mats easy to clean.) Cut the laminate so that it is the same size as your sheet of paper. Place the sheet of laminate over your drawing and staple together in the four corners. During a holiday dinner, put one place mat in front of each chair and set plates, forks, knives, and cups on top.

december 24

On Christmas Eve in France, after midnight mass, people invite their families and friends over and eat a large meal. In South America the midnight service is often called the "mass of the rooster." It's named after the rooster that announced the birth of Jesus. In Sweden a Christmas gnome, who lives under the floor of the house or barn, arrives with a bag full of presents. In many countries people joyfully sing carols to celebrate the holiday.

 Write about a time you felt happy and full of joy.

 On December 24 in the village near Lake Hallwil in Switzerland, a wienectchind, or Christmas Child, walks through the town wearing a white robe and carrying a lantern. Six girls wearing rose-colored dresses accompany her. They visit families, sing carols together, and give cakes and cookies to children.

To learn about how people around the world celebrate the holidays, read *Christmas Around the World* by Emily Kelley.

 Create a Christmas candle decoration. You'll need a toilet tissue tube; red, yellow, and green paper; scissors; and glue.

Cover the tube with the red paper and glue it in place. Cut out two flame shapes from the yellow paper and glue each one to the inside of the tube, one on each side. Cut ten leaf shapes from the green paper and red berries from the red paper. Arrange the leaves and berries around the bottom of the candle and glue them in place.

 Christopher "Kit" Carson was an American pioneer, soldier, trapper, and guide. He was born on this day in 1809 in Madison County, Kentucky. When he was 19 years old, he traveled west though the wilderness and became a skillful trailblazer.

A trailblazer marked paths through forests for other pioneers. Imagine when there were no roads, highways, streets, or sidewalks. Write about how you'd travel from one place to another. Would you want to be a trailblazer?

RESOURCE

Christmas Around the World by Emily Kelley (Minneapolis: Carolrhoda Books, 1986).

december 25

Today is Christmas. On this day, Christians believe, Jesus was born nearly 2,000 years ago in Bethlehem. All around the world, people who celebrate this day exchange gifts, get together with friends, and dream of peace on Earth.

 Write down your special holiday wish.

 Practice saying "Happy Holidays" in another language. Wish your friends a good holiday in Spanish or another language of your choice. **Italian**: Buon Natale (Boo-ON Na-TA-leh); **Danish**: Glaedelig Jul (GLA-da-lig U-el); **French**: Joyeaux Noel (Jo-Yeuh No-EL); **Finnish**: Hauskaa Joules (HAUS-ka U-loo-a); **German**: Frohliche Weinachten (FRO-leek-eh VY-nak-tehn); **Spanish**: Feliz Navidad (Feh-LEES Nah-vee-DOD).

 To learn about holiday symbols and celebrations, read one of these books: *Christmas* by Barbara Cooney, *Christmas Time* by Gail Gibbons, or *Holly, Reindeer, and Colored Lights: The Story of the Christmas Symbols* by Edna Barth.

Create a candy cane reindeer to use as a tree decoration or to give to a friend. You'll need a candy cane with a tight plastic covering, two tiny plastic eyes (which you can purchase at a craft store), glue, and a brown pipe cleaner. Find the middle of the pipe cleaner and bend it at the curve of the candy cane. Twist it once around the candy cane to hold it in place. Shape the ends of the pipe cleaner so that they are outstretched like antlers. Glue the eyes near the top of the candy cane's curve.

RESOURCES

Christmas by Barbara Cooney (New York: Harper & Row, 1967).

Christmas Time by Gail Gibbons (New York: Holiday House, 1982).

Holly, Reindeer, and Colored Lights: The Story of the Christmas Symbols by Edna Barth (New York: Clarion Books, 1981).

december 26

Kwanza is an African-American family holiday celebration that recognizes the traditions of African harvest festivals. Each day of the seven days of Kwanza stress a different life value. December 26 emphasizes unmoja, or unity.

 Write about how you and your family can work together to solve problems and communicate better.

 Families celebrate Kwanza by lighting red, green, and black candles, which are set in a *kinara*. The *kinara* is a candleholder that symbolizes the seven principles (unity, self-determination, group effort, group cooperative economics, creativity, purpose, faith). Pick one of the life values celebrated. Write about what that value means to you and why.

 On the seventh and final day of Kwanza, *zawadi* are opened. These are little gifts that family members make for each other. They share these gifts before *karamu*, the special meal. Create a gift of special meaning for one of your family members. *Examples*: Give a free homework-help lesson to a younger brother or sister. Make a bookmark for the person in your family who likes to read. Promise your parents you'll do a certain household chore.

 Ask people in your class if they celebrate Kwanza. If they do, talk about how their families celebrate this holiday.

december 27

Radio City Music Hall in New York City opened on this day in 1932. This auditorium is the world's largest indoor theater—it has seats for 6,200 people. One of the most famous acts at Radio City Music Hall is the dance team known as the Rockettes. In their popular dance routine, the dancers face the audience, link their arms, and do some high kicking.

 How would you feel if you had to perform in front of 6,200 people?

 Gather your classmates and try the famous Rockette kick. Push your desks to one side of the room so you have an open space. Ask everyone to line up shoulder to shoulder, facing forward. Now place your arms around the shoulders of the people standing next to you. Practice a kick by asking everyone to kick up their left leg at the same time. Now kick up the right leg. Keep kicking left leg then right leg. As everyone gets used to kicking together, try kicking faster. Now try hopping up and down and then kicking together.

One of the world's greatest astronomers, the father of modern astronomy, was German mathematician Johannes Kepler. He was born on this day in 1571. Kepler was the first astronomer to believe that planets move in oval orbits around the sun. Before his discovery, astronomers thought that planets revolved around the sun in a circular path rather than an oval- or ellipse-shaped path. If you're not sure what an ellipse is, look up the word in a dictionary or in a math textbook.

 If you've ever wondered what it would be like to be an astronomer, find out more about this science. You could look up the word "astronomy" in an encyclopedia or ask a librarian for some good books about how to become an astronomer.

december 28

Dr. William Finley Semple, a dentist from Mt. Vernon, New York, patented chewing gum on this day in 1869. He described his gum as a "combination of rubber with other particles." During World War II, Semple's gum was only given to soldiers in the armed forces overseas. In 1946, the Wrigley company introduced spearmint-flavored gum to everyone. Juicy Fruit came next with Doublemint in 1947. Wrigley's introduced Big Red Cinnamon Gum in the 1970s. During that time, they also created Hubba Bubba Bubble Gum.

 Do you think gum is fun? Why or why not?

 On this day in 1895 in Paris, a movie theater showed a motion picture in public for the first time. Write about the first time you went to a movie theater. What movie did

you see? Who took you? If you can't remember the first time, write about the earliest time you can remember.

 In four more days, a new year will begin. Think back on this year. What was the best day for you? The best time? Draw yourself enjoying that special day or time.

 Thomas Woodrow Wilson, the 28th president of the United States was born at Staunton, Virginia, on this day in 1856. He was elected president in 1912 and 1916. It was Wilson who asked the Congress to declare war on Germany on April 2, 1917. To find out more about Wilson's decision to enter a war, look up "Woodrow Wilson" or "World War I" in an encyclopedia.

december 29

In his teens, Pablo Casals often searched the music stores of Barcelona, Spain, for cello music. One day he discovered some music by Bach that might have been lost forever if he hadn't found it. Casals was later celebrated as one of the greatest cello players in the world. He made his first American tour in 1901 and continued giving concerts for 70 years. He was born on this day in 1876.

 Imagine that you have just discovered something very important—something that might have been lost forever if you hadn't come along. What did you find? Why is it important? What will you do first, and why?

 People who try to learn more about the past by looking at fossils are called paleontologists. These scientists search for buried fossils to figure out what kinds of animals and plants lived on Earth millions of years ago. Many paleontologists look for dinosaur bones and fossils, hoping to find out more about these gigantic creatures.

Write a few sentences on what you know about dinosaurs. What are the names of some dinosaurs? Do you have a favorite dinosaur? Why is it your favorite?

 Today is the anniversary of the massacre of more than 200 Native American men, women, and children by the U.S. Seventh Cavalry. The attack happened in 1890 at Wounded Knee, South Dakota. The Native Americans were preparing a religious ceremony called the ghost dance. Soldiers, however, wanted to prohibit all Native American ceremonies and fought anyone who tried to take part in religious dances and rituals. To find out more about this dark time of American history, look up "Wounded Knee" in an encyclopedia.

 On this day in 1952, transistorized hearing aids went on sale for the first time in Elmsford, New York. These small devices help people who are hard of hearing understand conversations. Write about the things you could do to communicate with a person who is hearing impaired. If you are hearing impaired, tell your classmates how they could communicate better with you.

december 30

Rudyard Kipling wrote several successful novels for adults and many poems, but his stories for children earned him an international reputation. He was born in Bombay, India, on this day in 1865. When he began to write for children, Kipling used events from his childhood in India. One of his stories is called *Rikki-Tikki-Tavi*. It's about a mongoose that saves a family from a cobra. In the story, the jungle animals talk to each other.

 Write a scene in which animals talk to each other.

 Some of Rudyard Kipling's stories are about Mowgli, a boy who grows up in the jungle. You can read about this boy who was raised by wolves in *Jungle Book Adaptations* by Robin McKinley. You might also enjoy *Just So Stories*. Read about this author's life in *Kipling: Storyteller of East and West* by Gloria Kamen.

 During this last week of the year, TV news shows, magazines, and newspapers review the past year's happenings. They show pictures of events that happened throughout the year.

Make a list of your accomplishments for last year. *Examples*: Include something fun you did last summer and the new grade you started in September. List the things you've learned in each subject so far. You could also include a good report card you had or the name of a club or sports team you joined.

 From 1966 to 1968, TV viewers watched the "Monkees," a show about four young men trying to make a living in California. (Today, you can still watch the reruns.) This zany group of four guys became a popular group on stage and played to sold-out concerts around the world. Davy Jones and Mike Nesmith, two of the Monkees, were born on this day (Jones in 1946 and Nesmith in 1942).

Design a concert stage. Create different levels on your stage for the performers. Include bright lights and special effects.

....

RESOURCES

Jungle Book Adaptations by Robin McKinley (New York: Random House, 1952).

Some books by Rudyard Kipling

Rikki-Tikki-Tavi (New York: Harcourt Brace Jovanovich, 1992) and *Just So Stories* (New York: Doubleday, 1972).

Kipling: Storyteller of East and West by Gloria Kamen (New York: Atheneum, 1985).

....

december 31

Today is Make Up Your Mind Day. It's a day for all those people who have a hard time deciding what to do.

 Write about a time when it was hard to make up your mind.

 In honor of Make Up Your Mind Day, make a decision and follow through with it. *Examples*: decide to baby-sit a younger brother or sister more often, make your bed when you get up, clean up your dishes after you eat, or make up your mind to arrive somewhere on time.

 Today, during the annual World Peace Meditation, people around the world focus their thoughts and energy on peace. The event begins at noon Greenwich mean time and lasts one hour. Take some time out today to think about peace.

 If you'd like to know more about the Peace Meditation, send a letter to:

World Peace Meditation
P.O. Box 1151
Coeur d'Alene, ID 83816-1151

index

TETON COUNTY LIBRARY
JACKSON, WYOMING

about the author

Lorraine M. Dahlstrom is a graduate of Delta College, Saginaw Valley State College, and St. Thomas University. She has been teaching middle school and high school since 1974.

She presently teaches English and Language Arts at the secondary level for the Rosemount/Apple Valley, Minnesota, School District #196. Lorraine also teaches for Project ReEntry, the alternative learning program for the Bloomington School District #272.

Lorraine is the mother of three sons. When not watching her youngest son play hockey or attending the drum corps shows of her two older sons, she reads, weaves, and writes.

She is also the author of *Writing Down the Days: 365 Creative Journaling Ideas for Young People*, published by Free Spirit Publishing.

Other Great Books from Free Spirit

Building Self-Esteem Through the Museum of I
25 Original Projects That Explore and Celebrate the Self
by Linda R. Zack, M.Ed.
The student-centered, open-ended activities in this book encourage divergent, original thinking and allow creative expression in varied media and forms. Includes dozens of reproducible handout masters.
For grades 4–8.
$18.95; 144 pp., softcover; illus.; 8½" x 11"

Growing Good Kids
28 Activities to Enhance Self-Awareness, Compassion and Leadership
by Deb Delisle and Jim Delisle, Ph.D., illustrated by Ken Vinton, M.A.
Created by teachers and classroom-tested, these fun and meaningful enrichment activities build children's skills in problem solving, decision making, cooperative learning, divergent thinking, and communication.
For grades 4–8.
$21.95; 208 pp., softcover; illus.; 8½" x 11"

Jump Starters
Quick Classroom Activities That Develop Self-Esteem, Creativity, and Cooperation
by Linda Nason McElhern, M.A.
Make the most of every minute in your classroom by keeping this book close at hand. Features 52 themes within five topics: Self-Awareness and Self-Esteem, Getting Along with Others, School Success, Life Skills, and Just for Fun.
For teachers, grades 3–6.
$21.95; 176 pp., softcover; illus.; 8½" x 11"

Writing Down the Days
365 Creative Journaling Ideas for Young People
Revised & Updated
by Lorraine M. Dahlstrom, M.A.
This revised and updated edition of a Free Spirit classic includes a whole year's worth of fresh, inventive creative writing assignments, all linked to the calendar year. For ages 12 & up.
$14.95; 184 pp.; softcover; illus.; 6" x 9"

To place an order or to request a free catalog of SELF–HELP FOR KIDS® and SELF–HELP FOR TEENS® materials, please write, call, email, or visit our Web site:

Free Spirit Publishing Inc.
217 Fifth Avenue North • Suite 200 • Minneapolis, MN 55401-1299
toll-free 800.735.7323 • local 612.338.2068 • fax 612.337.5050
help4kids@freespirit.com • www.freespirit.com